Lawrence
of Arabia

By the same author:

Isandlwana
Rorke's Drift
Crossing the Buffalo
Redcoats and Zulus
The Curling Letters of the Zulu War
Sister Janet: Zulu War Nurse
The Who's Who of the Zulu War

Lawrence of Arabia

MIRAGE OF A DESERT WAR

ADRIAN GREAVES

Weidenfeld & Nicolson

LONDON

First published in Great Britain in 2007
by Weidenfeld & Nicolson

1 3 5 7 9 10 8 6 4 2

A CIP catalogue record for this book
is available from the British Library.

ISBN-13: 978 0 297 84656 7
ISBN-10: 0 297 84656 6

Typeset by Input Data Services Ltd, Frome

Printed and bound in Great Britain
by Butler and Tanner Ltd, Frome and London

Weidenfeld & Nicolson

The Orion Publishing Group Ltd
Orion House
5 Upper Saint Martin's Lane
London, WC2H 9EA

The Orion Publishing Group's policy is to use papers that
are natural, renewable and recyclable products and made
from wood grown in sustainable forests. The logging and
manufacturing processes are expected to conform to the
environmental regulations of the country of origin.

www.orionbooks.co.uk

Contents

List of Illustrations

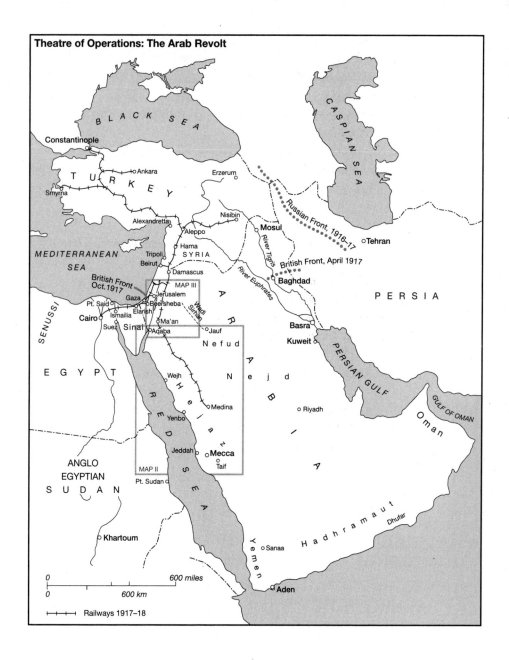

Theatre of Operations: The Arab Revolt

BLACK SEA

Constantinople

TURKEY

Ankara

Erzerum

Smyrna

CASPIAN SEA

Nisibin

Alexandretta

Russian Front, 1916–17

Aleppo

Mosul

Tehran

Hama

SYRIA

Tripoli

River Tigris

Beirut

British Front, April 1917

MEDITERRANEAN SEA

Damascus

River Euphrates

Baghdad

PERSIA

British Front Oct.1917

MAP III

Gaza Jerusalem

Pt. Said

Beersheba

Elarish

Wadi Sirhan

Cairo

Ismailia

Ma'an

Jauf

Basra

Suez Sinai

Aqaba

Kuweit

SENUSSI

Nefud

PERSIAN GULF

EGYPT

Wejh

N e j d

GULF OF OMAN

A R A B I A

Medina

Riyadh

Oman

Yenbo

Yenbo

Jeddah

Mecca

MAP II

Taif

Pt. Sudan

ANGLO EGYPTIAN SUDAN

RED SEA

Hadhramaut

Dhufar

Khartoum

Yemen

Sanaa

0   600 miles

0   600 km

Aden

├──┼──┤ Railways 1917–18

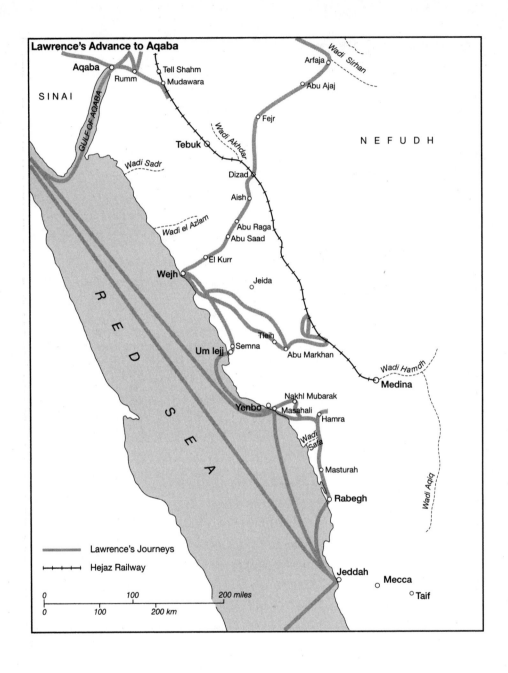

Lawrence's Advance to Aqaba

SINAI

Aqaba
Rumm
Tell Shahm
Mudawara

Arfaja
Abu Ajaj

Wadi Sirhan

Wadi Akhdar
Fejr

NEFUDH

Tebuk

Wadi Sadr

Dizad

Aish

Wadi el Azlam

Abu Raga
Abu Saad

El Kurr

Wejh

Jeida

R E D

Tleih
Semna
Abu Markhan

Um lejj

Wadi Hamdh

Medina

S E A

Nakhl Mubarak
Yenbo
Masahali
Hamra

Wadi Safa

Masturah

Wadi Aqiq

Rabegh

Lawrence's Journeys

Hejaz Railway

0   100   200 miles
0   100   200 km

Jeddah   Mecca

Taif

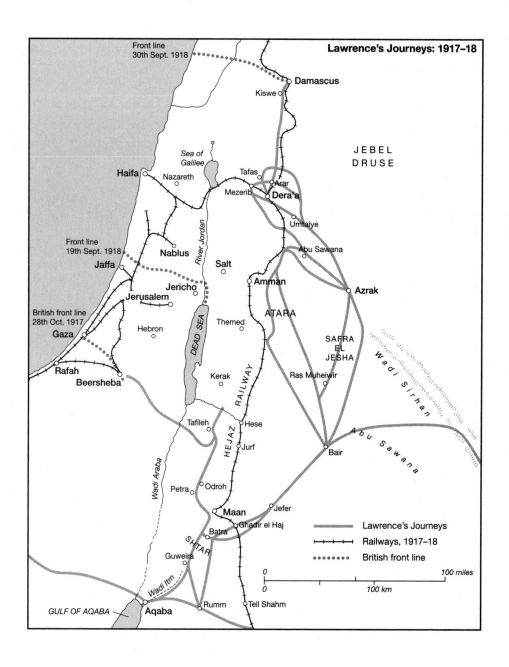

Lawrence's Journeys: 1917–18

Front line
30th Sept. 1918

Damascus

Kiswe

Sea of
Galilee

JEBEL
DRUSE

Haifa

Nazareth

Tafas

Arar

Mezerib

Dera'a

Umtaiye

Abu Sawana

Front line
19th Sept. 1918

Nablus

River Jordan

Salt

Amman

Azrak

Jaffa

Jericho

ATARA

Jerusalem

British front line
28th Oct. 1917

Themed

SAFRA
EL
JESHA

Gaza

Hebron

DEAD SEA

Ras Muheiwir

Wadi Sirhan

Rafah

Beersheba

Kerak

RAILWAY

Tafileh

Hese

Abu Sawana

HEJAZ

Jurf

Bair

Wadi Araba

Petra

Odroh

Jefer

Maan

Lawrence's Journeys

Ghadir el Haj

Railways, 1917–18

Batra

British front line

SHTAR

Guweira

0   100 miles

Wadi Itm

0   100 km

GULF OF AQABA

Aqaba

Rumm

Tell Shahm

INTRODUCTION:

T. E. Lawrence

*J*ust after the First World War, a young man became a national hero overnight. Known to his family and friends as Colonel T. E. Lawrence, he rapidly became the best known Englishman worldwide and his heroic and almost unbelievable exploits in the biblical deserts of Arabia inspired a flood of newspaper articles, books and films. Alone and wearing the flowing white robes of an Arabian prince, he led ferocious Arab raiders into battle against well-defended Turkish positions, he repeatedly crossed mighty waterless deserts by camel to dynamite enemy trains, bridges and heavily defended railway stations. These were refreshing, new and glamorous stories to inspire a generation still reeling from years of war in the trenches of France.

And yet, of all the material published about his role during the dramatic Arab Revolt, few researchers have looked at Lawrence as he really was, or attempted to understand the brutal battles he fought as a commander of the Arab army against the Turkish aggressors. As the years accelerate us away from the time when his famous exploits excited men around the world, it appears that less is known about this charismatic young Englishman than he deserves. This book seeks to redress these omissions.

By the opening stages of the First World War, Lawrence was a well-educated young archaeologist in his mid twenties. Although he was sensitive to his surroundings he nevertheless delighted in mixing the serious academic side of his life with adventures of his own making, firstly as a youth in France and later when exploring and excavating in Syria. He always had a flair for mocking officialdom, a psychological trait that he learned and cultivated in childhood, yet he always respected clever men - they, in turn, respected him. This respect grew inestimably after his untimely death in 1935 when he was killed in a motorcycle accident at the age of only forty-five.

Lawrence's own account of the Arab Revolt and his wartime experiences in the desert, *Seven Pillars of Wisdom*, is one of the most famous works ever written by an Englishman. It is an extremely complicated study and heavily slanted towards the Arab perspective of the war; its theme was developed from his personal war diaries and Lawrence redrafted the book many times before he was even remotely satisfied with its form and content. When *Seven Pillars of Wisdom* was eventually published it was widely acknowledged as a masterpiece, and indeed it is; but like many an academic work, it remains virtually incomprehensible to the average reader. It is a direct consequence of his deliberate use of high Victorian prose and enigmatic style that people in the twenty-first century more readily recall T. E. Lawrence as a result of David Lean's brilliant film, *Lawrence of Arabia*, rather than as a result of any biographers' work or even Lawrence's own writing.

His sudden death, and all the legends and mysteries that sur-rounded him during his short life, gave way to a steady stream of psychologists, psychiatrists and academics, all keen to use their professional skills to explain the inexplicable. How could a young man in his twenties know so much about Arabia and its way of life? And how could he have then overcome conventional British military protocol by riding off into the desert to unite the Arab nation – a nation of perpetually warring tribes – to the extent that most Arabs were effectively oblivious to the vicissitudes of a world war raging around them? Yet unite this fragmented nation he did; if only for a brief moment in time. Lawrence achieved something that no Arab leader even thought possible, he brought warring Arab leaders and their tribes together and assisted them first to thwart and then overwhelmingly rout their brutal Turkish occupiers. He then led the growing Arab army across vast unmapped deserts and into Palestine; he wrote that his aim was to 'establish them with arms in their hands, in a position so assured (if not dominant) that expediency would counsel to the Great Powers a fair settlement of their claims.' In other words, he sought not merely to defeat the Turks in battle but also to defeat his own country in the great council chambers of Europe. Towards the end of the war this tenuous Arab army soundly defeated a number of vastly superior Turkish armies, all commanded and trained by experienced German and Austrian officers. Lawrence's Arabs then supported General Allenby's advancing British attack in a series of successful actions that resulted in the swift destruction of the German-led Turkish Army in Palestine, a defeat that contributed to the final collapse of Germany in 1918.

But the miracle of Arab unification was only the first stage of Lawrence's long-held dream. The second vital stage, gaining international recognition of Arab unification, would prove impossible. For the leading Muslim Arabs who believed and trusted the assurances of Lawrence and the Christian British government throughout the war, their dream of lasting peace would turn into a nightmare of deceit, subterfuge and treachery – and set the scene for future generations of Arabs to mistrust Christian politicians.

Lawrence's strength and character came from his apparently traditional family background – although even this was not as conventional as it might seem to the casual observer. Of undoubted intelligence, Lawrence developed an unusually perceptive and life-long understanding of medieval tactics, which he studied during his years at Jesus College, Oxford and later in Palestine as a postgraduate archaeologist. He had learned the ancient theories of desert warfare during his archaeological studies and understood perfectly the unorthodox tactics of Hannibal, Belisarius, Mohammed and the Crusaders. He would soon put these tactics to good effect in numerous actions against the German-led Turkish Army. Lawrence had no military training yet he fought numerous actions and battles against the Turks, and fought them well. He only ever fought one battle using conventional tactics, at Tafileh, which resulted in another overwhelming Arab victory.

During his short military service, Lawrence's attitude to certain senior officers' inefficiency created many problems, usually for the officers in question; he despised officers and politicians who displayed a benign attitude to the war. He always believed steadfastly in the theory that attack is the best form of defence and stood out defiantly for the rights of the ordinary soldier, both British and Arab.

I believe Lawrence's story is more straightforward than previously portrayed by numerous authors and his biographers; it is definitely a more straightforward tale than Lawrence depicted. Winston Churchill wrote in *Great Contemporaries* that the idea behind Lawrence's desert campaign was simple:

> The Turkish armies operating against Egypt depended on the desert railway. The slender steel track ran through hundreds of miles of blistering desert. If it were permanently cut the Turkish armies must perish: the ruin of Turkey must follow and with it the downfall of the mighty Teutonic power which hurled its hate from ten thousand cannons on the plains of Flanders. Here was the Achilles heel, and it was upon this that this man in his twenties directed his audacious, desperate, romantic assaults. We read of them in numerous succession. Grim camel rides through sun-scorched, blasted lands, where the extreme desolation of nature appals the traveller … through these with infinite privation men on camels with shattering toil carried dynamite to destroy railway bridges and win the war, and, as we hoped, free the world.

In the same way that T. E. Lawrence was not truly a Lawrence (he was actually the illegitimate son of Sir Thomas Chapman), there was no 'Lawrence of Arabia' during the Arab Revolt or even immediately after the First World War. There were a number of young British officers deployed to Arabia, all performing a myriad of dangerous tasks. Lawrence's fame was generated by the enthusiasm of an American, a former professor from Princeton University, who spent several weeks with Lawrence in the desert. Lowell Thomas gained the young Lawrence's confidence, filmed him and then embarked on a postwar lecture tour of the world – much to Lawrence's amusement. It was Thomas who gave life to the 'Lawrence of Arabia' story, for that is what it is – largely a story, often being nearer to fiction than to reality.

Much that has been written about Lawrence has been exaggerated or fabricated; for example, Lawrence was not the first to start dynamiting Turkish trains – he learnt the skill from French officers already attached to the Arabs. The French had also been busy trying to ensnare the Arabs politically long before Lawrence came on the scene – itself an interesting insight into the complexity of French diplomacy, which Lawrence fought with as much passion as he displayed in his actions against the Turks. Secondly, much was made in the film *Lawrence of Arabia* about Lawrence's capture and mistreatment by the Turks at Derra. This incident made gripping cinema and subsequently gave the psychologists much to ponder – if only it were true. The story, believed by many authors to be genuine, spawned a host of psychological explanations for Lawrence's subsequent behaviour, especially when he refused honours, fame and offers from Winston Churchill of positions of high office. At Buckingham Palace he declined decorations and left the bemused king holding the box – and instead became a raw recruit in the Royal Air Force. The Derra incident comes from an account in Lawrence's *Seven Pillars of Wisdom* and is typical of Lawrence's vivid inventiveness and devious urge to shock. I will set out why I believe Derra was a figment of his imagination because there is evidence that, at the time he claimed to be under arrest in Derra, he was on patrol several hundred miles away near Aqaba, accompanied by British officers. No one will ever know the truth about Derra; Lawrence's tale is probably based on a minor incident when, as a trainee archaeologist in 1913, he was briefly detained while visiting Syria.

Today Lawrence is all but forgotten in Britain; he remains highly respected by Americans, whose army officers still study him as a role model, and he remains a legend in Jordan. His is a remarkable story. He was trusted by those he worked with and adored by the Arabs. Many still remember the tale of this young Englishman who wore Arab clothes and who went to war on their behalf in a Rolls-Royce, who dynamited Turkish trains, threw out the Turkish occupiers and was present when the new Arab army, which valiantly supported General Allenby's advancing army, managed to reach Damascus ahead of the Allies.

Over thirty years ago I wrote an investigative thesis about T. E. Lawrence as part of my higher police training. To write this book I used my original thesis as a framework and then broadened my research. I was privileged to visit a number of the battlefields fought over by Lawrence, and experienced the severity and hardship of desert life. I remain highly respectful of what this young man achieved. I also gratefully acknowledge my dedicated guide in Jordan, Ahmad Amrien, who accompanied me to the various locations and kept me safe.

Adrian Greaves

Chronology for
T. E. Lawrence

The chronology of Lawrence's activities and expeditions prior to and during the Arab Revolt, based on his account in *Seven Pillars of Wisdom*, is difficult to follow. I therefore supply brief details of his activities.

1888
August: Born at Tremadoc in North Wales.

1910
First travels to the Middle East.

1911
Works at Carchemish in Syria, walks to northern Mesopotamia (Iraq).

1912
Works as an archaeologist in Egypt.

1912–14
Works at Carchemish under Wooley. During his summer 1913 visit to Oxford, he is accompanied by his two servants, Dahoum and Hamoudi.

February 1914: accompanies Wooley and Newcombe across Sinai, returns to Carchemish until outbreak of war in spring 1914.

1914
Returns to Oxford due to outbreak of war. Refused permission to 'join up' due to his physique. Joins the War Office as a map maker.

26 October: is commissioned into the Special List (for officers unattached to a regiment or corps).

December: is posted to Egypt.

1914–16
British Intelligence Office Cairo.
March 1916: travels to Mesopotamia to negotiate release of British forces trapped at Kut.

June 1916: Arab Revolt commences.

October 1916: accompanies Storrs to Medina, goes on to have first meeting with Feisal. Is posted to the Arab Bureau then to Arab forces as liaison officer to Feisal.

1917
8 January: with Feisal's army to Wejh.

9 May onwards: Aqaba expedition begins.

6 July: seizes Aqaba, then goes to Egypt for first meeting with General Allenby.

26 July: is promoted to major.

October–November: unsuccessful raid on Yarmuk viaduct.

20 November: alleged capture by Turks at Derra.

21 November: tests newly arrived motor vehicles at Aqaba.

11 December: accompanies Allenby for entry into Jerusalem.

1918
15 January: battle of Tafileh.

March: is promoted to lieutenant colonel.

March–September: numerous raids against Turkish rail network.

19 September: Allenby launches Allied attack supported by Lawrence and Arabs.

1 October: Damascus falls to Arab and Australian forces.

4 October: Lawrence is promoted to colonel and returns to England.

October–November: attends War Office briefings.

November–December: with Feisal in France and Britain.

1919
January–October: attends Paris Peace Conference.

May–June: travels to Cairo by air, is injured in air crash.

1919–21
Oxford, Paris and London working on *Seven Pillars of Wisdom*.

1921–2
Appointed adviser to Winston Churchill at Colonial Office.

March 1921: attends Cairo Peace Conference with Churchill.

August–December: travels to Aden, Jeddah and Trans-Jordan.

July 1922: resigns from Colonial Office. Refuses all offers of senior government positions.

August: changes name to John Hume Ross and joins RAF. Lawrence is traced by the press.

1923
Dismissed from the RAF following the press disclosure of his presence. Joins the Royal Tank Corps as Private Shaw and purchases Clouds Hill in Dorset.

1925
Rejoins the RAF as T. E. Shaw and is posted to RAF Cranwell in Lincolnshire.

1927–9
Serves in India until December 1929 when recalled to England following press allegations of his fermenting revolt in Afghanistan.

1925–35
Works in England as an RAF mechanic on Schneider Trophy aircraft and then in the development of high-speed marine rescue craft.

1935
Retires to Clouds Hill.

13 May: sustains serious injuries in a motorcycle accident.

19 May: dies of injuries.

I

The Demise of the Ottoman Empire

In 1914 the Turkish-controlled Ottoman Empire was composed of the enormous landmass that today includes the countries of Israel, Palestine, Jordan, Lebanon, Syria, Saudi Arabia, Kuwait and Iraq. Since before biblical times the whole area had been a much fought-over battleground, a troubled area that had witnessed numerous human migrations criss-crossing its desert wilderness. Some of these migrations became settled, others were invariably displaced as a consequence of wars. The whole area is a vast desert, from the long and narrow coastal plain, which stretches northwards from the Suez Canal to Turkey, to the high mountainous flanks running along the Jordanian Valley and the vast high deserts of distant Iraq. To the south-east the desert extends towards Saudi Arabia. To outsiders this landscape appears to offer only unending sand with few features, apart from the distant holy city of Mecca and its small port of Jeddah on the Red Sea.

In the fifteenth century the coastal area experienced massive destruction wrought by the Christian Crusades, which were fought at such a terrible cost to both the warring factions and the small civilian populations of local Arab tribes. After the Crusaders departed the barren and war-ravaged region, life in the desert slowly returned to some normality. The nomadic Arabs resumed their timeless lives by following their whim or the lure of trade; some settled near the Mediterranean coast in small villages but by far the majority followed their chiefs and tribal elders living in tented towns in far-flung desert regions, vast wastelands they had controlled and wandered over since time immemorial.

In 1600 the armies of the Ottoman Empire, the most powerful and wealthy neighbour of Arabia, marched south and effectively annexed this vast and inhospitable desert landmass into the empire's sphere of political influence. The only group of immigrants that had any direct effect on the area at this time, and only in one small region abutting the Mediterranean, were the many thousands of Jewish settlers who had begun to arrive in the coastal region of the Holy Land from the 1600s onwards. Most had fled Russia and its surrounding satellite countries to escape the widespread savage pogroms and their associated mass murder, imprisonment and harassment. To prevent any dissension, Turkey's rulers placed the population under strict military control. No other military power had previously expressed any interest in this barren empty wilderness and so the Turks were left to reign supreme. Thereafter, in general, the Turks kept to the few coastal towns and so the desert Arabs were left to carry on their nomadic way of life relatively undisturbed.

Following the 1854–6 Crimean War, Britain, as the dominant colonial power, had remained wary of Russia and feared the possibility of Russian warships gaining quick access to the Mediterranean and beyond by passing through the narrow straits of the Turkish-controlled Bosporus. Passage for Russian warships from their home ports on the Black Sea to the open high seas necessitated negotiating the narrow straits – but it was impossible without the permission of the Turkish government. Britain did not relish Russian warships challenging British domination in the Mediterranean or the North Atlantic and so Britain attempted to bolster the overstretched Ottoman government with political and financial support in order to withstand Russian advancement into the area. Russia saw its plans for a sea passage through the Bosporus to the Mediterranean being permanently impeded so turned its attention towards India. The reaction of the British Viceroy to India, Lord Curzon, was to thwart Russia by expressing support for German expansion into Arabia; he believed that such economic development would bolster the Ottoman Empire and help persuade Russia to concentrate on its own domestic affairs and borders, rather than engage in military expansion towards India.

At the same time, Germany sought to extend its colonial and military influence on the Ottoman rulers by advocating the construction of long-range railway routes from Berlin to Baghdad and Mecca, via Constantinople. This would enable Germany to threaten British interests in both India and north-east Africa.

Meanwhile, in 1869, the Suez Canal was finally completed. It was an engineering feat that dramatically shortened the long sea routes between Europe and the Far East, India and Australia, and finally enabled trade and shipping to avoid the lengthy and costly journey round Africa's southerly and dangerous Cape of Good Hope. The British Empire was the greatest beneficiary of the Suez Canal and in order to protect its enormous trade interests, Britain occupied Egypt in 1882, albeit with assurances to Egypt and Turkey that it was 'only a temporary measure'. The Egyptians and Turks took no action but Germany responded by appointing senior army officers to the Turkish Army's General Staff; these included Colonel Koehler who was appointed deputy chief of the Turkish General Staff. He died within a year and was succeeded by Lieutenant Colonel Von der Goltz who was appointed a Turkish field marshal. The Germans also pressed on with their plans for the construction of two railways across Arabia and permits were obtained for these to be laid as far as the Persian Gulf and Yemen. In 1883 the direct rail link between Berlin and Constantinople was finally opened and the way was now open for extensions to Yemen and Baghdad.

Meanwhile, the Ottoman Empire had survived its first serious crisis: in 1878, when the Congress of Berlin terminated Turkish rule in the Balkans, and following a short war with Greece, Turkey lost control of Crete and some of its Aegean islands. And then Macedonia rebelled, supported by the might of Russia. Turkey slowly began to reel from the domino effect of this peripheral disintegration and it was not long before civil disobedience began to ferment within Turkey itself. In 1888 widespread unrest spread to Turkey's Armenian neighbours who, seeing Turkey weakening, began to voice rebellion. The Turkish sultan, Abdul Hamid, reacted by sending his army to face down the Armenian dissidents. Many thousands of Armenians were arrested, including anyone even suspected of association with the dissidents, and a series of brutal massacres followed. The intention was to intimidate the Armenians and dampen their expectations; the Turks viewed the repression as successful but it cost over a quarter of a million Armenian lives and inflicted enormous material losses on the Armenian population. The fate of the Armenians attracted little sympathy from the rest of the world and Turkey was temporarily able to slow the disintegration of its empire.

Germany was already a strong ally of Turkey and in 1898 the Kaiser visited the Padisha to sign the Anatolian Railway Concession, which would facilitate the completion of the Berlin to Baghdad railway; the next extension of the line, the Hejaz Railway, was built in 1903. The Hejaz line was ostensibly a pilgrims' railway to enable easy access to Mecca and was largely funded by pious Muslims across the world, yet most of the money was diverted to the Padisha's coffers. News of the systematic misappropriation of these moneys gradually leaked out and the Padisha's police responded by imprisoning thousands of innocent Muslims, which in turn led to the foundation of a number of secret societies across the Ottoman Empire, including Damascus.

In 1908, response to the ever increasing crisis across the Ottoman Empire resulted in the founding of a new political group, known as the 'Young Turks', who deposed the dictator, Sultan Abdul Hamid, in a military coup. A more democratic but chaotic form of government followed. Recognizing the opportunity caused by political confusion within Turkey, Russia reactivated its interest in obtaining access from the Black Sea to the Mediterranean and demanded of the Turks free passage for Russian warships. Britain countered by requiring access into the Black Sea, resulting in a stalemate. Towards the end of 1911 Italy invaded Libya, anxious to take a slice of the 'sick man's' legacy of failing Turkish domination. In October 1912 the situation deteriorated further when Bulgaria, Greece, Montenegro and Serbia all declared war on Turkey. Russia, anxious lest the Balkan armies reached Constantinople, intervened and settled the dispute by forcing Turkey to withdraw back to its original national boundary.

In 1913, Turkey was in a desperate state of political and financial turmoil and turned to its new ally, Germany, for help. But it was not immediately forthcoming as a cautious Germany waited to see how events in Turkey developed. With little or no political guidance, with financial stability within Turkey collapsing and with morale across the whole country at a low ebb, a small but influential section of the Young Turks group effected a coup and seized control. The coup brought the Committee of Union and Progress (CUP) to power and constitutional government to an end. The CUP was led by a triumvirate: Enver, Minister of War, a pro-German who had been educated in Germany; Talaat, Minister of the Interior (Grand Vizier in 1917); and Jemal, Minister of the Marine. The CUP espoused an ultra-nationalistic ideology, which advocated the formation of an exclusively Turkish state. It also subscribed to an ideology of aggrandizement through conquest directed eastward towards other regions inhabited by Turkish peoples, especially Armenia, and onwards to Russia.

The CUP steered Constantinople towards closer diplomatic and military relations with Imperial Germany and immediately sought financial assistance from abroad. The new finance minister, Djavid, had once met Winston Churchill when he had visited Turkey in his capacity as the President of the Board of Trade. Churchill agreed with the concept of assisting Turkey but the Foreign Secretary, Sir Edward Grey, rebuffed the Turkish request. Germany seized the moment and offered a large military mission to train the Turkish Army. Within weeks, General Liman von Sanders arrived in Constantinople with nearly one hundred highly qualified military advisers. The general was swiftly appointed Commander of Constantinople, to which the Russian government objected on the grounds that Germany would have control of the narrow access between the Black Sea and the Mediterranean. The Turks merely redesignated the German position and instead appointed von Sanders to the rank of field marshal in the Turkish Army. During the fuss, and to keep Turkey 'on side', Britain offered to retrain the Turkish Navy, an offer which was accepted by the Turks and caused no adverse response from Russia.

At the beginning of 1914 Europe was slipping ever closer towards war; Britain suspected Germany's growing association with the CUP and changed its mind about assisting Turkey. Having recently completed the construction of two large warships for the Turkish Navy, the British government secretly decided to keep the warships and reflag them into the Royal Navy. In June 1914, with hostilities imminent between Germany and Britain, two German warships, the Dreadnought cruiser *Goeben* and her escorting cruiser *Breslau*, were ordered to harass British shipping in the Red Sea in the event of war. Due to a miscalculation of German statesmanship, both vessels found themselves still crossing the Mediterranean when they were detected and chased by a tenacious HMS *Gloucester*. A number of well-aimed long-range shots damaged the *Goeben*, which fled at high speed to seek refuge in Constantinople; the only alternative open to the Germans was to risk further confrontation with HMS *Gloucester* and then attempt to run the gauntlet of the main British fleet at Gibraltar.

By the end of July 1914, senior Turks secretly negotiated a treaty of mutual support with Germany. In return, Germany tried to force Turkey into declaring war against the Allies on Germany's behalf, but the Turks stalled, only to have the *Goeben* threaten to shell the

Sultan's palace in Constantinople. Eventually, after Germany paid 2 million Turkish pounds for military equipment, Enver Pasha, Turkey's Minister of War, agreed that the *Goeben* and *Breslau* should be allowed to attack British and Russian ships off Turkey. The German commander of the *Goeben* was understandably reluctant to re-engage HMS *Gloucester*, which was still patiently waiting the reappearance of the German battleship back in the Mediterranean; instead, the *Goeben* went the other way and slipped into the Black Sea to bombard the Russian ports of Feodosia, Odessa and Sebastopol. This forced the Turks into war four days later.

When the First World War broke out in August 1914, the Ottoman Empire immediately declared war on Russia and its Western allies and became part of the German-led Triple Alliance along with Austria and Hungary. Meanwhile, with European governments diverted by war, the dominant Islamic Turks again focused their attention towards the Armenians, a Christian minority, who still lived as second-class citizens in the north-east of the land. Since the earlier massacres of Armenians, neither their lives nor their property had been secure. As non-Muslims they were obligated to pay discriminatory taxes and denied participation in government. By 1914 the Ottoman Empire had lost virtually all its lands in Europe and Africa and, understandably, Armenian and Greek aspirations for representation and participation in government began to ferment. This soon aroused suspicions among the Muslim Turks who had never tolerated any minority, other than from their brother Muslims, the Arabs.

Through the spring of 1915, the Turks used the confusion of pending war to kill off many thousands of Greek dissenters. Then the numerous Armenian soldiers who were serving in the Ottoman army were disarmed and either executed or sent to labour camps where they were deliberately worked to death. The Armenian civilian population, especially those in the Balkans and the Caucasus, were now in a high state of tension. The Turks reapplied the screws of massacre and oppression and gave the order for the Armenians to be deported en masse from their homes. When the Armenians were driven out, thousands of Muslim refugees were settled in the now vacant Armenian homes and farms and most Armenian disposable wealth was confiscated by members of the CUP. Some Armenians had a few days' notice to leave their homes, but the majority had little more than a few hours. They were not allowed to carry any possessions with them and most valuables were hastily sold to non-Armenians for a tiny fraction of their value. Some of the better-off were able to bribe the guards to allow them to take carts but once the carts were loaded the goods were usually confiscated by the very guards who had taken the bribes.

Across the Ottoman Empire, military units began collecting columns of tens of thousands of Armenian men, women and children and forced them to walk the hundreds of miles towards the distant Syrian desert regardless of age, gender or health. The Turkish people were told the Armenian deportations were part of a humanitarian resettlement programme and few voices were raised in dissent. Without shelter, adequate food or medical care, the elderly, children, the sick and pregnant women were the early victims of these marches. The deportees walked in convoys guarded by armed militia who alone decided if and where they could rest and drink. The routes had been carefully chosen so as to avoid witnesses, especially as bodies were abandoned where they fell. En route, the defenceless refugee convoys, in particular those from the eastern provinces, were deliberately attacked, robbed and slain by organized gangs drawn from the local Muslim population or by specialist murder squads, mostly prison convicts specifically released from prison into these death squads, known as the *Teshkilâti Mahsusa* and trained in the art of mass murder. To save money, the killing process was normally carried out by the sword. If there was ever doubt that the Turkish policy was genocidal then the mass killings that accompanied the deportations proved the point.

In a number of Armenian towns, young women were systematically selected for 'education', which was nothing more than an orgy of mass rape before the victims were taken off to 'houses' for use by the Special Organization militias or placed into slavery in Turkish homes. The remaining refugees, including women and children, were then herded together into one of the many convoys being assembled. Those deportee columns lucky enough to reach the desert were forced to walk deeper into the wilderness to their 'destinations', without shelter, medical care, food or water. In reality, there were no 'destinations' so there can be little doubt that the mass deportations were intended solely as death marches. The killer mobs, the desert and the deprivations ensured that few survived. One isolated group of about one thousand Armenians eventually reached the desert village of Tafileh and were taken in by sympathetic Arabs – and would shortly wreak terrible revenge on the Turks.

Any members of the Armenian population fleeing the mass evacuations were hunted down mercilessly by Turkish irregular forces. Inland towns that resisted, such as Urfa (Edessa), were first reduced to rubble by Turkish artillery before the traumatized survivors were rounded up and slaughtered or deported. On 9 October 1916, the police chief of Deir-ez-Zor, Zekki Bey, ordered great stacks of petroleum-soaked wood to be built by a group of male Armenian prisoners. Some 2,000 newly orphaned children were thrown into the pyre, which he personally ignited. At the same town, a Jewish officer of the Ottoman army, Eytan Belkind, reported 5,000 Armenian prisoners were bound and arranged in a huge circle before being sprayed with petrol and torched. He recalled that the screams of the unfortunate victims, burnt to death in the huge fire, could be heard for miles. Underground caverns in the oil-rich area of north Syria were used for the same purpose of mass burnings. In the caves of Shaddadeh, which are still known as the Ditch of the Armenians *(Chabs el-Ermen)*, 80,000 deportees were herded underground and burnt or suffocated in burning petroleum. For the Turks, the policy was successful; the bulk of the Armenian population was effectively eliminated and their property assimilated into Turkish possession.[1]

Unwittingly, swathes of the local Muslim population also became infected by the diseases carried by the wretched Armenian deportees. Typhus spread through the malnourished refugees and their bands of guards, infected corpses lay unburied, others were dumped in wells, streams and rivers, including the upper reaches of the rivers Tigris and Euphrates. Over the next three years an estimated one million Muslim Ottoman citizens fell victim to typhus. The Austrian Military Plenipotentiary, Joseph Pomiankowski, wrote, 'This was the vengeance of the murdered Armenians against their henchmen.' The steady elimination of the Armenians, and the crude methods used, was witnessed by many German officers serving with the Turkish Army; some reported the matter-of-fact success of the Armenian expulsion to their superiors in Germany.

Although the Allied Powers repeatedly warned the Ottoman government to halt its policy of genocide, it is estimated that up to a million and a half Armenians perished at the hands of Turkish military and paramilitary forces. The policy effectively eliminated the Armenian demographic presence in Turkey.[2]

Meanwhile, Turkish leaders were becoming alarmed by news of open dissension spreading across Arab towns, especially in Syria. Turkey now turned its attention to bringing its desert subjects to heel.

To define who these subjects were is a complex process and best attempted in terms of topography and language. Latitudinally, Arabia begins south of Turkey with the long range of mountains of northern

1 Arnold J. Toynbee wrote *Armenian Atrocities: The Murder of a Nation* (1915) in which American sources are emphasized. In the forward, Viscount Bryce estimated 800,000 Armenians had been killed in 1915. He emphasized that the killings were by government order, not by popular Muslim passion. Toynbee concentrated on the sufferings of women and children.
2 Despite international pressure, in 1915 alone the *New York Times* published 145 articles on the subject; this genocide was sustained until 1923. Each year, 22 April is an Armenian day of national mourning for the victims of the genocide.

Syria. It then runs into what Lawrence knew as Palestine, including Israel and Lebanon, then south through Arabia proper to the Hadramut Mountains. Longitudinally, its western boundary is the Suez Canal and the Red Sea; it then extends eastwards to include Mesopotamia, modern-day Iraq, and on to the Persian Gulf. Its area equals that of the subcontinent of India and has an average height of over 3,000 feet. In Lawrence's time, most of the inner area was unexplored. The most densely populated areas were Mesopotamia to the east, watered by the Euphrates and Tigris rivers, and Palestine's Mediterranean coastline followed by the mountainous area of the Hejaz and Yemen. The remote inner desert area was dotted with springs, fed by distant mountains, which gave life to scattered oases and sustained the tribes of nomadic Arabs. It was from the tribes of Syria and the Hejaz that Lawrence principally collected his army of Arab fighters.

In terms of nationality, the people were as diverse and divided as the Europeans in Europe, but without the complexity of starkly different languages. Arabia was and is still made up of differing groups of people, ranging from nationalities to tribes, but all speaking a version of Arabic, a language spread by Mohammed's conquests and the word of the Koran. Foreign invasions, and there were many, including those by Egyptians, Greeks, Romans, Persians and Christian Crusaders had little influence on the Arabic language. These invasions were always temporary and, after being repulsed by the Arabs, left few traces. The flow of war was not always one way; the Arabs also sought fresh land beyond their own shores as far away as France, India, Spain and Morocco – but these were always unsuccessful.

Syria was especially complicated; for thousands of years the land had been subjected to passing armies and numerous civilian migrations. The valleys of Syria were mostly categorized by reference to the nationality of the original settlers. They were predominantly Algerians, Arabians, Armenians, Circassians, Greeks, Kurds,

Persians and Turks with the sole common denominator being their use of the Arabic language. By the First World War the whole of Syria and the coastal region south of Aqaba as far as Yemen had been occupied by the Ottoman Empire for over four hundred years; these occupied Arabs were totally suppressed by the Turks and, as compliant subjects of their Turkish overlords, they lacked any form of collective bonding or national identity. Life for the struggling population was difficult; sanitation was negligible and many died at an early age as a direct result, their falling numbers only being replaced by nomadic Arabs who drifted into the towns for work. Arabs in the pay of the Turks spied everywhere and any Arab who dared to question Turkish rule would be arrested and disappear. Conditions in Lebanon were only marginally better. There the response of many of the young and still healthy people was to emigrate to America, which left a growing imbalance at home. But now the Arabs could see the fault lines appearing in the Turkish occupation, the people were gaining confidence and public disquiet was spreading.

However, the Arabs lacked leaders, weapons and training. Even at the height of the approaching Arab Revolt, Prince Feisal could call upon a fighting force of not more than 9,000 men. They came from a variety of tribes and each man served under his own tribal sheikh; few would serve beyond their own known tribal limits. In this way they could rely on their knowledge of water holes and friendly villages for food, fresh camels and supplies. When a large force was required, the sheikhs would be called for by a sherif, whose position, being a descendant of Mohammed, put him above all tribal sheikhs and beyond their inter-tribal rivalries and feuds. The Arabs were never a united nation, a situation that remains especially obvious in modern times. It was remarkable that Lawrence and Feisal could ever bring these disparate tribes and clans together; most tribes nurtured deadly feuds that had their origins hundreds of years earlier. By playing on the Arab hatred of the Turks, Lawrence and Feisal were able to suspend such inter-tribal feuding for the duration of the war and brought these discordant people together for the common cause of freeing Arabia. Tribes that were sworn enemies – the Ateiba, Billie and Juheina – cooperated for the first time in centuries and served under Feisal, so long as they were not required to combine or mix together in a raiding party or on the march. There were, nevertheless, occasional scores that were settled in the heat of battle and both Feisal and Lawrence frequently spent valuable time calming grievances.

Lawrence had quickly learned that the desert Arab was a brave fighter but not a regimental soldier. Born in the endless wilderness of sand, rock and shale, his whole life was geared to the camel, rearing, selling and using the beast for its milk, meat and transport. Camels were their currency and wealth. On raids, the desert Arab naturally preferred to fight as he had learned to hunt, usually in small groups. Being fully in harmony with the harshness and ways of the desert the Arabs were ideal for guerrilla warfare: sniping and sudden attacks were their forte. It was ingrained into their culture to attack small caravans, usually consisting of lost pilgrims or members of another tribe, and loot their victims' possessions and camels. Under Lawrence, their enjoyment and excitement when destroying Turkish trains, railway lines and stations, especially with dynamite, was almost childlike and equally uncontrollable. The subsequent killing of Turks was seen as a necessity and a means of exacting retribution but looting was always their greatest delight. After such an attack they would load their camels with as much booty as could be carried and, if unrestrained, they would head straight back to their home area without understanding the need for cohesion and debriefing. One serious problem for Lawrence and Feisal was the need to stimulate their groups of Arab fighters in order to keep them ready to fight. Long periods of either activity or inactivity frequently resulted in tribesmen drifting away and returning home. Such temporary deser-tion was socially acceptable to the Arabs: without the incentive of gold or the promise of immediate action and booty, they would invariably disappear until called upon to fight again.

For regular fighting, the British would have to rely on the Arab townsmen of Syria and Mesopotamia. Many had earlier been conscripted into the Turkish Army and there were thousands of such soldiers in captivity in Egypt, having been taken prisoner by the British in earlier engagements in Mesopotamia and against the Suez Canal. Given the opportunity of remaining in captivity or fighting the Turks, most chose to fight. Their leader, a senior Arab who had held high command under the Turks, Aziz el Masri, was given overall command of this force, which later gave loyal service to General Allenby in his coastal advance on Damascus. Lawrence realized at an early stage that, whether from the town or desert, Arabs were brave fighters and were equally prepared to die for their cause, so long as they were paid and were permitted to loot; they were, however, terrified of being subjected to Turkish artillery fire or aerial bombing. Lawrence cleverly countered this fear by supplying them with their own artillery – usually obsolete pieces sent from Egypt and last used in the Boer War, which they loved to fire off regardless of their efficacy. In action they would crowd round their guns and cheer with each firing. Lawrence had to ensure that such action would not invite return fire from the Turks, which would have been more accurate.

The finest description of Feisal's troops comes from Lawrence himself in *Seven Pillars of Wisdom*:

Most of them were young, though the term 'fighting man' in the Hejaz means anyone between twelve and sixty sane enough to shoot. They were a tough-looking crowd, dark coloured, some Negroid. They were physically thin, but exquisitely made, moving with an oiled activity altogether delightful to watch. It did not seem possible that men could be hardier or harder. They would ride immense distances day after day, run through sand and over rocks bare-foot in the heat for hours without pain, and climb their hills like goats. Their clothing was mainly a loose shirt, with sometimes short cotton drawers, and a head shawl usually of red cloth … They were corrugated with bandoliers and fired joy-shots when they could.

There was another group living among the Arabs who were equally down-trodden by the Turks. By 1914 there were 75,000 Jews living in Palestine, the vast majority having fled from Russia and Romania. With the certainty of an outbreak of war across Europe, the Ottoman government attempted to ban further Jewish immigration. With war declared, Turkey was faced with Russia as her main adversary and the Jews in Palestine, mainly those of Russian origin, were immediately subjected to stringent controls and food deprivation. Some 18,000 Jews were expelled from Palestine with around 10,000 being sent to Egypt. Many elected to travel to America. Those that remained encouraged their leaders to establish a number of discreet military training camps in order to protect the kibbutzim, should the need arise. The idea developed further and plans were secretly made to form a Jewish Legion to fight alongside the Allies. As soon as the opportunity arose, over 500 young Jewish men volunteered their service to the British and many went off to Gallipoli to serve in the vitally important Zion Mule Corps.

For those who remained behind, life was harsh. The people struggled, first through a drought and then a plague of locusts, which was followed by an unusually harsh and wet winter. Many of the elderly and young children died of cold and malnutrition to which was added the terror of attacks by emboldened Arabs keen to display their growing resentment against the settling Jews. Later, in 1917, the Turks would decree that all Jews were banned from Jerusalem and Jaffa, which gave rise to the worldwide campaign in aid of the Jews of Palestine, and in Britain to the Balfour Declaration, an agreement for a Jewish National Home in Palestine. The declaration galvanized Jews, especially in America, to volunteer for service with the Allies in Palestine. On 2 February 1917, a battalion of Jewish volunteers marched through the City of London prior to being sent to Egypt to support Allenby's campaign in Palestine. The unit was known as the 38th Battalion of Royal Fusiliers who were to see action in support of Allenby when he drove the Turks northwards across the river Jordan. In general, the Jewish community across Palestine willingly supported the Allied cause to defeat the Turks. Lawrence made no mention of the Jews in his writings, least of all in *Seven Pillars of Wisdom*, but made one generous comment about them in a letter, quoted in *Letters of T. E. Lawrence*. Referring to the lands they colonized he wrote, 'The sooner the Jews farm it the better, their colonies are bright spots in the desert.'

This then was the make-up of the southern part of the Ottoman Empire, the most successful empire of modern times since the four-teenth century, though for the previous twenty-five years, dissension and successful rebellion by subject nations within the empire began to reduce the Turks' influence. By 1913, the empire, ruled over by an insignificant sultan, had rapidly reduced to Turkey, Anatolia and the Arab lands westwards to the Suez Canal. But dissension was now spreading across Arabia – its complex mix of Arabs, Armenians, Jews, Turks and dozens of other ethnic groups and tribes began to rebel and turned to their elderly Emir Hussein and his four prince sons for leadership to throw the Turkish yoke.

2

Turkey Controls the Arabs

The Ottoman Empire had effectively occupied greater Arabia for some four hundred years. The Arab people were also predominantly Muslims and their combined numbers amounted to approximately half the total population of the Ottoman Empire's 20 million subjects. Turkish rule across the Ottoman Empire had long since been achieved by a combination of total military and political control and the slow but steady assimilation, by force if necessary, of all subject peoples. The Turkification of Arabia was nearly complete; street names and public places and announcements were in Turkish but due to the vast distances, the Turkish authorities had always been wary of exerting too much control over the majority of the Arab population who were mainly nomadic. The Turks could rule the major population centres of regional towns but there was no possibility that Turkish rule could ever extend into the deserts: the Arab population was simply too large, spread out and mobile to persecute. Many Arabs held senior positions within the Turkish administration and any widespread control would have created a serious rift.

It was better, for the time being, to pacify and encourage these pro-Turkish Arabs. The sultan, Abdul Hamid, variously known as 'the Damned', for his brutality to anyone he thought might oppose him, or 'the Recluse of Yildez Kiosk' for his refusal to allow Turkey to modernize, permitted his politicians to woo the Arab intelligentsia by building mosques and Islamic schools across the land. While these educated and important Arabs were groomed for positions within the Turkish administration and army, their assimilation was only achieved by becoming surrogate Turks. By the beginning of the twentieth century, the Arabic language was no longer used by the (Turkish) government in Arabia; its use was banned in schools, offices and courts. Young town Arabs joined the Turkish Army in their thousands and politically correct Arabs were commissioned into the officer ranks.

With the British controlling the Suez Canal, the German government now sought to modernize the Turkish Army. The Germans began building a new communication system across the Ottoman Empire,[1] their geologists were exploring for oil and, having persuaded the Turks to consider a narrow gauge trans-Arabia railway to by-pass the canal, the railway was being rapidly expanded southwards. The military benefit of rapidly moving troops and equipment between Constantinople and the two holy cities of Mecca and Medina had long been obvious and construction of the Hejaz railway extension was started in 1901, with the public reason of facilitating the annual Muslim pilgrimage, which every Muslim was and is expected to undertake at least once in their life.

Hussein Ibn Ali, Emir and Sherif of Mecca, a direct descendant from the prophet Mohammed through his daughter Fatima, was the most influential Arab leader at the time, though to render him politically impotent he had been a virtual prisoner of the Turks in Constantinople for fifteen years until 1912. Having originally been 'invited' to Constantinople as a 'guest' with his three small sons, he had been obliged to accept or risk suffering the alternative of 'disappearing' like other Arab leaders, whose bodies tended to reappear, trussed in sacks, from the deep waters of the Bosporus. Sherif Hussein and his family were obliged to live in Constantinople

---

1 The Germans also commenced building a radio station in Yemen in order to ferment anti-British sentiment in Sudan and Eritrea.

on a small salary and his third son, Feisal, would later speak of his childhood as one of some suffering, with meat featuring in their diet just once a week. When in 1912 the Young Turks again took control from Abdul Hamid, all senior political 'guests' were released including Sherif Hussein and his, now, four sons, who all returned to Mecca. These grown sons quickly found that life in Mecca was very different; there were no sporting afternoons or gala balls to attend, only spartan accommodation and no pleasant distractions. It was to get worse, for all the sons were soon attached to desert patrols to harden them for their future roles as Arab leaders. One son was about to have an especially important role to play; Emir Feisal was to create a strong impression on another young man, one from a totally different culture and background. The recently commissioned Second Lieutenant T. E. Lawrence was now on his way to Egypt.

Without doubt, the CUP believed that such a lengthy period of indoctrination had softened Sherif Hussein and converted him into becoming a loyal Turkish puppet. Their belief was in fact wishful thinking – but the sherif had no military resources to withstand the Turks. At the same time, talk of an Arab rebellion began to reach Turkish ears. The centre of unrest was Syria and the Turks' spies discovered a number of Arab secret societies operating across the country. In western Arabia the societies had disbanded the well-known *Akhua* and replaced it with the more militant and secretive *Fetah*, which had its base in Syria. In Mesopotamia many Arab army officers banded together in a new anti-Turkish secret society, the *Ahad*, whose role was to rebel against their Turkish masters when the revolution was eventually called. With their usual efficiency and brutality, the Turkish authorities arrested hundreds of suspects and the process of interrogation and execution began. Prisoners were tortured for information by burning with red-hot irons, beatings, mutilation and starvation. Some of the worst excesses and executions were carried out in front of recently arrested prisoners with the intention of quickly getting names of the societies' other members;

the Turks rarely obtained the information they sought. Few of those arrested survived their ordeals. As added security all Arab-speaking regiments, one-third of the Turkish Army of twenty-five divisions, were despatched to distant locations and placed in every firing line possible.

In January 1915 both *Fetah* and *Ahad* secretly proposed to Hussein that they were ready to rise against the Turks, but only under the leadership and authority of Hussein. News of the Turks' atrocities had already reached the Hejaz; escaping Syrians talked freely of the Turkish oppression and, possibly fearful that the Turks would soon behave similarly in the Hejaz, the Arabs finally agreed to make a stand against the Turks, subject to financial and military assistance from Britain. The effect that Turkey sought was becoming ever more unachievable; their persistence through brutality merely strength-ened the resolve of the Syrian people, a resolve that had begun in Armenia and was now spreading across Arabia.

Meanwhile, with war declared in Europe, Turkey pronounced a holy war against Britain and France. Emir Hussein, Sherif of Mecca, was ordered to extend the proclamation across Arabia; instead he queried the role of Turkey's own ally, Germany, which was just as Christian as the British and French. Turkey responded by blocking Arab use of the railway. Hussein quickly implored the British to supply food to the southern Arab ports and supplies were promptly sent from British-held Egypt with promises of military supplies to enable Arab troops to begin harassing the Turks. The humanitarian act of providing food was greatly appreciated by the Arabs and the promise of military support undoubtedly persuaded Hussein to side with the British. Hussein sent his eldest son, Ali, to sound out the Arabs at Medina – now under the control of the butcher of Armenia, Fakhri Pasha – while the third son, Feisal, went to Syria to assess the potential for a general Arab revolt. Feisal soon suggested that the British should place troops between the Arab and the Turkish main army but the Allies demurred as this was not part of their plan. To gauge the likelihood of Allied success, Feisal decided to assess British strength in the Dardanelles where British and Turkish forces had been locked in a brutal head-on struggle; he observed the massive Turkish losses and decided that the time for a Syrian uprising was right. Unfortunately for the leaders of the pending Syrian insurrection, Turkish intelligence had infiltrated Arab high society and was able to make a number of important arrests. Following interrogation of those arrested, usually to the point of death, the Turks gained the names of a number of leaders in the secret Syrian revolt. These named individuals, whether involved or not, and anyone connected with them, were quickly arrested. Scores were hanged and the opportunity for a Syrian revolt passed. To emphasize Turkish control, and to personally intimidate him, Feisal was escorted to witness some of the executions of those arrested, including hangings of significant Syrian leaders implicated in the unrest. The families of those killed amounted to several thousand people and the majority were exiled to North Africa. Feisal protested and the brutal Turkish commander-in-chief, Jemal, retaliated by threatening to hang Feisal. It was only due to pressure from Feisal's friends in Constantinople that he was freed; it was argued that Feisal would be needed to lead his Arabs against the British at Suez.

Days later, Feisal learned that his father, Emir Hussein, was about to release the Arab Revolt in the southern cities. Unaware of events and believing Hussein would support a Turkish war against Britain, Jemal announced his immediate visit to Medina, and Feisal was to accompany him. Tension ran high at Medina; Jemal and Feisal were taken to watch Arab troops manoeuvring but while Jemal thought they were preparing to support the Turkish Army the Arabs knew that they were shortly to be launched against the Turkish occupiers. A number of senior Arab leaders implored Feisal to allow them to kill the visiting Turks – Feisal refused knowing such action would alert the Turks and lessen Arab chances of success. Jemal returned north without ever realizing how close he came to being assassinated;

in his *Memoirs of a Turkish Statesman* he wrote: 'Had I known the facts, I would have taken Feisal prisoner in Damascus and Ali in Medina. I should have sent a Turkish division to Mecca, seized Sherif Hussein and his sons and nipped the hateful rebellion in the bud.'

Overnight, the military significance of the Suez Canal became of paramount importance to Britain, whose military policy in Europe was seriously dependent upon its ability to bolster its fighting forces with additional troops and supplies from Australia, New Zealand and India; all would need to take the short route via the Suez Canal. Equally determined to thwart Britain was Germany, in accordance with its policy of *drang nach Osten*' or 'push to the East'.

Britain's Suez garrison was small. Under Major General Sir John Maxwell, just four battalions of infantry and one battery of artillery and a company of Royal Engineers were tasked with defending the Suez Canal against any Turkish threat and to ensure that Turkey didn't foster anti-British relations with the Arabs. On 5 November 1914 Britain declared war on Turkey and to ensure that the canal remained totally under British control, Britain deposed the Egyptian government and declared that both Egypt and Cyprus were annexed to the Crown.

Maxwell had much to do; Turkish troops had moved quickly and already occupied El Arish to the east of the canal and Nekhl – an isolated desert village that lay some sixty miles from the British line and now blocked the only overland route to Aqaba. Both Britain and Turkey reinforced their respective positions along the canal, a difficult activity over sandy terrain. Britain soon had over 75,000 troops available, many from India and Australia. The Turks, commanded by Colonel Kress von Kressenstein, Chief of Staff of the VIII Ottoman Army Corps, possessed a similar number of troops and over 100 field guns. The British lacked artillery but relied, instead, on British and French warships at each end of the canal. On 3

February, following several diversions, the Turks led by one of the leaders of the Young Turks group, Jemal Pasha, took advantage of cool weather and a sandstorm to launch a major attack on the canal from Beersheba. The advance across the desert took ten days and most movement took place at night to avoid detection. Just before dawn on 2 February the Turks appeared before Ismailia and advanced on the thin line of British defenders. At the time it was a common joke that the Suez Canal was protecting the British, not the British protecting the Suez Canal. Due to the skill of the British general commanding the line, Major General Wilson, the attack was repulsed at enormous cost to the Turks who lost nearly 1,500 men compared with a loss of 158 British troops. The Turks had deliberately been allowed to reach the canal in one zone, only to find themselves a concentrated target for long-range fire from two French warships, the *Requin* and the *d'Entrecasteaux*. Only four Turks reached the British side of the canal, all were found hiding miserably the following morning. One aim of the Turks and their German commander had been to impress their military might on the Arabs; they failed, and no further all-out attacks were made on the canal. Meanwhile, the British remained on the defensive and easily repulsed a number of minor raids on the canal led by Turkish and German officers. To assist their defence, the British began to build a railway and road that followed the coastal plain north – it was a construction that would greatly assist Allenby in two years' time. As recorded by Jean Beraud Villers, an insignificant intelligence officer in Cairo, Lieutenant T. E. Lawrence, commented at the time:

> The Canal is still holding out and we are forgetting all about it. Turkey, if she is wise, will raid it from time to time and annoy the garrison there, which is huge and lumbersome and creaks so loudly in the joints that you hear them eight hours before they move. So it's quite easy to run down, chuck a bomb at it, and run away without being caught.

General Lord Kitchener knew that the Hejaz was vital to British interests; whoever dominated the area would have control over the vital Red Sea passage. Under Britain's control, Turkish and German plans to infiltrate agents beyond Arabia would be hindered and it would negate the strategic importance of the Turkish railway through the Hejaz to Mecca and onwards to distant Yemen. The British decided to offer Sherif Hussein money and weapons to initiate Arab rebellion against the Turks; the Sherif responded by requesting confirmation of the creation of an Arab state, with himself as sovereign. However, the British offer was restricted to money and weapons. The message was passed to Sherif Hussein, who, without funds or modern weapons, decided to watch and await the outcome of the spreading conflict before declaring his allegiance to one side or the other. Forced into a stalemate, Britain also watched and awaited developments.

Meanwhile, Britain and her Allies became bogged down in Gallipoli and the war on Europe's Western Front was proving impossible for either side to advance without unacceptable losses. Germany was proving a difficult adversary and this gave the Turks greater faith in their ally and encouraged them to make a stand; they badly misread events and accordingly allowed themselves to be sucked into allying themselves with Germany.

In 1915, an Allied expedition was prepared to seize the Bosporus Straits with the intention of capturing Constantinople and opening a Black Sea supply route to Russia. The First Lord of the Admiralty, Winston Churchill, promoted the plan to open the straits using the Royal Navy but execution of the plan failed. In April 1915 a force of British, Australian and New Zealand troops landed at various points on the east coast of the Gallipoli Peninsula while a French force landed on the Asian side of the straits. Meanwhile, the Turks had not been idle; alerted to the threat, they reinforced the whole coastline with five times as many troops as had previously guarded the area. The following landing in August at Suvla on the west coast of the peninsula resulted in severe Allied casualties preventing the Allies from making any important gains. Allied cooperation was chaotic; there was lack of coordination between land and naval forces, which resulted in a premature naval attack without adequate support from the army. After months of increasing Allied casualties and no territorial gains, the Allied commander, Sir Ian Hamilton, was replaced by Sir Charles Munro and the Allies withdrew from the area on 9 January 1916.

Britain's Sir Mark Sykes and France's M. Georges Picot had not been idle in anticipation of their countries' eventual victory over Germany and Turkey. Both worked on a plan for the division of Syria following the eventual Turkish defeat. France desperately wanted Syria to complement her North African territories; Britain had no such territorial intentions. By the time of the First World War, the French language was the language of culture and commerce across much of the near East and French language schools abounded. France was the strongest trading nation throughout the area and with its generous finance it controlled the banks, docks, the tobacco industry, railways, electricity and mineral mines. In the spring of 1916 the Sykes–Picot agreement was secretly signed, which would reward France with the greater part of Syria. Post conflict, Britain would take Mesopotamia (Iraq) while Palestine would be controlled under international agreement. No thought was given to the Arabs having any say in the division of spoils, perhaps because the negotiators believed that as the Hejaz was more than 1,000 miles from Syria the Arabs would not be interested in the outcome. The overall scene was set for a long period of deception and notwithstanding the secret Sykes–Picot agreement, the Arabs would be encouraged to revolt against the Turks in the erroneous belief that they would have a strong voice in their own post-war destiny. The promises by the British to the Arabs were now nothing more than dead paper and the aftermath of the Sykes–Picot deception would undermine Arab trust in European politicians for decades.[2]

2 Dr Abu Jaber Karmel, ex-Jordanian Foreign Secretary: 'It was the biggest betrayal between the British and Arabs in history.' Personal comment, Channel Four Television.

In May 1916, a totally unexpected event forced Emir Hussein and his sons to decide where their loyalty lay; the British had just suffered a serious defeat at Kut in Mesopotamia, which encouraged the Turks to strengthen their positions throughout Arabia. Sherif Hussein was not prepared to tolerate such a strengthening of Turkish control and with his sons' cooperation, though without much military skill or weaponry, they prepared to attack the Turkish garrisons stationed at the holy cities of Mecca, Medina and Jeddah. On 9 June, Emir Hussein gave the order for the attack to begin. The revolt began by the besieging of the Turkish garrisons at Mecca and Jeddah and, at the same time, the revolutionary forces of the Hejaz attacked the Turks wherever they could, notwithstanding the small quantity of arms and ammunition that they possessed. In the stifling heat, the Turks were taken by complete surprise, as was the British High Command when the news eventually reached them.

The Arabs, brave as they were, were unprepared for modern warfare and their eventual victory took several weeks and cost many lives. Sherif Hussein personally supervised the attack on Mecca, a city of narrow streets and low mud-brick buildings, and although most of the city quickly fell to the Arabs, the Turks were able to hold two well-built stone forts from which they constantly fired artillery shells into the Arab positions, including Sherif Hussein's palace. Then, some two weeks into the fighting, the Turks made the mistake of firing into the mosque of the Kaaba, the most sacred Muslim shrine. The shell damaged the holy black stone and killed a dozen Arabs at prayer. The sherif's subjects were so incensed that, armed only with swords and daggers, they rushed the two Turkish forts and after much hand-to-hand fighting the Turks were overrun and the position taken from them.

The outcome of the battle for Jeddah was more positive. Being assisted from the sea by Captain Boyle and his five armed merchant ships, the British and Arabs were able, over a period of two weeks, to bombard the town. The shell-shocked Turks duly surrendered and over one thousand Turks, together with their German officers, were taken prisoner. All were handed over to the British for a period of lengthy imprisonment in Egypt. Due to the presence of German officers at Jeddah, the Arabs immediately set about destroying the sacred Tomb of the Grandmother as the holy shrine had been seen and touched by German Christians. The significance of the tomb was reflected in the name of Jeddah, which means 'grandmother'.

The Arab attack on Medina was less successful. Under the command of Emirs Feisal and Ali, the attack commenced on the same day as that on Mecca. They initially attacked the Turks' railway line into the city destroying sufficient lengths of track to render the garrison immobile. The Arabs quickly took control of the outlying area and occupied the town's perimeter before they became pinned down by heavy Turkish firepower. The Turks then withdrew to a position in the town centre around the sacred Tomb of Mohammed, which they hoped the Arabs would not shell, and awaited the outcome. The Arabs believed they were in control of the siege but as dawn broke, the besieged Turks mounted a well-organized counterattack on the main Arab force camped near the suburb of Awali. First they attacked Awali itself, firing machine guns into the flimsy houses and then into the fleeing women and children. The Turkish general and his troops were veterans of several Armenian massacres and proceeded to slaughter the inhabitants; some fled to their homes only for the Turks to fire the houses and, faced with death by gunfire or death in their own homes, those that had tried to hide were burnt to death. In the tradition of the Turkish method of controlling rebellious people, there were no survivors. News of the massacre rapidly spread among the armed Arabs who regrouped then attacked the main Turkish position, which is what the Turks had intended. The guns opened fire on the frenzied Arabs, who had never previously experienced artillery fire, and the Turks' accuracy quickly decimated the attacking Arab force. The Arabs nevertheless maintained their attack until nightfall but by then they were running low on ammunition and withdrew, unable to continue the fight. The Turks quickly repaired the damaged railway line and were soon able to receive supplies and reinforcements. To assert their total control over the city, and with the suburb of Awali and its people destroyed, the Turks then drove most of the remaining 30,000 Arab inhabitants out of the city and into the desert. Over time, these refugee people made their way to a number of Arab towns and cities.

Meanwhile, the local Arab chief at Rabegh, the port where British supplies were being landed, had decided that the Turks were most likely to win any war and so stopped supplies to Medina and Mecca. Feisal sent his elder brother, Ali, to Rabegh to rout the rebellious chief, who promptly fled into the hills. Surrounded by stores, Ali also chose to do nothing rather than support the growing Arab cause, which left a discouraged Feisal to carry on the revolt single-handed. Aware that things were not going as planned, Feisal's army quickly lost enthusiasm for the fight and began to return to their homes.

Fortuitously, just as Feisal's enthusiasm was faltering, a number of strong personalities arrived, including Lieutenant T. E. Lawrence, General Allenby and two French Army officers, Captains Raho and Pisani. All were to play a significant part in the Arabs' war against the Turks, and all were aware of the Arabs' sincere belief that they were fighting for their future – freedom from the oppressive and cruel Ottoman Empire and for the freedom to run Arabia as their own country according to their own laws and customs. It was a cause with which these players in the theatre of the forthcoming desert war were to have considerable sympathy, but neither they, nor the Arabs, suspected that the British and French had already signed the Sykes–Picot agreement, which had set in motion the plan to dispose of much of Arabia without consulting the Arab leaders. With the Arab Revolt under way and with thousands of Turkish troops now engaged against the Arabs, influential British military figures began to consider the possibility of attacking Turkey and Germany through Palestine. They advocated that it would be a quicker and less costly resolution, both in terms of finance and human lives, than seeking to defeat Germany solely along the Western Front. Once in place, the Palestine force under Allenby would rapidly expand and soon become the second largest force of the Allies, after the Western Front.

To the Arabs, the single most important motive that caused the Arabs to revolt was the sincere belief that they would obtain full independence once the war was over. Emir Hussein and his advisers believed the promises given by Britain were firm and beyond doubt, especially as the promises were backed up in the form of official documents. Conversely, to the Allies, the Arab Revolt was little more than a helpful sideshow to distract Turkish troops, and promises could be broken if circumstances changed.

3

T. E Lawrence: An Apparently Insignificant Englishman

*L*awrence was not Lawrence. He was born the illegitimate son of Thomas Chapman, an aristocratic landowner with an extensive estate at Castletown Devlin in Ireland. The Chapman family believed their estate had originally been given to their ancestors at the instigation of a distant and famous relative, Sir Walter Raleigh. In 1885, Thomas Chapman abandoned his strictly religious and generally unpopular wife Edith, who was known locally as the 'Holy viper', together with their four dour daughters and his family estate. The cause of Thomas Chapman's desertion was the arrival from Scotland of the family's new, fresh-faced and cheerful young governess, Sarah Maddern. Sarah's mother was a Miss Maddern, who had become pregnant with Sarah after meeting a Scandinavian sailor named Junner or Junnor. It is believed Sarah used her mother's surname when seeking employment.

It was not long before Thomas and Sarah resolved each other's loneliness and despite an age difference of fifteen years, their relationship soon became one of master and extramarital mistress. The young governess was illegitimate and had initially been brought up by her ageing grandparents following the death of her mother when Sarah was only nine years old. Latterly, Sarah had lived with her uncle, a church minister, and his wife, until she was accepted for the position of governess with the Chapmans. Having lived in a strict religious household during her formative years, Sarah was perfectly familiar with a regime of authoritarian rules and discipline – qualities she never gave up – so her intense dalliance with her new employer, especially as he already had a wife and four daughters, was all the more inexplicable.

When the heavily pregnant Sarah could no longer fulfil her duties, she was required by an increasingly suspicious Mrs Chapman to resign her position. Instead of returning to her family in Scotland, she took rooms in Dublin, forty miles from the Chapman estate. Mr Chapman then found it necessary to make frequent business visits to the city and with classic inevitability, their relationship soon formally came to the attention of Mrs Chapman. Unfortunately, Sarah was seen shopping by Mrs Chapman's butler who, tasked with tracking down where the pregnant governess was living, secretly followed her home; there he observed his former master and Sarah effectively living together. The butler reported back to Mrs Chapman and the deceit burst into the open. Mrs Chapman went into a rage and her husband had no option but to abandon his family. Legally, Mrs Chapman could sue for divorce but would not; it was against her moral beliefs and according to the Matrimonial Causes Act of 1857, Thomas could not obtain a divorce as his wife had not engaged in any extra-marital misconduct. This uncomfortable and irresolvable stalemate forced Thomas and Sarah into the only course of action available to them, which was to flee. They randomly took the surname Lawrence as their new family name and registered it by deed poll.

Over the next few years they could not settle anywhere for long lest they were discovered so they moved house regularly. They nevertheless had five sons, the first, Montague Robert, was born in Dublin in 1885, Thomas Edward at Tremadoc in North Wales in 1888, William George at Kircudbright in Scotland in 1889, Frank Helier in the Channel Islands in 1893 and finally, Arnold Walter in 1900 in Oxford. It was at 2 Polstead Road in Oxford that the 'Lawrence' family finally settled and made their home. The concept of living together and having children outside wedlock would have been totally unacceptable to Oxford's 'decent' middle-class society so they posed as a discreet married couple and kept a low social profile. Money was scarce as Thomas still had to support his family in Ireland. Sarah had become a strict disciplinarian and ran the household on a tight reign, alcohol was banned and Thomas travelled on foot or by bicycle. Apart from their love for each other, they shared a mutual passion for books and learning, which all the Lawrence boys inherited; this was a most useful asset when the boys attended the High School in Oxford. The family's financial plight was eventually eased in 1914 when Thomas's wealthy cousin died, leaving Thomas to inherit the family baronetcy and considerable assets; there was then sufficient money available for the five Lawrence sons to be given £5,000 each, a large sum of money at the time.

The young Thomas Edward had few friends at school. His main friend was Charles Beeson, a quiet lad who readily attached himself to the more exciting Thomas. The two spent much of their time visiting churches around Oxford making brass rubbings and then scraping and digging around the numerous building sites across the city looking for buried artefacts. The two sixteen-year-old lads began to run a profitable business paying workmen a few pence for their finds and then selling them on to such respected outlets as Oxford's famous Ashmolean Museum; Lawrence's interest in archaeology had begun. The Ashmolean was to record its appreciation when its Annual Report for 1906 stated that 'owing to the generosity of Mr T. E. Lawrence and Mr C. F. Beeson, who have by incessant watchfulness secured everything of antiquarian value which has been found, the most interesting finds have been added to the local antiquities in the Museum.' The two boys' finds can still be seen at the museum today. It was at this time that Thomas Edward, known to his family as Ned, only answered to 'Lawrence' to everyone outside the family home.

Two events then occurred that greatly affected Lawrence's self-perception. Firstly, he broke a leg in an informal wrestling bout and it appears the accident stopped his growth, leaving his body slightly lop-sided and never to catch up in growth with, as Lawrence perceived it, his large head. His head size was normal and in perfect proportion with his body, but he did have a shovel jaw, which would have given him the impression in a mirror that it was disproportionate. Secondly, he appears to have suddenly rebelled against his parents. The discovery of his birth circumstances may well have been the cause of his unforeseen and rebellious behaviour. In 1906, aged 16 years, he disappeared and enlisted as a boy soldier, until his father discovered his whereabouts and collected him. Lawrence was greatly relieved; he had been severely shaken by the army's bullying discipline, which was mindless and overpowering, even compared with that of his authoritarian mother. It is possible that he could not cope with army life and so contacted his parents; in any event he was grateful to be able to return to Oxford. Perhaps he had tried to flee disharmony at home; Lawrence alludes to this in his later letters but there is little evidence to indicate why he should want or need to escape an apparently stable family home and possibly end his on-going friendship with Beeson. And besides, it is by no means certain that Lawrence knew he was illegitimate at this time, and if so, whether it had any effect on him. Although he later claimed that he had known of his illegitimacy from an early age, he never divulged how he knew.

Like most children struggling for attention within a large family, Lawrence had learned how to fabricate and embellish minor events and stories. As a child, he learned that extroverted behaviour, such as engaging in hazardous tree climbing and swimming across rivers and lakes, would earn his parents' approval. Lawrence's propensity to 'gild the lily', especially when recalling interesting events, was to develop and become an important characteristic of his life and, being one of a houseful of children competing for attention, he would have seen nothing wrong in what he was doing.

Lawrence's brief encounter with the army as a boy soldier was one of the first where his accounts of the experience are deliberately contradictory. He either admitted his army experience and told various lurid tales of bullying or denied it completely, depending on how impressionable his audience was. He then frequently claimed that Lord Morris, who went on to open the Morris car factory, had personally constructed his bicycle when Morris had earlier owned a cycle shop in Oxford. Lord Morris always denied the story. Lawrence the youth successfully created a personal smokescreen around himself, perhaps because he so disliked being below average height at five feet four inches. He overcame his shortness by teasing, irreverence and story-telling. At school he had been popular but disdained popularity; he focused on lone activities such as cycling or walking long distances while eschewing all forms of organized sport. Meanwhile, the pomposity of youth and a penchant for teasing and practical joking were strong traits in him. For example, he would show off human bones taken from crypts and he enjoyed secretly rabbiting in other peoples' gardens.

Familial frustration brought about by his mother demanding that the Lawrence household was run on strict biblical lines may have led Lawrence into undertaking blatant or unusual physical exercise, possibly as a distraction; these daredevil experiences would set the pattern for his adult life. He once explored the underground watercourse that ran beneath Oxford. He repeatedly canoed the flooded river Cherwell in the bleakest depths of winter and broke the ice on ponds to go for a swim, seeming to his friends not to care whether he would survive a particular test. He was physically, and sometimes psychologically, the boy who never grew up. These developing characteristics of Lawrence's behaviour would soon stand him in very good stead in the appalling conditions he would later face in the vast and arid deserts of Arabia.

His life-long interest in antiquities began to develop into a fascination with castles, especially those of the Crusaders. Through his prodigious reading he had already developed an early affinity with the Arab people and wrote: 'The Arabs made a chivalrous appeal to my young instinct and whilst still at the High School in Oxford, already I thought to make them into a nation.' In 1907 Lawrence pursued his interest in the ancient and medieval world and enrolled at Jesus College, Oxford to read history. He soon became known as an eccentric and a non-conformist; he joined the Officers Training Corps where he displayed a casual attitude to discipline and an inability to appear smart – yet he became a first-class marksman and could effortlessly out-perform the other cadets in matters requiring physical endurance. While an undergraduate, his bizarre behaviour continued to ensure his isolation. He could behave evasively and avoid contact with strangers, only opening to them once he felt safe, and he often used his intellectual prowess to remain aloof or dominate a conversation, as it suited him. He attended college dining halls for meals but not to eat. He would put in an appearance at sports events but not participate, work at night while others slept. He never drank alcohol, which he regarded as a poison and he had little respect for anyone who over-indulged in his presence. Certainly, his fellow students never understood him; many avoided him while others accepted that behind his eccentricity there was a possible genius. His behaviour and dress marked him as 'different' and some of his activities caused the university authorities the occasional headache. He would climb the university's spires, which was forbidden, and on one occasion fired off a revolver in another student's room – the rounds were blanks – and as no damage was caused, no action was taken. One stunt that especially amused him was to gain entry to the college wine cellar and randomly move around rare wines from their allocated racks. Without seeking permission, he also corrected some of the stone carvings outside the Iffley Road church in Oxford, which he knew were inaccurate.

He soon realized he was the intellectual equal of the best Oxford academics; he could read several books a day and possessed a prodigious memory, which enabled him to easily 'hold his own' in any conversation or debate. He studied the military classics including Clausewitz, the twenty-five volumes of Napoleon's despatches and then moved on to the work of Bourcet, Guibert and Saxe, who all advocated indirect and unconventional warfare, before taking on the eighteenth-century manuals of arms and the theories of the Roman military secretary, Procopius. His mentor at Oxford, the noted archaeologist and Keeper of Oxford's Ashmolean Museum, Dr D. G. Hogarth, wrote of Lawrence, 'to think as fast or as far as he thinks is not easy, and still less easy is it to follow up with swift action.'

Lawrence was also different because he was remarkably free of the conventional restrictions of the age. Most young men of his class were destined for formal careers and they accepted the rigidity of an army commission or profession, they married and had families, and they accepted financial liabilities or inherited the traditions and responsibilities of their age. Lawrence had none of these restrictions. His wanderings in France and then Syria gave him his freedom and this made him different from his peers. He would later use his intellectual acuity to belittle those in authority whom he could not respect, while at the same time his perceived odd behaviour, developing powers of endurance and prodigious memory (he could quote the classics and archaeological works word perfectly), ensured he was ever-prominent and eminently suitable for the task he would soon undertake.

Lawrence's real interest, however, was archaeology, especially that of castles. Initially, tales of crusading knights were a powerful diversion from his mother's strict rule at home and deepened his interest. Having visited and studied every twelfth-century castle of France, it was natural that he would be drawn to those of the Middle East, especially the Crusader castles. At Jesus College, Oxford he developed his own theory that the castles of the Middle East were all of original design at a time when academic historians collectively believed they had been copied from the earlier European design; he chose as the subject for his final degree thesis the title 'The influence of the Crusades on the medieval military architecture of Europe'. To obtain definitive proof, he gained official permission from the occupying Turkish authorities to travel around the Middle East to conduct his research. He sought out Dr Hogarth for advice on travelling the area. When Hogarth strongly advised taking a guide and carriage, Lawrence's response was typical: he said he would guide himself and walk everywhere.

However he travelled, his tour was remarkable. In the summer of 1910 he travelled from Haifa on Palestine's north coast to the Taurus Mountains and then trekked to Urfa near the river Euphrates in northern Mesopotamia. During his time there, his final long holiday from university, he initially claimed he walked everywhere in European clothes wearing stout brown walking boots. He later maintained he wore Arab clothes while learning Arabic as he went, though as late as 1912 he wrote that he could still not speak Arabic. In any event, in conducting his research he must have covered well over 1,000 miles, and if it was on foot in the height of summer then it was an even more astonishing achievement. He visited some forty castles, claimed he was attacked and robbed and, having suffered several bouts of malaria, he arrived back in England late for the beginning of his next term at Oxford. Lawrence's assertion of robbery was certainly one of his better stories and the tale would grow in complexity and bravery depending on the enthusiasm of his audience. Lawrence's own letters are at variance with the tale; he confirms wearing European clothes, hiring guides and a carriage, staying in hotels and being slightly injured – or seriously injured (depending on which letter one reads) – when the carriage overturned.

Lawrence's account, and the effect he intended it to have on others, is a classic behavioural trait of Lawrence. It is possible that it was the development of this story that made him aware of the power of exaggeration and embellishment as a means of influencing others; it certainly proved to him that such behaviour brought considerable gain. The initial exciting tale told on his return to Oxford soon spread beyond Lawrence's friends and one person who was deeply impressed was Dr Hogarth, who had tasked Lawrence with collecting Hittite seals on behalf of the museum. Lawrence was aware that Hogarth was a potential sponsor. He had collected the seals for Hogarth but the unwitting price would be a future obligation for the Ashmolean Museum to sponsor Lawrence.

As far as the university was concerned, it mattered not that Lawrence returned late for his college term because everyone was in awe of his adventures. His completed thesis was widely acclaimed and resulted in the award of a First Class degree and a postgraduate scholarship worth £50 per year to prepare a thesis on medieval pottery. The study of pottery was not what Lawrence intended. Hogarth was meanwhile in Carchemish, the ruined Hittite city on the Syrian bank of the Euphrates, where he was in charge of excavations and already working with a full team. In some desperation Lawrence offered his services free of cost to the museum but his request was declined. When Hogarth returned to Oxford, Lawrence was poised ready to have his obligation to Hogarth redeemed. Hogarth had been completely taken by Lawrence's earlier story and not only offered him a position at Carchemish, but gave him a four-year £100 Magdalene College research grant to work there on behalf of the British Museum. Lawrence set off towards the end of 1910 and would spend the next four years working primarily as an assistant at the British Museum's excavation at Carchemish and on other archaeological sites across the Middle East such as the Egyptian site run by Sir Flinders Petrie. Lawrence was able to memorize every artifact and its history. Robert Graves recorded in *Lawrence and the Arabs* that Field Marshal Allenby, a keen amateur archaeologist, wrote during the war: 'When Lawrence and I talked archaeology it was always Father Lawrence talking to a little schoolboy, I listened and learned.'

His initial role at Carchemish was as the odd-job administrator with responsibility for keeping records and managing the local labour force, which he relished as he was able to learn local Arab dialects. As the excavations progressed, more secure rooms were required to house the growing number of artefacts and visitors, who occasionally included the wives of officials and the explorer, Miss Gertrude Bell. The archaeologists' accommodation came under increasing pressure. In 1911, prior to one of Miss Bell's visits, an application was made to the local Turkish administrator for additional buildings, but permission was granted only for one room. Lawrence interpreted the permission by having a large U-shaped building constructed that contained numerous rooms, but all having access onto a central amenity area so as to comply with the exact Turkish permission. The central meeting area was temporarily relaid with a recently discovered mosaic floor and the whole room then decorated with appropriate artefacts. Miss Bell's visit caused great interest among the numerous Arab workers who all knew Lawrence and Miss Bell were unmarried. They drew the wrong conclusion from her visit and prepared a marriage celebration for the unsuspecting couple. When Miss Bell departed the same evening, without the anticipated wedding, there was a 'great clamour' and Lawrence was hard-pressed to restore order in the village, where it was believed Lawrence had been rejected; it took many years before Hogarth let on to Miss Bell what had happened that day. It was a tale which greatly amused the intrepid lady explorer.

By 1913 Lawrence was gaining experience as a professional archaeologist, now working under Leonard Wooley, Hogarth's deputy. It was in October that one of Lawrence's brothers visited him at Carchemish; Will was passing through on his travels to India and spent several days being shown the sights by his brother. Lawrence recounted the implausible tale that one of his friends, Busrawi Agha, had been responsible for the massacre of some 8,000 rebels just four months earlier and that Lawrence and Agha had been planning the sacking of Aleppo. The massacre referred to had indeed taken place but in 1909, when Lawrence was still in England. Such a lurid tale was another early example of how Lawrence embellished the truth to impress those around him. In any event, Lawrence was in his element and in December 1913 wrote of his contentment:

> Then there are the digs, with dozens of wonderful things to find; and hosts of beautiful things in the villages and towns to fill one's house with. Not to mention Hittite seal-hunting in the country round about, and the Euphrates to rest in when one is over-hot. It is a place where one eats lotus every day.

Wooley and Lawrence were both adept at gaining the support of their growing workforce; such was the local confidence in the two Englishmen's fairness that they were unofficially appointed as local judges in order to resolve disputes. They also paid for their workers' finds – the greater the value of the treasure, the greater the financial reward – and the excavations accordingly progressed with vigour and enthusiasm. Notwithstanding his personal prejudice, Lawrence made the effort to make the acquaintance of some nearby German archaeologists; he disliked their arrogance and formed strong negative views about German support for the Turks, believing German interference was to the detriment of the Arab people. The Germans paid their men a minimum wage, didn't bother to learn their names and treated omissions or mistakes with a beating. On one occasion, following a dispute concerning deductions from his pay for bread not received, a worker in the German camp protested, which resulted in an overseer whipping the protester. The man's Kurdish friends retaliated by hurling stones at the overseer who sought to defend himself by wildly firing his revolver and the German onlookers joined in the battle. Hearing the firing, Wooley and Lawrence rushed to the scene and after a good hour of negotiation, peace was restored. Meanwhile, the Germans had telegraphed their base at Aleppo for help but the message was misinterpreted – 'Firing' was read as 'Fire' – and in due course the local fire brigade attended. The whole incident petered out and Lawrence and Wooley were later nominated for a Turkish award for their bravery; both refused. Lawrence wrote an anonymous letter to *The Times* bringing to the attention of the British public news that German engineers were 'taking' stones from the archaeological site at Carchemish for their Berlin to Baghdad railway. Regardless of the substance of his allegation, the British people were taken in and seeds of anti-German sentiment had been successfully sown.

Lawrence took every opportunity to wander further afield; in the winter rainy season between December and March he visited Syria and, apart from studying antiquities and preparing notes for a proposed book, he began to meet members of the various Arab groups who were secretly preparing resistance to Turkish rule. Their ideas and controlled fanaticism sparked his enthusiasm for the concept of an Arab revolt; it was a concept that would soon become an obsession for Lawrence and world events were about to facilitate the conversion of this dream into reality, but for the moment, how to achieve his dream continued to elude Lawrence. For the time being he concentrated his mind on his new book, which he had decided would be named *Seven Pillars of Wisdom*. It was to be a guidebook about the main Near Eastern cities of Aleppo, Beirut, Cairo, Constantinople, Damascus, Medina and Smyrna.

In January 1914, having returned to work at Carchemish, Lawrence learned that his superior, Wooley, was to undertake a survey of the Sinai desert. The expedition leader would be Captain Newcombe of the Royal Engineers. When it was realized that Wooley was unable to complete the whole expedition due to the busy schedule at Carchemish, Lawrence persuaded Hogarth that he should be allowed to go too. And so Lawrence became acquainted with Captain Newcombe who was already well known as an accomplished expedition leader and competent mapmaker. Newcombe was to survey various biblical routes that lay in a particular area of Turkish-administered Sinai, which controlled the desert approaches to the British-controlled Suez Canal. To the alarm of the British in Cairo, the Turks had earlier surreptitiously moved their border posts nearer to the canal and banished a civilian survey team from the area. Lawrence was in no doubt that the purpose of Newcombe's intended survey was military with the archaeologists acting as a civilian front. Newcombe's group were, as far as the Turks knew, tasked with tracing biblical routes and sites where Moses had kept his people in hiding but, according to Lawrence, he was to prepare up-to-date maps for the army. The expedition was able to travel widely and even managed to visit the ruins at both Petra and Maan, places that would become significant once the Arab Revolt commenced. Lawrence was especially fascinated by the hidden city of Petra, then virtually unknown to the outside world; he spent a day digging near the front of the main Treasury building – and missed finding the disguised entrance to the secret vaults by just a few feet. The entrance was to remain hidden until accidentally discovered in October 2004.

Lawrence's Sinai experience resulted in his first attempt at publishing. The work was co-written with Wooley and titled *The Wilderness of Zin*; it was well received. Lawrence had enjoyed the Sinai venture and its associated secrecy made the whole trip stimulating and very different from conventional archaeology by being quasi-military yet 'unofficial'. There can be little doubt that being 'behind enemy lines' stimulated Lawrence's enthusiasm for excitement. Whether or not Lawrence obtained sufficient material and data for mapmaking remains open to doubt; he claims he did, yet in 1915 when General Murray was planning his attack across Sinai there were no accurate maps readily available and Murray was obliged to organize an aerial survey to rectify the deficiency. The deficiency was most probably a simple case of one army department not knowing what another possessed. Nevertheless, Lawrence admired Newcombe and got on well with him; he had persuasive skills that were new to Lawrence, skills based on sound military training but highly flavoured with boldness and a flair for audacity that Lawrence admired. Lawrence avidly learned as much as he could from New-combe and the two became friends for life.

At about the same time, Lawrence was indirectly involved in another event of considerable military and political significance. The northern Turkish town of Erzerum was being besieged by the pro-Russian Armenians and since Carchemish, Lawrence knew the various personalities involved on both sides. By unknown means, Lawrence was asked for this information via discreet official sources in London. The information was passed on by the British government to the Russians who were able to make contact with the main Turkish players and, having bribed them, Erzerum subsequently fell without a battle. Little is known of this matter other than a brief mention by Lawrence in *Seven Pillars of Wisdom* and by Graves and Hart in their biographies. In any event, the Russians expressed their gratitude, which improved Lawrence's standing in London's corridors of power.

Before departing Sinai, Lawrence fortuitously visited Aqaba, home of a small Turkish garrison and a site of genuine archaeological interest to Lawrence. Being situated at the head of the Red Sea corridor and a significant port in historical terms, Aqaba was now derelict and deserted apart from a small resident Turkish garrison. Lawrence was uncertain of Aqaba's time-line but he knew it had been an important trading crossroads for thousands of years. On a more practical note he also needed to take bearings at sea level to substantiate the survey records. Naturally the Turkish commander was highly suspicious of this English archaeologist who spent time walking around the Turkish position and taking photographs and measurements. Lawrence was swiftly banned from using his camera and ordered from the vicinity. Just eight miles south-west of Aqaba and only a quarter of a mile offshore lay the tiny Pharaoh's Island; it was once a Crusader fortification but now lay in ruin. On his arrival at the shoreline, and with the island tantalizingly close, Lawrence had his plan to cross to the island impeded. The local Turkish officer ordered all the available boats to be hauled away from the waterline to prevent Lawrence reaching the ruins; Lawrence responded by swimming out to the island supported by a makeshift raft. He took his banned camera and spent several hours examining the ruins before returning to the mainland. Lawrence later told his friends, untruthfully, that the waters were 'shark infested'. Lawrence's intention was then to travel back to Carchemish but, with war imminent, the party returned to England in the spring of 1914.

Without doubt, Lawrence had developed a strong fascination with Syria and the desert, he had spent valuable time talking to the Arab workers and supervisors and learned to fluently speak the various local Arab dialects. Lawrence found inner peace living among the Arabs; to them he was a flamboyant and important person, and few Arabs were taller. He absorbed both their culture and their hatred of their Turkish overlords; slowly the people's cause, freedom for the Arab people, was to become his cause. Lawrence had earlier fallen in love with France where he spent many happy holidays, until he realized that the French were intending to control Syria. He discussed the problem with Wooley, who later wrote in *Lawrence by his Friends*:

> He hated the Turks because they were the masters of Syria and treated the Arabs as inferiors; that their place was to be taken by a non Arab power was monstrous. Long before the Sykes–Picot agreement drove him into a deliberate policy of frustration, Lawrence was an enemy of France.

Back in England, a country now feverishly preparing for war, Lawrence went home to Oxford where he attempted to join the local Officers' Training Corps, but was rejected on medical grounds. He then travelled to London with the same intention – only to be rejected on grounds of height and weak stature, along with Jimmy Wilde, who was deemed by the army doctors to be of 'emaciated appearance' despite the fact that Wilde was then the unbeaten World flyweight boxing champion. The two rejections depressed Lawrence who responded by burning his initial draft of *Seven Pillars of Wisdom*. The unfinished manuscript was never rewritten. This draft was a book about travel in the desert but it was clearly very different from the post-war versions of the same title; nevertheless, Lawrence had already decided on the title of his book even if subsequent events were to force a change of content. This act of self-punishment might well have created an unwitting pattern for the later 'loss' of his *Seven Pillars of Wisdom* manuscript of the Arab Revolt. Lawrence would later claim that it had been stolen at Reading railway station. At the time he was similarly depressed by events after the desert war.

October 1914 found Lawrence in the Geographical Section of London's War Office engaged in drawing road and track maps of Sinai. Lawrence's life was about to change irrevocably. The British Army urgently needed people with Lawrence's skills and local knowledge of the Sinai region to update the military High Command, now busy preparing to embark for Egypt, which was officially known as the English protectorate of Egypt and commanded by Lord Kitchener. At the time it was anticipated that Turkey would soon formally ally itself with Germany. With Turkey controlling the Sinai desert, this alliance placed the Suez Canal in grave danger. Hearing of Lawrence's plight, Dr Hogarth of the Ashmolean Museum in Oxford, and recently appointed to British Intelligence, recommended to the Head of the Geographical Section of the General Staff, Colonel Hedley, that Lawrence should be recruited. A few weeks later Hogarth enquired into Lawrence's progress; he was informed by Hedley that Lawrence was running the entire department; it was news that came as no surprise to Hogarth. Now twenty-six years old, Lawrence was duly appointed to the army as a second lieutenant, though without having undergone any military training. On 1 November Turkey declared war on the Allies and Lawrence was sent to the General Headquarters at Cairo.

He was billeted at the Savoy Hotel, which had been commandeered for the growing number of British officers and advisers. He was to spend the next two years working in the army's Intelligence Department map room where his knowledge of Arabic and the area were invaluable. He found himself under the command of Colonel Clayton, whom Lawrence liked and respected, and Lawrence's friend, Newcombe, who was now a major and Clayton's deputy. Clayton was a highly regarded and competent intelligence officer who would render expert service to the local commander, General Maxwell and his successors, including General Allenby. Lawrence matched Clayton for intellectual acuity and respected him greatly; Lawrence knew Clayton was the eyes and ears of those in authority and accordingly followed his master's footsteps with care. Although soon promoted to the temporary rank of staff captain within the headquarters, Lawrence always insisted that he was a civilian, and to the annoyance of the military establishment wore his uniform in such a way that brought little grace to its wearer, usually without the appropriate hat or Sam Browne belt.

Lawrence's open lack of tact and respect for certain senior officers around him irritated many, but the game amused Lawrence and his close friends. Lawrence's circle of friends included Stewart Newcombe and Leonard Wooley, Philip Graves, *The Times* correspondent from Turkey, and two Members of Parliament, George Lloyd and Aubrey Herbert. He was also friendly with Major Stirling DSO, MC, who was an intelligence officer at Ismailia. The group were known as 'the intrusives' and 'academic thinkers'; they were distinctly unpopular with the gin-drinking social scene-stealers who made up the bulk of British officers in Cairo, men who were enjoying a comfortable war and thought that the awaited advance against Turkey would be 'fun'. They resented any analysis of their military competence, especially by academic civilians freshly into uniform. They were men, Lawrence wrote, who made trivialities into man's work and when more important work arrived they made it trivial.

Invariably his masters overlooked this boyish trait of not

respecting rank, simply because Lawrence's outstanding ability at overseeing the printing of maps, decoding Turkish military telegrams and his skill when interpreting prisoners' statements was way beyond the skills of most of his colleagues. Probably due to boredom, Lawrence began collating obscure but interesting details of military intelligence, which Newcombe edited and then published as the *Cairo Review*. Specialists like Cornwallis, Philip Graves (author Robert Graves' older brother) and MacDonnell all contributed to the publication, as did Lawrence, some under their own names, some anonymously. Lawrence duly published sketches, usually about the Turks, which showed the depth of his knowledge concerning the Turks and their allies.

His incisive comments, which he added to senior officers' reports, caused equal annoyance to the unwary. He frequently added personal details relating to Turkish officers or dismissed suggestions by senior officers by adding remarks such as 'impossible', especially if he thought a senior officer was lazy, or 'nonsense' where they were clearly wrong. Lawrence would also refer to historical facts to prove his point and senior officers were often uncertain whether Lawrence was serious or joking at their expense. With over sixty colonels and general officers and their staff now in Egypt, all convinced of their collective and absolute excellence and busy sending each other memoranda, Lawrence became seriously frustrated by the malaise of their inaction. He avoided the eternal rounds of card games, parades and official lunches for senior officers and steadily gained a reputation for being a snob. He always had the perfect and truthful defence for his unusual behaviour – he was a civilian without any form of military training, earning Lawrence and other academics working in army intelligence the label 'temporary gentlemen'.

But Lawrence knew more about Arabia than anyone else in Cairo. He understood the Arabs and knew full well that the vast deserts were not open spaces for whosoever wanted to roam. Every stretch of desert, each range of hills and especially the water holes and oases all belonged to one tribe or another and were strictly controlled. Temporary passage would be permitted but for no more than three days and then permission would be required, plus appropriate payment. There was no common purpose or ideology between the various Arab tribes. There was even less tolerance for the hazardous annual pilgrims' progression to Mecca: the majority of the pilgrims were city dwellers from Syria, Turkey and further afield, all were subject to extortionate fees for the freedom of passage and the Arabs were not averse to attacking and robbing small groups of pilgrims and leaving them to die in the desert. It was only when the Turks built the so-called Pilgrims' Railway that these people could travel to Mecca in some safety.

As an Arab linguist, Lawrence began to take his turn interrogating prisoners, usually captured following minor raids against the Suez Canal. Many of the prisoners were Arab Syrians who had been forcibly recruited into the Turkish Army. His gift of understanding their local dialects ensured him considerable success. Once he could identify a prisoner's home district Lawrence would discuss domestic issues with the prisoner; with the occasional cigarette and a modicum of kindness, Lawrence invariably obtained the information he sought. By August 1915 Lawrence had been employed in a variety of positions and his senior officers were all aware of his capabilities.

The British then learned of a series of secret visits by certain senior Arabs to the French and Turkish embassies in Athens. Lawrence was despatched to Athens to ascertain the nature of the visits but little is known about his activities and at the end of August he returned to Cairo. He arrived in time to claim a role in a rescue mission to save the crews of two British freighters following their capture by Sanussi tribesmen after their vessels had been sunk by German U-boats off the coast of Libya. Lawrence later related to Robert Graves how he had been part of a rescue mission; that such a mission had taken place and succeeded is not an issue, but there is no evidence that Lawrence was in any way involved and his role in this episode seems to extend only to his vivid imagination. The Duke of Westminster's motor squadron equipped with stripped down Rolls-Royce cars had undertaken the rescue; it involved an exciting foray across the desert – an event that deeply impressed the army and Lawrence. Apart from occasional tales of derring-do, life went on; Lawrence's boredom was eventually shattered by the news that two of his brothers had been killed in France; Frank had been killed as he accompanied his unit marching to the front line and Will, who had just taken up his duty as an observer in the Royal Flying Corps, had been shot down. Lawrence was devastated by the news; it was an event that hardened him against German participation in the desert war.

Then, in March 1916 Lawrence seized the opportunity to accept an invitation to accompany a fellow officer, Colonel Aubrey Herbert, to review the situation at Kut al Amara, a small town north of Basra in Mesopotamia. Herbert was the Member of Parliament for South Somerset and equal to Lawrence in his eccentricity by wearing a homemade corduroy uniform. Their task was both military and humanitarian: to rescue an isolated force of British and Indian soldiers at Kut. This force, under the command of Major General Townsend, had been sent from India to strengthen the British garrison at Kut. It has to be said that it was an expedition undertaken against the wishes of the Mesopotamian Arabs. Initially everything went well, apart from a policy of non-cooperation from the Arabs who were just as happy to slit the throats of British soldiers as Turkish soldiers; there was little opposition from the Turks, but inefficient transport within the expeditionary force meant supplies were muddled and delayed. Due to the oppressive heat, heatstroke was usually fatal and general sickness quickly set in among the British troops. Morale deteriorated, army discipline was fierce and executions for sleeping on duty were not uncommon. To the growing frustration of the troops, who were frequently expected to mount cavalry charges with sabres drawn against Turkish positions defended by machine guns and artillery, the British commanders appeared to lack a positive strategy. The capture of Baghdad was uppermost in the minds of the British generals, not their supplies, which were woefully inadequate, or the welfare of their men. Then the weather turned cold and, with the British dithering, the Turks seized the opportunity to counterattack. With local Arabs looking on, the British force was blocked, surrounded and then repeatedly attacked by the Turks. With nearly 4,000 British casualties and provisions failing, the sick began dying and, with no available reinforcements able to go to their rescue, Lawrence and Herbert were sent by the British High Command to assist in obtaining suitable surrender terms.

Sadly, the British were as optimistic as their intelligence was seriously flawed. British intelligence had claimed that the Turkish troops were in an equally bad way, that Turkey's Arabian regiments were about to mutiny and most significantly, Russian and Armenian troops were about to take Erzerum, the Kurdistan capital to the north of Kut, before marching on the Turk's home province. The intelligence was only partially correct; Erzerum had been taken but the Russians were not marching on Turkey. More seriously, the morale of the Turkish troops facing the British was still high and at Kut the Turkish commander's resolve for an early and easy victory was strong.

Lawrence and Herbert each considered the other to be especially useful for the task. Lawrence was chosen following his recent assistance to London, due to his knowledge of senior Turkish officials, which enabled the Russians to take Erzerum, whereas Herbert spoke fluent Turkish. The pair's negotiations were handicapped before they began – the two British generals conducting operations in Mesopotamia believed their own faulty intelligence rather than responding to the approaching disaster unfolding in front of them. They were vehemently opposed to any thought of surrender. The two junior negotiators pressed on and discussions took place at the

Turkish headquarters, which involved Lawrence and Herbert being blindfolded and then taken through the Turkish positions to the Turkish general's headquarters. But their attempts to negotiate failed. In vain they offered £2 million but General Khalit Pasha, a wealthy nephew of Enver, the leading 'Young Turk', refused. By the conclusion of their negotiations, only the wounded and sick soldiers were released, in exchange for many more unwanted Turkish prisoners. The Turks informed Lawrence that the remaining British prisoners would be taken back to Turkey; what they kept secret was the fact that there was no transport available and Turkish supplies were diminishing. In the increasing heat of an early summer, the demoralized British force of 20,000 would shortly be forced to surrender. Apart from the sick and wounded, most would be marched, at bayonet point, first to Baghdad and then on to Turkey, a distance of nearly 1,000 miles.

Lawrence pleaded for the Arab prisoners serving with the British to be humanely treated but the Turks despised the Arabs and Lawrence was ignored. The pair were still at the headquarters of the Mesopotamian garrison when Kut was surrendered on 29 April 1916. After mercilessly hanging the senior Arabs, the Turks began to force-march the British and Indian survivors to Turkey; medical facilities and supplies en route were virtually non-existent and many died following the horrific rigours of the march and their subsequent imprisonment at Yozgat, about 140 miles to the east of Ankara. The Turks took over 13,500 prisoners to Turkey and the survivors were eventually released after the war; over 4,000 British soldiers never returned home, having died on the march or in captivity. Lawrence and Herbert returned by ship to Cairo disheartened by what they had witnessed while the remainder of the British Army in Mesopotamia spent another two desperate years struggling to reach Baghdad. Lawrence had made his dislike of the senior officers responsible for the fall of Kut well known; he had openly ridiculed them and wrote stinging reports concerning their incompetence.

Although he was correct in every detail, his attitude created much animosity among senior officers in Cairo and made Lawrence numerous enemies, which he relished. Lawrence's report was summed up by Major Stirling who wrote:

> The document that he produced for us on his return was an amazing document, considering the author was only a second-lieutenant. It was a violent criticism of the mental capacity of the draughtsmen and map-makers, of the quality of the stone used in their lithography, of the disposal of cranes on the quayside, of the system of mooring the barges and of the shunting operation of the railway, of the medical arrangements, particularly of the provision for the wounded, and even of the tactical dispositions of the commanders in the field and of the general strategical conception of the campaign. We dared not show it to the Commander in Chief, but had to water it down till it was considered fit for the great man's perusal. I have regretted ever since that I never kept a copy of the original; it was Lawrence at his best.

The official account of the disaster and surrender at Kut remains one of the saddest and blackest episodes in British military history.

As Lawrence settled back into his mundane Cairo duties in June 1916 Sherif Hussein of Mecca fired the long awaited symbolic shot from the balcony of his royal palace to signal his authority for his sons to unleash the Arab Revolt against the Turks. It was initially difficult for the British in Cairo to evaluate the success or otherwise of the fledgling revolt and without doubt, many senior British officers were uninterested and quietly sided with the Turks, who they viewed more favourably for being 'more European' than the Arabs. Worse, in Lawrence's eyes, were the French who were endeavouring to establish a military mission in both Jeddah and Mecca. Lawrence realized his outspokenness was now playing against him; he was being marginalized to the point where he would have no more influence in supporting the Arab Revolt. Lawrence rebelled by maintaining his insubordination, which continued to infuriate those immediately senior to him.

During the uncertain opening stages of the Arab Revolt the British commanders in Cairo did not want to send troops to the Hejaz to support the Arabs. They were still smarting from their appalling and embarrassing reversal at Kut in Mesopotamia and besides, putting Christian soldiers on the ground near the Muslim holy cities of Mecca and Medina could well incite a religious uprising by Muslim countries against the Allies instead of the common enemy, Turkey. Indeed, Sherif Hussein had already banned a British ship from landing at Jeddah to pick up Turkish prisoners, purely on religious grounds.

There was a sorry stalemate developing; the Arabs' progress against the Turks was beginning to loose its impetus while, at the same time, the British in particular were unsure how to render appropriate help. Rumours reached Cairo that the Arabs were running low on ammunition and that without urgent assistance, the Turks would swiftly regain the initiative. The British High Command, meanwhile, needed accurate intelligence on the progress of the revolt and so Ronald Storrs, the Oriental Secretary at the British Agency, who had previously liaised with the Grand Sherif Hussein, was the obvious person to task with the mission. It was duly decided to send Storrs to Jeddah to seek clarification of the Arabs' actual needs and his mission was supported by Major al Mizi, Sherif Hussein's chief of staff. Storrs was a shrewd politician who had been greatly impressed by Lawrence when the two had worked together in Cairo; Storrs also knew that Lawrence's understanding of Arab politics was superior to that of the Allied military leaders, who tended to think more in terms of a military solution rather than considering the possible success of a political approach. Lawrence had already expressed the wish to seek permission to travel inland to meet Sherif Hussein but no one thought that it would be possible either to obtain permission from the sherif or safely undertake the journey.

Now Lawrence's dream of escaping Cairo for the open desert began to take on a positive form. Using official channels, Lawrence attempted to join Storrs but was refused permission by the same officers Lawrence had for so long irritated. So in typical Lawrence style, he took ten days' leave to unofficially join Storrs, who discreetly managed to get Lawrence transferred to the new Arab Bureau under the control of the British Foreign Office; he never returned to his normal duties. The bureau was a political intelligence centre and dealt with all Arabic-speaking countries of the Middle East under the command of General Clayton as head of the unit.

Lawrence's fellow officers were pleased to see him go and, apart from his immediate friends, few wished him well. His contemporaries were annoyed by his air of superiority and overtly relaxed and indifferent attitude to all things military, while senior officers found his constant correcting of their written reports more than annoying. At the age of twenty-eight, Captain Lawrence was still a junior officer, but because he spoke Arabic and knew the area, he was indispensable; Storrs was happy to have his company and the party set off by steamer for Rabegh with orders to ascertain what exactly was happening with the Arab Revolt in the Hejaz region. So Lawrence was now on his way to the Hejaz, he was part of the new Arab Bureau specially formed to assist the Arab Revolt and his senior officers including Hogarth, the elder statesman of the group, were all well disposed to him. Lawrence's game plan could now enter its second stage.

On 16 October 1916 Lawrence and Storrs arrived at Jeddah where Abdullah, Sherif Hussein's second son, met them. Abdullah was mounted on a fine white mare and resplendent in his white robes. He had just returned to Jeddah following a successful attack on the Turks at Taif. While British intelligence reports intimated that Abdullah was the leader of the Arab Revolt, Lawrence was unsure. Abdullah appeared to lack the necessary overall vision and drive that

Lawrence sought in a leader; nevertheless, he was able to inform Lawrence that the Turks had managed to amass sufficient troops and equipment to retake and reinforce Medina before driving the Arabs further back to Rabegh and, in so doing, they would probably undo the initial progress made by the revolt. Abdullah requested more guns and ammunition and the assistance of a whole British brigade, especially one composed of Muslim troops, which he requested should be sent to bolster the Arab force before they could again attack the Turks. Lawrence responded by pointing out there were no brigades manned by Muslim troops and that the defence required by Abdullah could be equally well provided by the Royal Navy, as they had recently proved when the British fleet had bombarded the Turks at Jeddah. Fearing this young British officer was outflanking him, Abdullah tried to lay the blame for the lack of Arab success on British lack of support and supplies, and furthermore that the British had neglected to cut the railway line, which had enabled the Turks to amass reinforcements and supplies. Lawrence was able to inform Abdullah that his brother, Feisal, had specifically requested the railway be left intact and that Feisal had declined any further offers of supplies. From Lawrence's conversation with Abdullah, and his lieutenants, it was obvious to Lawrence that his commitment was suspect whereas his brother, Feisal, was more deeply engaged in actual military action against the Turks.

With Storrs' agreement, Lawrence resolved to cross the desert to seek out Feisal. Having obtained the permission of Sherif Hussein and armed with a letter of authority from Abdullah to travel to Feisal's camp, Lawrence set off to Rabegh to inform Ali, the oldest of Sherif Hussein's sons, that he proposed travelling the 120 miles through the territory controlled by Ali to visit Feisal's camp at Hamra. Lawrence liked Ali but realized he was unambitious. With the necessary formalities completed and with great secrecy lest spies should compromise the mission, Lawrence set off from Rabegh into the desert night accompanied by two trusted guides. They took with them a supply of fresh dates and bread, the staple diet in the desert, which if the riders were lucky, could be supplemented with melons, cucumbers and grapes that could occasionally be found growing in isolated villages. As the Arabs at Rabegh were known to include a number of Turkish informers, and the local Arab chief was pro-Turkish and currently in hiding from his brother Arabs, Lawrence was given Arab clothes and a shemag headdress to wear lest his journey to Feisal be detected.

Lawrence was in his element; two years of boredom and frustration appeared to be at an end. He was now free of military discipline and heading off into the desert on an important mission. But the reality of two years of soft living now struck home; Lawrence was riding a prince's camel, which was used to covering long distances without a pause, as was his escort. Lawrence said nothing to his guides and all maintained the same swift progress towards their next watering place at Masturah. Having ridden through the night, the party arrived at the well by mid morning. One of Lawrence's escort clambered down the steps into the well and brought up water for the riders and camels. Two other riders arrived at the well and, not being of the Harb clan, watered their camels without acknowledging Lawrence's party. It later turned out that these two riders were both nobles of the Harith tribe who were in a tribal feud with the Harb; Lawrence would be amused to later learn the true identity of the two noblemen and would, indeed, befriend them during the later stages of the Arab Revolt.

They pressed on; with over sixty miles of inhospitable desert behind them Lawrence was feeling stiff and tender from the hours in the saddle. Each mile of sun-baked desert was different and took his mind off the growing discomfort, the terrain would rapidly turn from sand to shale, to grit and then back to sand with perplexing irregularity. By evening they reached a hamlet of some twenty huts where they were provided with water to mix the dough carried by the guide. After a meal of freshly cooked unleavened bread they again set off into the darkness. Lawrence recalled that he kept dozing in the saddle until, at midnight, they stopped for a few hours of welcome sleep. As soon as the moon came up, the party continued with the journey. Dawn came and by mid morning they entered a long valley and passed a small hamlet tucked under the rising precipice of cliffs that rose out of the desert. They continued past tamarind and acacia trees, through the long valley and on into yet another ocean of desert until, late in the morning, they came across a low saddle of hills. They stopped at a small village where they were given water and fresh dates. A few miles further on they came across more tents and saw numerous armed Arabs patrolling the area. Clearly they were getting close to Feisal's camp. An Arab guide came and met Lawrence's party and led them through Feisal's main camp and on to Feisal's personal tents. *Seven Pillars of Wisdom* tells us that with no time for refreshment, a large black slave, complete with a silver-hilted sword, escorted Lawrence into the presence of Feisal.

Lawrence always claimed that he knew instantly that Feisal was the man to lead the Arab Revolt and this may well be true; it certainly turned out to be so. Lawrence's account in *Seven Pillars of Wisdom* is clear yet stunning. It reads:

I felt at first glance that this was the man I had come to Arabia to seek – the leader who would bring the Arab Revolt to full glory. Feisal looked very tall and pillar-like, very slender, in his long white silk robes and his brown head-cloth bound with a brilliant and scarlet and gold cord. His eyelids were dropped; and his black beard and colourless face were like a mask against the strange, still watchfulness of his body. His hands were crossed in front of him on his dagger.

I greeted him. He made his way for me into the room and sat down on a carpet near the door. As my eyes grew accustomed to the shade, they saw that the little room held many silent figures, looking at me or Feisal steadily. He remained staring down at his hands, which were twisting slowly about his dagger. At last he enquired softly how I had found the journey. I spoke of the heat and he asked how long from Rabegh, commenting that I had ridden fast for the season.

'And do you like our place here in Wadi Safra?' he asked.

'Well; but it is far from Damascus.'

The word had fallen like a sword in their midst. There was a quiver. Then everybody present stiffened where he sat, and held his breath for a silent minute. Some, perhaps, were dreaming of far-off success: others may have thought it a reflection on their late defeat. Feisal at length lifted his eyes, smiling at me, and said, 'Praise be to God, there are Turks nearer us than that.' We all smiled with him, and I rose and excused myself for a moment.

If Lawrence used the actual words 'Well; but it is far from Damascus', then it was a bold statement of intent. All those present knew that Damascus was the true Arab objective, but none had dared make the statement openly as this would have been a criticism of the Arab leadership, which had hitherto focused on attacking the Turks around Mecca and Medina.

Whether the first meeting of Lawrence and Feisal was as charged as Lawrence portrays in *Seven Pillars of Wisdom* will remain unknown; this account had been redrafted and written many times so it is possible that the final account has been heavily embellished for effect. There is no surviving Arab account. The American reporter, Lowell Thomas, recorded a different version, given to him by Lawrence; it has much the same result but without the drama:

After exchanging the usual oriental compliments over many sweet-ened cups of Arabian coffee, the first question Lawrence asked Feisal was, 'When will your army reach Damascus?' The question evidently nonplussed the Emir who gazed gloomily through the tent-flap at the bedraggled remnants of his father's army.

'In sh' Allah' replied Feisal stroking his beard. There is neither power nor might save in Allah, the high, the tremendous. May he look with favour on our cause. But I fear the gates of Damascus are farther beyond our reach at present than the gates of paradise. Allah willing, our next step will be an attack at Medina where we hope to deliver the tomb of the Prophet from our enemies.'

Lawrence's own diary version reveals a more likely scenario. He wrote that on his arrival, Feisal met him in a mud hut situated on a low rise, the hut was busy with visitors and following a brief exchange with Feisal, Lawrence found him 'unreasonable'; Lawrence went off for a wash and a well-deserved sleep. The following morning the two had a long conversation, which Lawrence described as a 'hot discussion' but there then followed an evening session where the two appeared to agree on the way forward

It is always possible that Lawrence found Feisal inscrutable, and if he was, then it must be stated that Feisal was fully aware that Lawrence was just another junior British officer. Lawrence had arrived unannounced; he had no written authority to negotiate, no diplomatic credentials and had simply ridden out of the desert and sought to engage the slightly bemused Feisal on important military matters.

Regardless of whose account is correct, the meeting certainly occurred and it boded well for further discussions. If Feisal thought it odd that such a junior officer as Lawrence should be sent by his seniors to discover Feisal's view about the Arab Revolt, he never showed any misapprehension; Lawrence certainly impressed Feisal.

4

The Arab Revolt Takes Hold

For a number of hours Lawrence was deeply engrossed with Feisal, discussing the subject of the Arab Revolt and it was late before Lawrence was permitted to sleep. The following morning he wandered among the Arab tribes assembled at Feisal's camp in an attempt to gauge their support for the revolution. During his inquisitive perambulations among Feisal's followers, Lawrence was impressed by the relaxed temperament of the various groups of Arab fighters. The artillery, manned by the Egyptian Army, was openly less confident. They distrusted Feisal's men who in turn mocked them for their military bearing and behaviour, which the Arabs thought irrelevant in their hit-and-run style of desert warfare. It was soon obvious to Lawrence that Feisal was being advised by an Arab officer, Maulud, who was clearly a shrewd politician. Maulud had previously served as commander of a Turkish mounted regiment but had been captured by the British during an engagement in Mesopotamia. In captivity he expressed his allegiance to Feisal who, on learning of his capture, requested his services.

Maulud asked Lawrence why the British were being reticent in helping the Arab cause. Lawrence neatly sidestepped the trap and reminded Maulud that this was his task – to assess the requirements of the Arabs. Well versed in military matters, Maulud suggested that the British were starving the Arabs of food, ammunition and guns; Lawrence responded by saying that the British were fully aware of the Arab needs but needed to know what and where to send them. This was a perfectly truthful answer, which also served to calm Maulud and the pair then discussed the issue with Feisal. Lawrence reiterated his role and his response satisfied Feisal who pointed out even he, as the Arab leader in the field, could not succeed without adequate help from Britain. In the meantime, Feisal indicated that he wished to sit tight until the Arabs were strong enough to defend Mecca from the Turks' expected attack. The only alternative was to launch an attack against Medina to deter the Turks from advancing against Mecca. With the immediate discussion over, Lawrence was dismissed from Feisal until later that evening. Walking round the camp Lawrence noticed the steady arrival of several more Arab sheikhs, complete with bodyguards and entourages.

At sunset the Arab dignitaries were again summoned to see Feisal and an hour later Lawrence was invited to join them. Although he was wearing British uniform, most thought him to be an Arab officer in the Turkish Army who had defected to the Arab cause, especially when he spoke to them in the dialect of northern Syria. That evening, the assembled sheikhs had much to discuss; all were in favour of making life as difficult as possible for the Turks. Lawrence's presence and mission was known only to Feisal and Maulud and he kept in the background to assess their willingness to fight the Turks. The complicated politics of Arabia soon became evident to Lawrence and difficulties unimagined by a European mind were already at the forefront of Arab thinking. One serious matter related to their new British ally being Christian. So how, they mused, could Arabs fight the Turks when both shared the same religion? Yet to everyone assembled, the acceptance that the Turks had oppressed the Arabs for over four hundred years was overpowering, whereas the British sought, or so the assembled Arab leaders believed, to make them free again by driving the Turks back to Turkey. Another question taxed their minds: if the concept of freedom was alien to most Arabs, so too was the concept of goodness. Defeating the Turks would be good for the British but would it be good for them? They pondered long. Enforced goodness could be just as painful as enforced badness, they said, but in the end they were all prepared to consider the concept, especially as it was espoused by Feisal.

Seeking their views on the pending revolt, Lawrence asked a number of pertinent questions about the recent and brutal Turkish treatment of Syrian prisoners. He was surprised that the collective response of the assembled Arabs was one of indifference; after all, they pointed out, the Syrians were in the pay of the despised French and would sell their country if given the chance. It was also pointedly insinuated that the British might also take over Arabia once they had sufficient troops to remove the hated Turks. Lawrence countered by informing the audience that thousands of young British soldiers were dying in France – and did they think Britain's objective was to occupy France? Not to be outdone, Feisal reminded Lawrence that Britain had occupied Sudan without wanting it or intending to occupy the country, and yet was still the occupying power there. Lawrence was temporarily checked and realized the Arab leaders were far more astute than he had earlier acknowledged. All present agreed that if the Muslim Turks could ally themselves with the Christian Germans, then there was nothing to stop the Muslim Arabs fighting alongside British Christians – so long as the end result was the permanent removal of the Turks from Arabia. There was also consensus, which Lawrence strongly approved of, that once the Turks had been removed, Arabia would go back to its pre-Ottoman era of Arabia ruled by Arabs. At the end of the conversation, Feisal intimated to Lawrence that he was ready to continue the revolt but needed gold to pay his commanders, food to feed his troops and weapons to arm them. That night Lawrence pondered the Arab Revolt; his youthful dreams back in Oxford were rapidly taking real shape and at last he was in a position to influence the future of the revolt and eventual unification of the Arab peoples.

Before he departed from Feisal, Lawrence promised supplies of equipment, food and some machine guns complete with properly trained crews. He also suggested that some Arab-speaking British Army officers might join Feisal's headquarters to help him coordinate forthcoming Arab attacks on the Turks. Feisal hinted that Lawrence might like to return in this capacity, but Lawrence reminded Feisal that he was only a junior officer, untrained in warfare, and that others would be better suited to the task. Feisal let the comment pass, for the time being.

Feisal left Lawrence in no doubt that without adequate supplies of arms and money, even the most loyal of his supporters would not remain in camp forever. All had families to go to and Feisal made it clear that without regular payments, any form of military retaliation against the Turks would be minimal. And without the probability of action and being able to loot Turkish positions or trains, his warriors would inevitably drift home; the message was not lost on Lawrence.

Lawrence proposed to return directly to Cairo so that he could break the news of the imminent Arab Revolt to his superiors – and ensure the promised supplies were sent without delay. With an escort from the Juheina tribe, Lawrence set off back into the desert for Yenbo where he knew he could take a boat for Egypt. On his arrival at Yenbo Lawrence was housed with a trustee of Feisal to await a ship; one was due in four days' time, which gave Lawrence adequate time to prepare his report. Lawrence was pleased when the vessel arrived, as it was under the command of Captain Boyle who had earlier assisted in the capture of Jeddah, and it was to Jeddah that Boyle was about to sail as Admiral Sir Rosslyn Wymess, commander of the Red Sea Fleet, was presently visiting. From Jeddah, the party then sailed for Port Sudan from where Lawrence travelled on to Khartoum for a meeting with the new High Commissioner for Egypt, General Wingate, who strongly supported the idea of an Arab revolt. Lawrence travelled on to Cairo and during the journey finished his report.

On arriving at Cairo, Lawrence soon learned of a new plan,

sponsored by France, to send an Allied force of British and French troops to support Sherif Hussein. This new task force was to be under the command of a senior French army officer, Colonel Brémond, and was designed to help prevent the Turks massing around Mecca for a counterattack. Fortunately, the British commander-in-chief, General Murray, was sceptical of the plan. Murray's orders from London were to attack to the north and drive the Turks back to Turkey; he saw the French plan as nothing more than a side-show. Lawrence redrafted his report and fiercely protested that the French were not operating in the British interest but were plotting to further their own plans to colonize the area. He pointed out, rather strongly, that Christian troops would never be permitted near the Muslim holy city, and further, that with suitable supplies, the Arabs could do the job more efficiently and at no cost or risk of losses to the British. He sent the report direct to Murray.

Murray was deeply impressed by the argument and called for Lawrence to attend his headquarters. Lawrence's report was far reaching and made strong sense, but he was still a junior officer and, apart from his reputation for eccentricity, he was personally unknown to Murray. The result of their initial meeting was that Lawrence swayed his commander-in-chief; all supplies requested were urgently despatched to Feisal and the Allied mission to Jeddah was cancelled, to Lawrence's relief. Murray was later asked what he thought of Lawrence at this first meeting, and he replied, 'I was disappointed: he did not come in dancing pumps.' Lawrence was instructed to return to Feisal but he was led to understand that, due to his lack of military training, the posting would be temporary pending the arrival of suitable British officers from London, who would then relieve him.

At the end of November 1916 Lawrence arrived back in the Hejaz and went to war. He took a ship for Yenbo to supervise the delivery of supplies for Feisal's army and was pleased to see that two ships were already at the port unloading the equipment that Feisal had requested from Murray. Lawrence was already planning an attack against the Turkish-held port of Wejh. The port was lightly defended but until the Turks could be removed they would all too easily be able to interfere with the Arab supply line, and the port's strategic position nearer Aqaba would also be ideal for unloading the growing amount of supplies needed for the developing revolt. It was at Yenbo that Lawrence met another British officer, Captain Garland of the Royal Engineers. Garland had been at Yenbo for two months and had already made a name for himself with the local Arabs. Skilled in the destructive use of dynamite, Garland had twice made the week-long camel ride to the Pilgrims' Railway where he had wreaked havoc by blowing up miles of track, a bridge and a train carrying Turkish troops. In between these adventures, Garland instructed selected Arab troops in the art of using explosives.

In anticipation of receiving the promised supplies, the Arab troops under two of Feisal's brothers, Zeid and his half-brother Abdullah, kept up the pressure on the Turks still holding Medina. Four British aircraft, complete with their pilots and maintenance crews, arrived at Rabegh along with a quantity of obsolete guns for the Arabs' use. At nearby Yenbo, the Arab regiments of 2,000 Mesopotamian Arabs were being trained by Zeid – an experienced Arab leader who would become a firm friend of Lawrence. Lawrence's plan was for a major assault on Wejh, which was located some 200 miles northwards along the coast towards Aqaba. Late in the afternoon, intending to travel in the cool of the night, Lawrence and his bodyguards, including Sherif Abd el Karim of the Juheina, set off along the coast to find and liaise with Feisal who was already at the camp of the Billie tribe. On arriving at the outskirts of the village, they heard gunfire and a general commotion; thinking the Turks were mounting an attack, Lawrence and his party crept forward – to find that the villagers were welcoming Feisal into their midst. As soon as Feisal heard Lawrence had arrived he called for him to attend his tent and, in the presence of Maulud and a cousin, Taif, updated Lawrence with recent events.

The Turks had managed to cut the Arab defence line between Feisal and Yenbo by attacking Zeid's headquarters and putting his men to flight. Untrained, they had not stood their ground but had fled in disarray towards Yenbo. Realizing that the Turks' success gave them an open road to Yenbo, Feisal had brought his army of 5,000, together with Egyptian machine-gunners, to block and protect the road back to Yenbo. Feisal knew that, with Yenbo unprotected, the Turks would otherwise be able to advance unmolested along the coast to Rabegh – and then press on to Mecca. The situation was highly dangerous for Feisal. Lawrence decided to return to Yenbo to help strengthen their defences and he reached its outskirts just as Zeid's defeated army arrived back at the port. Lawrence immediately telegraphed Captain Boyle at Jeddah with an urgent request for naval support to prevent Yenbo being taken by the Turks; within minutes Lawrence received the reply he wanted – Boyle was on his way. His relief was short-lived; Feisal had earlier come under a heavy attack when the Turks took his camp by surprise. Now Feisal's Arabs were in complete disarray and falling back on Yenbo; with the advancing Turks clearly gaining control, the Arab Revolt was coming perilously close to a dangerous end. During the evening, some 2,000 survivors from Feisal's force drifted back into Yenbo and it was immediately obvious that a large part of Feisal's force was missing; indeed, it soon occurred to the leaders present that there had been treachery.

The entire Juheina tribe was missing. Lawrence sought out Feisal who gave him an account of the Turkish attack. Just as it seemed to both men that the Juheina tribe had indeed mutinied, the Juheina's emir and his deputy, Abd el Kerim, arrived at Feisal's tent. It turned out that the Juheina, armed with obsolete rifles and guns, were unable to make any headway against the advancing Turks and had withdrawn to a position of safety to make coffee and consider their position. Meanwhile, Feisal and his force had also retreated so when the Juheina returned to the fray they found Feisal gone, and naturally broke off their engagement. The story had a ring of truth and both

Feisal and Lawrence saw the funny side of the misadventure. But what could now be done to save Yenbo? In the light of the Arabs' recent misadventures, Lawrence had clearly decided that the Arab Revolt was coming to a swift end and wrote: 'Our war seemed entering its last act – I took my camera and, from the parapet of the Medina gate, got a fine photograph of the brothers coming in.'

The Juheina were requested to return into the desert and attack the Turk's supply line, now strung out and dangerously stretched. The Turks had to leave isolated groups of soldiers to garrison their ever lengthening line, which made them easy targets for the fast moving Juheina camelry. They attacked the Turkish supply line with alacrity; seeing they were outnumbered the Turkish recruits surrendered but the Arabs took no prisoners, the luckless Turks were relieved of their boots, firearms and ammunition, and whatever else the Arabs fancied, then they were butchered on the spot. The Turks never took prisoners except to interrogate and torture them; the Arabs had no time for such revenge, they were simply content with quickly killing their prisoners.

It was with considerable relief that Boyle and five large supply ships arrived at Yenbo just two days before the anticipated arrival of the Turkish advance. Immediately Arab morale soared and there was feverish activity to unload the stores which, this time, included a large supply of modern British rifles, machine guns and ammunition. Captain Garland worked all day and night supervising the rebuilding of the old town wall; barbed wire was strung along the perimeter and machine-gun posts erected to protect the outer limit of the defence. With the ships' guns covering the dead ground between the port and the distant hills, everyone eagerly anticipated the arrival of the Turks. Just before midnight Turkish patrols reached the outer limit of Yenbo; the word went straight back to headquarters and the town garrison was quietly roused to man the wall. Suddenly the ships' searchlights pierced the black of the night and began playing to and fro across the open desert ready to highlight any movement. This alarmed the gathering Turks who, unaware of the ships' arrival, presumed Yenbo was well defended. They retreated and began to withdraw back to their forward base at Nakhl Mubarak. Yenbo was saved. Sadly, Garland died shortly afterwards. He had not been well for several months and due to the exertions of protecting Yenbo, became fatally ill. Garland should be remembered for his pioneering demolition work along the Turks' Pilgrims' Railway; it was Garland who first saw the value of such destruction and who undoubtedly inspired Lawrence to develop his mine-laying skills.

With Yenbo saved and the Turks now in retreat, Boyle withdrew his ships on the understanding that he would return if required. The Juheina had got over their embarrassment and returned to harass the Turkish withdrawal. As soon as they caught up with the Turks, they made the Turks' line of retreat a rout; the Arabs repeatedly attacked the strung-out column and with constant sniping at their outposts the inexperienced Turks had nowhere to hide. As their losses increased so did the Arabs' enthusiasm for attacking them. At this point the Turkish commander decided to throw the weight of his army at Rabegh; his logic was to force the Arabs onto the defensive.

Feisal, meanwhile, was at Rabegh so Lawrence took a ride in one of Boyle's ships to meet with him in order to prepare the next step in the revolt. With the Turks now slowly advancing on Rabegh, Feisal sent his army to discourage and slow them down. Lawrence met with the French commander, Colonel Brémond, who was still seeking an Allied landing near Medina to finally remove the Turks from Mecca. Lawrence and Brémond never got on, Lawrence saw to that. Brémond was on solid ground when dealing with Arab affairs; he had served among the North Africans, sometimes in disguise, and knew the Muslims thoroughly, which Lawrence resented. He was also a professional soldier, which Lawrence was not. Lawrence duly complained to London that Brémond was compromising him in Arabia and within days Brémond received a severe rebuke from the French government; it was a rebuke that terminated

Brémond's plan for an Allied advance southwards. At this point Murray's staff officer, Colonel Wilson, also arrived at Rabegh and, at a meeting with Feisal and Lawrence, persuaded them to ignore the Turks to the south; instead, they should turn their combined attention northwards to attack Wejh.

Wilson's plan was to move the whole Arab army to the outskirts of Wejh – the bulk of the Arab force would be transported along the Red Sea coast by the Royal Navy but many would have to ride across vast tracts of barren desert. Feisal politely asked what would happen to undefended Rabegh, which, under Wilson's plan, would be abandoned and thereby easily taken by the Turks. Wilson promised that the Royal Navy would remain at Rabegh until Wejh had fallen; Feisal saw the logic of the plan and Lawrence agreed; both were far more interested in taking the battle north towards Syria, and having Feisal's army on the Allied front line was far more important than supporting the dubious French far to the south near Mecca. Wilson's assessment was soon proved correct when the Turkish advance on Rabegh began to flounder. By having to provide troops to protect their supply depots the Turks were unable to maintain their front-line strength and, without loss to themselves, Feisal's marauders and snipers continued to pick off more than twenty Turks each day. The Turkish commander then learned that British planes were bombing his forward base at Nakhl Mubarak, which concerned him greatly. At the same time the lack of water in the desert wreaked additional destruction on the Turkish Army's soldiers and draught animals and, under such unremitting pressure, their advance on Rabegh eventually ground to an exhausted halt thirty miles from the town. On 18 January 1917 the troops withdrew to the relative safety of Medina where, trapped, they spent the remaining two years of the war unable to contribute to the Turkish war effort.

5

The Hejaz Campaign

*L*awrence spent the first day of 1917 at Rabegh pondering the logistics of advancing the Arab army north to Wejh. The agreed date for the Arab attack on the Turkish-held port was 23 January. With over 6,000 mounted warriors and an even greater number of camels poised ready to undertake the journey, supplies and water were of paramount importance if the army was to safely cross the inhospitable and largely uncharted terrain that lay across its 150-mile journey. Both Lawrence and Feisal knew that any bond between the gathering tribes was tenuous and only held together due to their own calming presence and the figurehead leadership of Feisal. The fact that the might of the British Royal Navy was supporting Feisal was also a major factor and added greatly to Lawrence's prestige – the navy's recent display of guns and searchlights had deeply impressed the Arabs who were hitherto unused to seeing such large ships. The Arab army's military skills were also improving since its recent experience of the half-hearted Turkish attack on Wejh and the Arabs were becoming more amenable to undergoing basic military training, such as advancing in line and not bolting when the first Turkish shell landed. Lawrence knew the few Egyptian gunners with the Arab force were far more professional than the Arabs, who would tend to stand around watching the Egyptian guns in action rather than follow their own orders. After consulting Feisal, the Egyptians were returned home in exchange for more Arabs who were now keen to fight the Turks. With his total force now virtually independent of the Allies, Lawrence's future plan for Arab unity under Feisal began to acquire even greater credibility.

To support the massive marching column, Lawrence arranged with Boyle for all the heavy supplies to be taken by the Royal Navy ship, the *Hardinge*, to Wejh. Equally vital, the *Hardinge* would land food and water at strategic points along the coast. Boyle was enthusiastic about the plan and generously arranged for half the Red Sea Fleet to arrive off Wejh and, in support of the proposed Arab attack, commence a bombardment of the town in order to demoralize its Turkish garrison. Landing parties would then land on the seaward side of the town in support of Lawrence's attacking Arabs. In case the Turks did succeed in taking Yenbo in their absence, Lawrence prudently arranged for all the spare guns and ammunition at Yenbo to be removed from the town armouries to the holds of the *Hardinge*. With plans made and agreed, the loading of supplies commenced; this gave Lawrence a few days for a different adventure.

Up to this point, attacks on the Hejaz Railway had all been carried out by a number of British or French officers. It was time for Lawrence to gain his own experience by leading such an attack and, on 2 January, he set off on a hundred-mile journey south-east with some thirty tribesmen to inflict some devastation. They crossed the Hejaz mountain range and descended onto the more level gravel and lava desert that led towards the distant railway line and a known Turkish army post. On reaching the line of low hills that ran next to the rail line, the party waited for dawn. The night-time temperatures on the high altitude plain were always bitterly cold and Lawrence was pleased when he could leave half his shivering force to guard the camels. He and the remainder of his small force scrambled down the far side of a rocky ridge to a vantage point overlooking the hollow that protected the sleeping Turkish camp from the prevailing desert wind storms. From a range of 100 yards the Arabs opened fire into the tents, which sent the sleepy Turks rushing to collect their rifles before running to the nearby trenches. The echoes of Arab fire rebounded round the surrounding hills giving the impression to the hapless Turks that they were surrounded by a strong attacking force.

In fact Lawrence's force had inadvertently attacked a strong Turkish position and was seriously outnumbered by more than ten-to-one. With his force becoming increasingly likely to be cut off Lawrence ordered an orderly withdrawal and captured two Turks who had been asleep on guard duty. Not prepared to allow the Arabs to kill the prisoners, Lawrence ordered the prisoners to be taken back to Yenbo. He then set off ahead of his party and as he approached the coast he was pleased to see that the march to Wejh had already begun. The *Hardinge* was about to sail north and Feisal was in the process of leading the huge procession away from Yenbo. Ever the shrewd politician, Feisal had arranged with Boyle to take two groups of Arab tribesmen on board to accompany the naval landing party; they would be able to take much credit for the operation and Arab fears of a 'Christian' assault would be negated. Feisal also ensured that the main marching force was inter-tribal and he gave each sheikh equal acknowledgement. The force consisted of some of the most important desert tribes including the Ageyl, Ateiba, Billie, Harb and the Juheina; collectively, it was the largest Arab force ever assembled. Feisal was making a powerful political statement – the Arab Revolt was united, national and now underway.

Equally astute was the decision to attack Wejh. Both Lawrence and Feisal knew that the small coastal town was unlikely to be strongly defended – it was too remote and unimportant for the Turks to maintain a large garrison and there was every likelihood that the Arab attack would be unexpected. Furthermore, with the Turks fully occupied at Medina and Mecca, and having to constantly patrol the Hejaz Railway, there would be no available Turkish troops to counterattack.

On 16 January and now halfway to Wejh, Lawrence was joined by Major Vickery of the Royal Artillery. He was to assist Feisal as staff officer and being a fluent Arabic speaker he was ideally suited for the task, except that he and Lawrence were never compatible. To Lawrence, Vickery was a typical army officer who did everything correctly and by the book. This approach was perfect in a European army fighting a conventional war but the Arab army was everything else, and so was the fighting. Like many senior officers before him, Vickery found Lawrence confusing; although warned of Lawrence's arcane ways, he could not understand Lawrence's flexible approach to serious matters and, impossibly, Lawrence appeared to be operating to his own private agenda. Vickery's suspicion was further aroused when Lawrence openly stated that the Arabs would take Damascus within the year. Vickery knew this was not part of the British overall objective and quietly fumed at this junior officer's perceived arrogance. Poor Vickery never came to terms with the subordinate Lawrence; he was an experienced staff officer who saw Lawrence as 'untrained', yet it was well understood that Lawrence made most of the decisions for Feisal and had the support of General Allenby – a difficult concept for a conventional staff officer to grasp. But Vickery had arrived at an opportune moment. Feisal and Lawrence decided to divide their huge force into smaller units so as not to overwhelm the scattered watering holes and so Vickery was tasked with making the detailed arrangements and planning to get everyone moved, fed, watered and into their attack position by 23 January. Lawrence would have just allowed all these things to happen, Vickery made sure they did. The huge Arab force departed Wejh on time.

After a short pause to replenish supplies, the advance continued on 18 January. In the middle of an open section of desert two camel riders were seen from afar approaching Lawrence's group. Due to the enormity of the gently loping army no one took much notice – until Lawrence realized that one of the riders was his long-time friend Colonel Newcombe. The two then rode side by side and exchanged news and views; Newcombe had been sent by the British headquarters to assume the position of chief military adviser to Feisal. Lawrence was aware that Newcombe sympathized with the true reason for the Arab Revolt, namely Arabia for the Arabs, and New-combe quickly became a strong friend and confidant of Feisal.

Conditions on the long march were more difficult than expected; the route was especially hot, rough and stony and the huge column of camels was only able to slowly pick its way across the difficult terrain. Due to the unexpected heat, the army ran out of water earlier than expected and although extra supplies were dropped off by the *Hardinge*, the delay forced Lawrence to accept they would miss the deadline of the 23rd. Meanwhile, Nasir arrived, the younger brother of the Emir of Medina and now the commander of the Arabs surrounding Wejh. He reported some unexpected bad news: the Turks were aware of the Arab army's approach and were preparing themselves for the attack and had withdrawn back into the town to concentrate their defences. Because the shortage of water was so severe it was arranged for the *Hardinge* to deliver more water-tanks, but the sea was too rough and everyone had to go without – and there were still three days march until Wejh. Next day, Lawrence received a message that the landing parties had been dropped as arranged and that Wejh had been taken, but as the *Hardinge* had left before confirmation had been received, no one knew for certain.

Lawrence's force arrived on the 25th and found most of Wejh had indeed fallen and of the Turkish garrison, those who had not been killed or captured had scattered into the desert. As the Arabs advanced towards the town they came across small groups of Turkish soldiers who willingly surrendered rather than fight such over-whelming odds; at this early stage of the war such prisoners were sent on to detention camps in Egypt. Lawrence and Feisal were dismayed that the attack, though successful, had cost the lives of over twenty Arab fighters and one English flying officer. Gunfire from the ship had smashed most of the town's buildings and sunk the majority of Arab boats in the small harbour. Lawrence then dis-covered that the attack had been carried out under the supervision of Vickery. Perhaps Lawrence was jealous of Vickery's interference or he genuinely thought the loss of lives and damage to the town had been unnecessary; in any event, Vickery was calmly informed by Lawrence that he should have waited two days for Feisal's army to reach Wejh, those valuable lives would not then have been lost, nor the town wrecked. Lawrence was probably correct as the Turks would certainly have surrendered. In any event, Lawrence had to admit that Wejh had been taken from the Turks, against the expectations of the British High Command in Cairo. It was a masterful victory for the Arab cause. Nevertheless, it was a reflection of Lawrence's displeasure that Vickery received no recognition for a very successful operation.

Lawrence immediately went to Cairo to report to General Murray who gracefully accepted that the Arab Revolt was indeed meaningful and viable; it had not escaped the notice of Murray that more Turks were now engaged against the Arabs than were facing his army, a concept that the general was keen to promote. Accordingly, fresh supplies of gold to pay Feisal's army, rifles, machine guns and vast quantities of ammunition were promptly despatched to Wejh. Murray thanked Lawrence for his role in the Arabs' advance and sent him straight back to join Feisal.

Before he left Cairo, the French again attempted to foist a revised version of their plan on the British; they were indignant that French troops had not participated in the taking of Wejh and immediately proposed another joint British and French expedition, again under a French officer, to force a landing at Aqaba. Lawrence saw this as yet another ploy to divert the Arab cause and politely pointed out that, while landing a brigade of troops might be feasible, it would not be possible for the brigade to advance beyond the town due to the rocky mountain range that surrounded and dominated the port, especially as the Turks controlled the only pass through the mountains. The French plan had a number of serious defects that Lawrence exploited: they had not been to Aqaba, they had no concept of the terrain and their maps were inaccurate. Lawrence had visited Aqaba when he

Colonel T. E. Lawrence in 1918.

Far left Captain Lawrence, Intelligence Officer in Cairo, 1917.

Left Auda, the sheik who led the charge at the wells of Abu el Lissan.

The two leaders – Allenby and Feisal.

Leonard Woolley and Lawrence (left) with a Hittite slab, Carchemish, 1910.

Pharaoh's Island and the restored Crusader castle.

Left Feisal and bodyguard at Yenbo.

Above Feisal and the Arab army approaching Yenbo.

Below The Arab camp at Wejh.

Fakhri Pasha with Emir Abdullah after surrendering at Bir Derwish.

Nuri Bei Said commanding Arab troops at Aqaba.

Left to right: Captain Furness Williams, Lieutenant Tookey, Lieutenant Lanham, Bimbo Peake and Captain Hornby at Aqaba, 1918.

Emir Zeid's army arriving at Aqaba.

Lawrence ready to set forth on a raid.

The wild desert tribesmen from when Lawrence built up the Arab army.

surveyed the area in 1913 and his opinion held sway. This French notion had come perilously close to wrecking Lawrence's own secret plans for the Arabs to take Aqaba from the desert, which would then strategically place them in the perfect position for their onward march to Damascus. Lawrence then learned that the wily French Colonel Brémond had attempted to sell his plan to Murray who, in turn, referred him on to Feisal. Before Lawrence could intervene, Brémond had set off for Wejh to solicit Feisal's support. Lawrence made haste and arrived before the Frenchman who, on meeting with Feisal, found Lawrence already sitting in the corner of Feisal's tent wearing the half-smile that so irritated the Frenchman; Brémond immediately knew his long journey had been wasted. There was to be no Allied invasion of Aqaba.

Feisal's position as leader of the Arab Revolt was now undisputed. He had total control over all the tribes between the Hejaz and the Red Sea and from Wejh southwards along the coast to Medina. To the far north, the Ruwalla tribe, led by the old and experienced Emir Nuri, were not yet committed to the Arab Revolt; messengers travelled regularly between Feisal and Nuri and each leader respected the other. Feisal now considered the time had come to seek Nuri's permission to advance through his northern territory, which contained the only desert water holes across the inhospitable Sirhan desert. The reply came swiftly, along with a gift of fine racing camels; permission would be granted but further assistance would be limited until the revolt spread north. The Turks were in force throughout Nuri's area and could easily quell an isolated mutiny – unless supported in strength by Feisal. The other northern tribe, the Abu Tayi of the Howeitat tribe, were led by Auda, a famous warrior who controlled much of northern Arabia. Feisal had sent a number of requests to Auda and on 17 February he received the awaited reply: Auda would support Feisal. By sheer patience and the skilful use of his diplomatic skills, Feisal achieved something previously unheard of, a powerful united Arab force. There were still on-going feuds to settle and Feisal would spend much time soothing anxieties and healing grudges, but the uneasy alliance of sworn enemies looked as though it would hold for the time being.

Lawrence's plan for an Arab advance on Aqaba was delayed when, at the beginning of March 1917, Allied intelligence in Cairo intercepted secret messages passing between the Turkish commander-in-chief and his commander at Mecca in the far south. The messages had been seized when Newcombe and Garland blew up a Turkish train; they discovered and recovered official despatches relating to the Turks' secret operation for an imminent withdrawal of the whole Turkish brigade from Medina. This force numbered thousands of well-trained Anatolian troops and supporting artillery. The Turks' plan was to march the army out of Medina in close columns supported by armoured supply trains. Their intended objective was the small town of Tebuk on the railway line near Maan, where they could reorganize and then pose a serious threat to the British desert flank. By closely following the Pilgrims' Railway, the Turks could easily supply and re-equip this force from Maan, which lay further north. An urgent message was sent to Feisal and Lawrence either to attack Medina or destroy the column en route.

In order to prevent the Turks harassing Feisal's growing force, sporadic raids on the railway line and its isolated fortifications were a consistent feature of Arab tactics, so the orders from Cairo were already being complied with. This southerly shift in emphasis back to Medina frustrated Lawrence, who believed that the weight of the Arab attack should be directed at Damascus in the north. With Feisal's approval, Lawrence decided to travel south to meet with Abdullah, now encamped just to the north of Medina, to assess the situation.

Once the journey was underway, Lawrence was faced with a personal crisis from which he would never totally recover. Most of the Arabs had been feuding during the ride and at an overnight camp an Ageyl and a Moor had come to blows, which resulted in a fatal shot being fired. Lawrence intervened to prevent a major sectarian fight developing. He was faced with one dead body and the culprit being pinned down. Both sides lined up facing each other while their leaders looked to Lawrence with much consternation; he did the only thing possible, he shot the offender himself.

The incident shook him to his core, especially as he was becoming desperately ill, but the journey had to continue. Only when he reached Abdullah did the caravan halt. Lawrence, now seriously ill with fever, was moved to a lone tent to allow the fever to run its course. During this period he had time to recover and, while doing so, he spent his time analyzing the military effectiveness of the retrogressive change of plan. As the days went by it became clear to him that he could achieve both the British order and his own plan for the Arab capture of Damascus: not attacking the Turks at Medina, where a wasteful loss of Arab lives would surely ensue, but by totally destroying the railway line both in front of and behind the Turkish advance. If executed carefully, the Turks would be trapped. They would be forced to defend themselves against surprise Arab raids as well as having to rely solely on the supplies they carried with them. The Turks could be forced back to Medina, which was now of no use to the Arabs; the civilian population had largely been removed and it would be too far south, by a thousand miles, to have any effect on the forthcoming British advance.

So Lawrence developed a new strategy, approved by Feisal and Abdullah. The Arabs would continue with their indiscriminate raiding, blowing up trains, railway tracks and stations on the approach to Medina. This would be more than an inconvenience to the Turks: repairs and replacement lines would have to be organized from Maan, hundreds of miles away to the north requiring a Herculean effort on the part of the Turks to maintain the line. Once repaired, the Arabs would allow minimal supplies to get through and then destroy the line again. Lawrence decided that such frequent and unpredictable Arab raids carried out at isolated locations would inflict more than sufficient damage on the trapped Turks, both physical and psychological, and render them militarily ineffective. To keep the line open, even for a few days, would require the attention of a vast number of the besieged soldiers and any thoughts by the Turkish High Command for a withdrawal from Medina would have to be delayed. This strategy was put into effect and from that time on, the Turkish force in Medina was successfully kept from interfering with the Allied advance. The lot of the Turks trapped at Medina was unenviable. With the fear of constant Arab attacks and few replacement supplies available, they were soon reduced to eating their pack animals for food.

Lawrence had, meanwhile, toyed with the statistics; he knew the disposition and strength of the Turkish Army and calculated that the Turks would forever be under strength. He estimated that they would need a force of 600,000 men to hold Arabia whereas they had 100,000 available. By fighting the Turks with rebellion, they would never know where the Arabs would strike next and this would seriously damage their morale and wear them out. In his work *Oriental Assembly* Lawrence described the Turks' frustrating situation as akin to 'eating soup with a fork'. The food analogy was relevant because Lawrence knew that the Turks' food supply line would bind them to the vicinity of the Hejaz Railway; there was no possibility that they would be able to move far from the line, which left, according to Lawrence, 99.9 per cent of Arabia free of Turkish influence. Lawrence understood the value of his Arabs knowing the location of water holes and on their attack missions, they could carry food for up to six weeks giving them a range of 1,000 miles; he commented that tinned bully beef had modified the fighting of a land war more than the development of gunpowder. Lawrence reasoned that by keeping the railway working, but only just, he could tie the Turks to less than 1 per cent of Arabia, leaving the remainder under the control of his Arabs. Lawrence described his tactics, as he neatly put it, 'in fifty words'. They were tactics that the Arabs would use successfully into the twenty-first century. In his *Oriental Assembly* he wrote:

> Granted mobility, security (in the form of denying targets to the enemy), time, and doctrine (the idea to convert every subject to friendliness) victory will rest with the insurgents, for the algebraical factors are in the end decisive, and against them perfections of means and spirit struggle quite in vain.

Lawrence was about to enjoy himself. Once recovered from his fever, he decided to accompany one such raid by Ateiba tribesmen with a machine-gun team led by Sherif Shakir. It was to attack the line about 100 miles distant and the party set off in high spirits, Lawrence relishing the chance to practise his recent lessons in mine-laying. It was not long before they saw an approaching train and after the explosion, the machine-gunners opened fire. Lawrence's first attempt was only partially successful; the mine had been incorrectly laid and despite a huge explosion, it had only blown off the train's front wheels. With the train able to reverse out of danger, and because it was more than adequately defended by the Turks, Lawrence's raiders withdrew. He returned a few days later, this time accompanied by a party of the Juheina, so as not to show favouritism to any one tribe, and relaid his mines. The group hid in the dunes and after a short wait, they saw the distant smoke heralding the approach of a train and anticipated the explosion. The charge was fired but nothing happened, which was fortunate as the train was a decoy train carrying a large number of displaced Arab women and children from Medina.

When the train had disappeared, Lawrence examined the mine. Due to heavy rain the night before, the mine had sunk into the moist sand and the electrical contacts had become dislodged. To distract the Turks, he led a night attack on the nearby guard post then returned to the line and reset the mine. The following morning an unsuspecting train went over the mine and the engine was totally destroyed. The Arabs rushed forward, slaughtered the stunned Turkish survivors and loaded their camels with all the loot they could carry before heading back to camp. Such random raids now became the main feature of Arab guerrilla warfare; it was a policy that sapped the Turks and rendered their Medina garrison impotent. Few Arab casualties were reported.

Satisfied that the Arabs could continue without him, Lawrence returned to Feisal at Wejh, arriving there on 10 April 1917. Feisal had requested the other British officers at Wejh, Hornby and Newcombe, to undertake similar attacks along the line but to focus their attention more to the north. British supplies were continually arriving at Wejh from Egypt and the time was fast approaching for the Arabs to commence their advance northwards, but the Turks still held the area through which they would have to advance. The Turkish held the port of Aqaba, which dominated the area, and the whole region between the port and Maan was still heavily defended. Lawrence began to formulate an audacious plan to attack Aqaba, not from the sea as advocated by the French, but from its unprotected rear, the desert. Lawrence knew this would involve a dangerous march across many hundreds of miles of unexplored desert but the more he thought about the plan the more the idea grew on him. It was everything that was Lawrence – it would be dangerous, audacious and spectacular. It would be a totally unexpected victory, both political and military, for Lawrence's British masters and seriously disrupt the whole plan of Turkish defence across Arabia.

6

Spying in Damascus and the Taking of Aqaba

While pondering the logistics and plans for such a venture, the northern Howeitat leader, Auda, unexpectedly arrived at Wejh. This powerful Arab figure had received numerous reports of Feisal's successes and was impatient for the revolt to spread to his own homelands in the north. There was immediate respect and rapport between Auda and Lawrence and they spent much time sitting in Auda's tent discussing Arab and world history. Lawrence also used the opportunity to gauge Auda's willingness to support his proposed adventure to Aqaba. He explained that with Feisal's army in Aqaba, Feisal could more speedily be supplied from the Red Sea by the Royal Navy; Aqaba was closer to Cairo for the British and closer for the Arabs to make their final advance in support of the Allies and thence on to Damascus. Auda took the bait and Lawrence unfurled his plan: Auda and Lawrence would travel north where, unsuspected by the Turks, Auda could raise a force of Howeitat to ride on Aqaba. By travelling lightly and swiftly across the vast desert area to the north and rear of Aqaba, taking the wilderness route east of Maan and Damascus, they could then, with Auda's fresh tribesmen, ride on the unsuspecting Turks at Aqaba and seize the port. In the event that Lawrence's group was spotted or reported moving north, the Turks would presume the Arabs intended liaising with General Murray's force or were even attempting to rally the northern Arabs for the same cause. They would not be anticipating the following reverse move south-west on Aqaba.

Lawrence convinced Auda the plan would work; it was based on Lawrence's knowledge of the terrain around Aqaba where he knew all the Turkish defences were directed seawards. Protected by Aqaba's steep and mountainous hinterland, there was little need for additional defences. The only narrow pass leading inland from Aqaba to Wadi Itm[1] was easy to defend and there were only two small Turkish garrisons at Aba el Lissan and Guweira situated between Aqaba and the main Turkish base at Maan. Neither post had more than two hundred troops present. Lawrence anticipated that, faced by a totally unexpected and sizeable force of Arabs approaching from the desert, the Turks in these two small outposts would probably surrender or flee to Aqaba itself; if they fought then so be it. There was no way the Turks would ever anticipate an attack from the desert as they knew it was largely unexplored and rarely visited, even by Arab nomads. This particular area of desert lacked any viable water holes for hundreds of miles; the Turks felt totally safe with their backs protected by this wilderness.

Out of courtesy – after all he was the junior British officer at Wejh – Lawrence discussed his plan with Colonel Newcombe; this was slightly disrespectful to his senior officer as Lawrence had earlier briefed Feisal, who had willingly approved the plan. Lawrence went into greater detail with Newcombe and explained his fears that the Turks could soon move troops down to Aqaba and, by using the port as a strategic base, launch attacks against the Suez Canal. Such a deployment would also place a sizeable force of Turks behind British lines. Newcombe saw the logic of the plan and, because it would not affect his order to maintain attacks on the Hejaz Railway, gave Lawrence his full backing. Lawrence had explained to Feisal that the

---

1 Wadi Itm (Yutum) roughly translates into 'orphan'. This had special significance following the battles of the Arab Revolt. Today it refers to the results of numerous road accidents along the pass.

expedition was to be an independent Arab venture and without any Allied assistance; if it was successful, it would boost Arab credibility with the Allies, open the route northwards to Damascus and, of secondary importance to Lawrence, allow the Arab army to cover the eventual British advance towards Turkey from the desert.

Auda knew that the plan's success would enable him to extend the revolt to his own area; his people would enthusiastically rise against the Turks, for so long their oppressors. He insisted in accompanying the venture in order to assist Lawrence in recruiting sufficient tribesmen for the expedition, although the actual force was to be led by Sherif Nasir, who knew the area well, with an escort of about twenty Ageyl riders. Two important Arab leaders from the Damascus area accompanied the group, Zeki and Nesib, and it was anticipated that they would meet up with Maulud, Feisal's deputy, and Sherif Sharraf, Feisal's cousin. Feisal gave Lawrence some £25,000 in gold coin, which he shared between the three leaders and Auda. It was anticipated the journey would take up to six weeks and each man carried his own supplies, there were six additional camels laden with spare rifles and, in order to impress the northern tribes, enough explosives to blow up suitable Turkish targets en route. On 9 May 1917 the fledgling expedition was ready to depart; Feisal bade them farewell and they discreetly departed Wejh. The first part of their perilous journey was across the many miles of rough shale that formed the lower Hejaz slopes, then the rocky mountain range itself was traversed, always a slow and difficult passage due to the steepness of the track. This journey was no different and they lost two camels in the process, but as nothing could be wasted, each was cut up and the meat packed away to supplement the group's rations. Once on the far side of the mountain range they rode onto the upper plateau, which consisted alternatively of red and black sandstone hills interspersed by long ranges of sandy desert, but thankfully the going eventually became easier. As they descended from one shale escarpment they unexpectedly saw, in the far distance, three camel riders approaching. As the two groups closed with each other Lawrence was delighted to see that one of the group, in full Arab dress, was none other than an old friend, a fully bearded Captain Hornby, looking more like a brigand than a British officer. He was returning from a successful series of raids on the Turkish railway under the command of Colonel Newcombe; they paused long enough to exchange pleasantries and news before going their own way. Hornby and Newcombe had already both earned fine reputations for driving the Turks to distraction by repeatedly blowing up trains and track along the Pilgrims' Railway.

From then on the days passed slowly, the solitude of the baking desert and chilly nights changed little other than for the texture of the wind-whipped sand or shale beneath them; distant hills came and went, only to be replaced by more distant hills. Occasionally they came across clumps of thorn bushes, which they collected for their fires and it was on these occasions that they were able to make camp and enjoy the luxury of baking fresh bread. They continued on, each day much the same as the day before, and at last the rough terrain gave way again to open desert and fine sand to enable faster progress. To remind Lawrence of the frailty of Arab unity, the party was ambushed by an unknown group of some twenty raiders. Auda guessed they were of the Shammar tribe, a remote people. After a short skirmish the Shammar quickly retreated, not having anticipated such a determined response from a smaller group. Later that day their journey took them through a maze of low red sandstone hills and on to a water hole known to Sharraf. Lawrence saw empty sardine tins round the obvious fireplace, evidence of Newcombe and Hornby having used the well during their raiding. They pressed on the next day and crossed the Pilgrims' Railway near the village of Dizad. They had been warned by Newcombe that the Turks regularly patrolled the line with camel-mounted troops and railway trolleys protected with machine guns, but they saw no sign of any Turkish activity so Lawrence set a number of charges along the line. Auda was disappointed when he saw the size of the charges being laid but he had never previously experienced the effect of dynamite. Lawrence activated the fuses and the party rapidly withdrew towards the safety of some nearby dunes. Auda was invited to watch the blast – which he did by boldly standing in the open. The explosion was loud and blew much sand and sections of rails and sleepers high off the ground. A shaken Auda was deeply impressed by the explosions and thereafter waxed lyrical as to the value of dynamite. Fearful that the explosions would alert the Turks, the Arabs cut the telegraph lines and by hitching their camels to the telegraph poles, they hauled a number of them several hundred yards into the desert. By now they could hear the Turks coming, unaware of what had happened or the cause of the explosions, and they were approaching the scene firing wildly into the hills. Lawrence's group slipped away into the gathering shadows and disappeared.

By the end of the second week all needed a rest. They arrived at an ancient well that was full of brackish water, but it sufficed and camp was made. Auda went hunting and later returned with a gazelle that fed the whole party. The following dawn they moved on to avoid the blistering heat of the day and two hours later approached the great desert of towering dunes, known as the Nefudh, previously crossed only by a few intrepid explorers, including the audacious Gertrude Bell. Lawrence suggested a short cut across the dunes but this was unacceptable to Auda; the camels were nearing exhaustion, most were suffering mange that they had picked up at Wejh and the Nefudh was no place for anyone unless mounted on a healthy camel.

They started their third week by crossing the vast area of pure white sand known locally as the 'Desolate'; the blinding glare caused everyone in the party considerable discomfort and the only relief to be obtained was by wrapping the loose headdress worn by all Arabs over and below the eyes leaving the smallest slit through which to peer. The party had virtually run out of water and the hot wind slowed the camels to a mesmerizing walking pace; there was nothing else to do but continue plodding on. Then the soft underfoot sand turned to hard flint, which caused the camels great discomfort. Out of the haze came a rider who offered Auda two ostrich eggs; one turned out to be addled but the other made a welcome meal, even though most Arabs normally disdained eating eggs. Auda spotted an Oryx and, being unused to humans, it watched the party for a few moments too long – it fell to Auda's first shot and the party looked forward to dining well that evening. It was at this point that one of the camels was seen to be loose. On inspection the camel was still carrying its rider's rifle and equipment and Lawrence realized that Gasim, one of the escort, was missing. The Howeitat thought Gasim was with the Ageyl contingent, they thought the opposite. Lawrence had especially brought Gasim along as he hailed from Maan and it was intended that he would guide Lawrence around the Turkish-held town. Everyone agreed that he had most likely gone into a stupor during the intense heat of the day and fallen from his camel. To the Arabs, such an event was to be expected and none of them felt it their duty to go back for Gasim. To return into the desert without water would be certain death; instead, they looked to see what Lawrence would do.

Lawrence quietly turned his camel round and pointed her nose back into the searing heat of the white 'Desolate'. The camel pro-tested bitterly, her day's work was nearly over and the beast clearly knew that heading back into the desert did not bode well. Lawrence reckoned that their day's march had already covered nearly twenty miles and he hoped that Gasim had managed the greater portion of the journey before whatever had befallen him. As it was, Lawrence had been retracing the group's footprints for just over an hour when he saw a black dot through the heat haze. It was indeed Gasim, exhausted from following on foot, now highly confused and delirious with thirst. Lawrence dismounted and gave him the dregs from his own water bottle then pushed and pulled him onto the protesting camel. It was as if the camel understood the situation for as Lawrence turned her round she broke into a willing trot. Using his compass, Lawrence tried to ride directly towards the day's intended campsite; he had travelled for about four miles when he saw Auda riding towards him. Auda rode up greatly relieved to see Lawrence but chastised the hapless Gasim unmercifully. They continued together for another mile and caught up with the main caravan just as the group had paused to make camp on the edge of the Sirhan. The feared, barren and waterless 'Desolate' was behind them, well-watered Syria beckoned. Only during their evening meal was it noticed that Auda's slave and camel were also missing. Being mounted on a good camel no one bothered unduly but a fire was lit to act as a beacon; it was still burning at dawn but there was no trace of the hapless slave. His mummified body, blasted dry from the hot wind, was found months later beside that of his camel; both had apparently got lost and died of thirst.

Sixteen days into their journey they reached the wells at Arafaja, a small scrubby oasis where the water was unpleasant to drink, but they had no option except to fill their empty water battles from the strange-smelling well. While they were all occupied, three men of the Shammar tribe were discovered watching them from the cover of some distant scrub. Auda's cousin took a few men and pursued the scouts, only to quickly give up the chase as their camels were too weak from the long march. All was not well for Lawrence's party. That night a shot rang out from the blackness of the desert and one of the Ageyl riders screamed and fell; he died within minutes. The campfire was doused and rifles made ready but the raiders, perhaps from the earlier group of Shammar, were long gone. The events of the day reminded Lawrence of the brittle fragility of Arab unity; if an Arab could still wantonly kill another in the middle of a desert, then all his efforts were still needed to unite the tribes in their common cause against the Turks. With no further alerts, the group slept before resuming their intolerable march.

On 30 May Lawrence's group was joined by warriors of the Abu

Tayi and when the whole caravan moved off it was a spectacular sight. Accompanied by their servants and women, each family was grouped together within their allocated tribal group. Lawrence had taken two Arab boys as servants, Daud and Farraj and they had quickly become devoted to their master, although their pranks – hiding kit belonging to sleeping Arabs was a favourite – frequently got them into trouble. The Sirhan area through which they were travelling was notorious in the springtime for its deadly selection of reptiles, which habited the scrub needed for campfires. At night the snakes were especially feared as they would gather for warmth among the sleeping tribesmen. Rising each morning was a cautious affair, with each man relying on his neighbour to watch for him. Numerous snakes were killed each day and despite all their caution, three Arabs died of snake bites. The only cure was to bind the wound and recite the Koran. If the victim survived, then it was thanks to the Koran, if his sins were apparently unforgivable he died. But the caravan pressed on regardless and at last they reached Nebk, a homestead of the Ruwalla, and their long journey could now safely pause. Nebk was well sited to resupply the large caravan and possessed numerous wells and adequate grazing for the camels and mules; it was the ideal place for the central assembly point for neighbouring tribesmen to rally to the new cause, the forthcoming march on Aqaba. But with Aqaba less than 200 miles away, dissension once again threatened to breech the temporary truce throughout the Arab ranks.

The Syrian tribes, stirred on by Nesib al Bakri and Nasir, hankered to march directly on Damascus, especially as the more northern tribes, the Druse and Shaalans were ready to join an attack on the city. With their avowed objective almost in sight, the northern Arabs saw little need to go back into the desert and take Aqaba, just to assist the British. Their logic failed to take account of the Turkish fortifications just north of Aqaba and reinforcements of Turkish army units assembling at nearby Aleppo. Furthermore, the overall Arab leader, Feisal, was still back at Wejh; even if the new Arab army were to march successfully on Damascus, the British could not supply them and they had no means of maintaining communications. All logic was inconsequential to the rebels so Lawrence had to devise an alternative plan. He suggested that Nesib should indeed go to Damascus, but only with a small escort and a limited amount of gold. Nesib took the bait, not realizing that a lone Arab could do little harm to the Aqaba venture. On the other hand, Nesib could divert the Turks into believing him and sending search parties on a fruitless search for the non-existent force. If captured and forced by torture to speak, Nesib's tale of Aqaba would be so implausible as to be disbelieved. The Turks believed that not even the notorious Lawrence would come so far north just to turn back to Aqaba – and by then it would be too late.

Lawrence now made a most questionable decision. While the caravan rested and prepared for the march on Aqaba he decided to go and scout the Turkish occupied zone around Damascus, including the rail links that supplied the city. To write authoritatively on this venture is difficult; Lawrence's *Seven Pillars of Wisdom* is deliberately vague and no account is given of the trip. He later gave a number of differing accounts of his movements. It is known that he departed Nebk on or about 3 June and was accompanied by only a few body-guards. He took few stores and little money. Later accounts tell of him being transferred from tribe to tribe, entering Damascus to meet with senior officials, meeting and socializing with the Turkish appointed Arab governor, Ali Rida al Ricabi, sitting in British uniform at a café beneath a reward sign complete with his photo-graph, killing and burying some Turkish soldiers who attempted to arrest him, spying out the city's rail network and visiting a Turkish army academy (that didn't exist); these accounts are all typical Lawrence 'stories' and unverifiable – especially as he was unaccompanied at this point. He also claimed to have blown up the railway at Ras Baalkek, but this is even further north than Damascus. How this was achieved is unknown though an explosion was reported in the vicinity at the same time. Whether Lawrence was responsible, merely claimed the credit or just improved on a good story with each telling will probably never be known. What is certain is that such a mission would have been absolute folly if, indeed, it ever took place as Lawrence described. Furthermore, had he been captured the whole Aqaba expedition would certainly have failed, as would his dream of unifying Arabia. As far as this author is concerned, his two week disappearance has to remain something of a mystery.

In an account given to the historian Suliman Mousa, Nesib claimed Lawrence never left the Arab camp. Lawrence comments briefly in *Seven Pillars of Wisdom* that he undertook this long and dangerous mission to visit the more important of Feisal's secret friends and to see the key positions of their future campaigns. On the strength of his own report, uncorroborated, Lawrence received the decoration of the Companionship of the Bath. He later told Robert Graves that his account was 'part truth'.

The Arab task force to take Aqaba was now ready to depart. It consisted of over 500 tribesmen with Auda its nominated leader. They set off on 17 June and headed back into the desert, a long stony stretch of which slowed their initial progress, although everyone remained enthusiastic for the coming fight. The following day progress was still difficult so Auda took Lawrence ahead to visit the grave of one of his sons killed in an earlier tribal dispute. Lawrence was pleased to be relieved of the boredom of accompanying the plodding caravan and the pair sped off towards Bair. This suited Lawrence who was keen to check the location of the wells: with such a large party to be watered, the wells were of vital importance. As they approached the vicinity of the grave, they saw smoke rising from the wells. They scoured the vastness of the surrounding desert but could see no trace of human activity. They raced to the wells to discover the Turks had smashed the well heads and dynamited the well shafts. There were three main wells at Bair and all had been virtually destroyed; Auda then remembered a fourth a few miles distant and to their relief it was untouched, obviously this outlying well being unknown to the Turks. One well was not enough for the whole caravan so Lawrence returned to the largest of those destroyed and, descending in a bucket, found it still accessible. It was not badly damaged as one of the charges had failed to detonate. Lawrence carefully dismantled the dynamite charge, added the explosives to his supplies and declared the water fit to drink.

With the wells repaired, it was decided to rest the caravan at Bair, which gave Lawrence time to reconnoitre ahead and check the wells at Jefer. This would be an important watering place for men and camels alike, being the last known water before their intended attack on the Turkish garrison at Aba el Lissan, just forty miles inland from Aqaba. By seizing Aba el Lissan, Lawrence could cut the Turks' supply and communications line between Aqaba and Maan; this would further demoralize the Turkish garrison at Aqaba and render them more likely to surrender than fight.

It was important to decoy the Turks into thinking that Lawrence's force was little more than a raiding party, otherwise it might occur to the Turks to reinforce Aqaba from Maan. To lessen this possibility, Nesib was now active in the north near Damascus and busy spreading the word that Damascus would soon be attacked. Lawrence had also intimated at this during his recent Damascus adventure and even more convincingly, Newcombe had allowed some fake orders referring to Damascus to be found by the Turks.

To leave the Turks in no doubt that Damascus was the target, Lawrence decided to accompany a fast raiding party north to destroy the railway line at Minifer near Derra. The trip consisted of a hundred Arabs and took two days to reach its objective where the Arabs succeeded in destroying several sections of rail before laying a train-destroying mine. But no train came because they had deliberately alerted the Turks to their presence and patrols had begun to scour the surrounding area. Though many of his men were for attacking the passing Turkish patrols, they heeded his order to desist;

instead, Lawrence bribed the local peasants to inform the Turks that the saboteurs were from Azrak in the north. The deception succeeded; the Turks maintained their attention on the desert area east of Damascus, especially as three days later a supply train detonated the earlier Minifer mine causing the Turks serious problems and occupying even more troops to search the now empty desert for the long-gone raiders. In some panic the Turks destroyed water supplies along the major caravan routes, blindly sent patrols into the vast deserts and reinforced their guard posts along the railway line, all in the hope of deterring the Arabs, who were proving beyond any doubt that they could attack at will. On the return journey the Arabs captured two wounded Turkish deserters who gave themselves up. One soon died of his wounds and the other was left alongside the railway line. His dried-out skeleton was found when the Arab advance on Damascus later passed through the area.

Lawrence's raiding party followed the railway line south and at dusk came upon a small Turkish outpost guarding the refuelling station and rail store. They crept through the dunes to gain a better vantage point; having noticed some sheep tethered to a nearby post, the hungry Arabs needed little persuasion to attack. The Turks were totally unaware they were being observed until Zaal took aim at the nearest of them, an overweight officer slouching in his chair. The shot rang out and the Turks watched with incredulity as their officer slowly slipped to the floor, shot through the heart. This was the signal for Lawrence's men to charge the post; the Turks fled inside the stone building and barricaded the door. The Arabs, now unmolested by the terrified Turks, plundered what they could and rounded up the flock of sheep. Lawrence, meanwhile, supervised the Ageyl to lay out explosive charges and, on detonation, a stretch of line, a small bridge and a quantity of railway stores were blown sky high. Not wanting the Turks to follow them or open fire as they left, the barricaded blockhouse protecting the Turks was doused with drums of paraffin found in the store and set on fire. Later that evening the raiders rewarded themselves with a feast of roast mutton.

They rode on to Bair and rejoined the main force steadily moving southwards towards Aqaba, where Lawrence learned that his decoys in the north were working well. A large force of Turkish cavalry had been formed to comb the Sirhan area – they could not be further from Lawrence's force, which suggested strongly that the Turks along the route to Aqaba were unaware of their pending plight. As a precaution, the Turks had attempted to destroy the wells at Jefer, Lawrence's final water hole before the planned attack on the Turks at Aba el Lissan. Lawrence received news that the destruction of the wells had been bungled and on arrival the Arabs were able to restore the well, raising all the water they needed. They sent a small group ahead to assist the local tribesmen to take the Turkish blockhouse guarding the pass; unfortunately the Turks had been warned of the pending attack and drove the local tribesmen off before Lawrence's group could reach them. Thinking the attack had been purely a local matter the Turks sent a detachment of soldiers to exact revenge against the nearby Arab settlement; they did so by killing the inhabitants – old men, women and children – and leaving their mutilated bodies along the track. The Arab advance party came across the ravaged settlement and saw the Turkish detachment retreating ahead of them. The Arabs gave a fearful chase and fell upon the stumbling Turks slashing and stabbing at them with their swords and long knives as the ill-shod Turkish soldiers vainly attempted to flee the onslaught. It was all over in minutes.

With their blood lust inflamed, the Arabs continued on to the Turkish blockhouse and fell upon the unsuspecting defenders. Every Turk present was mercilessly slain and the blockhouse was then destroyed. The Arabs began their return journey to report to Lawrence that the way was clear. But it was not; they ran into a large Turkish force which, by a stroke of bad luck for the Arabs, just happened to have been on its way to Maan when it learned of the Arab attack on Aba el Lissan. The Turks immediately advanced in support of their colleagues guarding the pass and finding them all dead they chased off the Arab attackers. The sight the Turks found was appalling, dead soldiers lay around the smouldering blockhouse, all had been stabbed to death and most were stripped of their uniforms and weapons. With dusk falling the Turks were uncertain what to do; they gathered round the blockhouse well and settled down for the night to await orders from Maan.

Unaware of the day's events at Aba el Lissan, Lawrence had detached himself from the advancing column and accompanied a small group bent on wrecking the stretch of railway line south of Derra. With their mission successfully completed they turned back to join the main Arab force and en route they learned that the Turks had retaken the pass. Lawrence's approaching force was still unknown to the Turks, who were now inadvertently blocking the force's only route to Aqaba. With his stores running low and no opportunity to obtain fresh supplies, Lawrence found himself faced by a large, unwelcome Turkish contingent equipped with machine guns, artillery and cavalry. There was only one option, a surprise attack.

Auda agreed with Lawrence that they should ride through the night and attack the unsuspecting Turks at dawn, otherwise their mission was doomed to fail, or worse, they would all be trapped in the desert and at the mercy of the Turks. They rode through the night and by the break of day the Arabs had climbed the ridge overlooking the Aba el Lissan pass. The Turks had not deployed sentries and Lawrence was able to destroy the telephone line to Maan. Although heavily outnumbered, the Arabs quietly surrounded the sleeping soldiers from a distance of about 100 yards.

As the first rays of daylight illuminated the narrow ravine that served as the pass, the signal was given and the Arabs opened fire into the packed clusters of sleeping Turks. Confusion reigned; with the sound of rifle fire echoing round the hills, the Turks could not locate their attackers' positions or determine the strength of their force. The Turks fired wildly into the surrounding cliffs until they began to run out of ammunition. Within an hour, carefully aimed Arab sniper fire had decimated the Turkish force and panic set in. The Turkish survivors would sortie in one direction only to take fire from their rear; they would then try in a different direction and were rewarded with the same treatment. By mid morning the remaining survivors resorted to hiding among the rocks that littered the pass while the Arabs continued sniping at every movement. As the day wore on the heat in the pass rose inexorably and began to take its toll on both Arab and Turk. Each attempt by the Turks to get water from the well was met with accurate sniper fire and the growing pile of bodies around the dried-out water buckets acted as a strong deterrent to the survivors, now seriously wilting from thirst. Lawrence realized he had to act, but how? He sought out Auda and following a meaningful tease from Lawrence, the old Arab chief ran to his camel and rode off down the ridge towards a hidden gully. Lawrence guessed it led directly into the pass below, where the surviving Turks were huddled together for mutual support. Unbeknown to Lawrence, Auda had already assembled his best 300 riders in the gully and at Auda's signal, they charged down the slope and into the astonished and now exhausted Turks. A feeble volley of rifle and pistol shots was fired at the charging Arabs and four fell, two fatally.

Lawrence had in the meantime mounted his camel and gave chase, firing his revolver wildly as he went. As the Arab riders set about the remaining Turks Lawrence was thrown from his camel, forcing those following him to veer either side. He later discovered that, in his excitement, one of his pistol shots had hit the back of his own camel's head and killed the beast outright. Lawrence staggered to his feet expecting to be attacked by Turkish soldiers but the Arabs were already among the Turks and occupied with their slaughter. Fortunately for Lawrence, the only Turks near him were dead or seriously wounded. A handful of mounted Turks managed to flee from the pass but most of the Turkish soldiers were trapped and began paying the ultimate price for the slaughter of the Arab village the day before.

Few shots were fired, the Arabs preferring to use their swords and long knives; in less than five minutes, over 400 dead Turks lay around the well. Exhausted with the effort the Arab attackers heeded Lawrence's call to halt the slaughter and so one hundred or so Turks, many wounded, were pulled from their hiding places and taken captive. Some of the Arabs were all for killing them but, on this occasion, they obeyed Lawrence.

With their lives and drinking water on offer, the Turks readily talked; they admitted that they had no idea Lawrence's force was nearby and better still, the garrison at Maan was now reduced in size to less than one regiment. This news excited the Howeitat who wanted to go straight to Maan. The thought of taking a major town and looting the shops and stores was almost too much for Auda's men, who knew there was nothing at Aqaba except the derelict port. To the Arabs the tactical advantage of Aqaba paled into insignificance compared with the lure of looting Maan. But Lawrence and Auda resolved the situation by giving promises of gold at Aqaba and their argument won the day. For the moment the Arabs contented themselves with stripping the dead and wounded Turks of the few valuables they possessed. Lawrence knew that some of the Turkish escapees would report his presence to the two main Turkish outposts of Guweira and Kethera, which lay between the pass and Aqaba. He confidently expected their surrender.

Lawrence and Auda walked round the battlefield; it was a sight few men would ever want to see and Lawrence had to accept responsibility for the deaths of the hundreds of young Turks now lying still before him. But he had lost only two men in the attack and knew that the battle could easily have gone the other way. Had Lawrence lost the fight, the Turks would have shown his Arabs even less mercy. The Arabs were exhausted and that night slept where they could among the carnage. As the sun rose from behind the mountain range they wearily mounted their camels and set off towards Aqaba.

The Turks at Guweira had already surrendered to a local Howeitat sheikh and, with another 140 prisoners added to those already in tow, the Arabs pressed on and by nightfall were within three miles of Aqaba. They could now look down on the small port of Aqaba from the mountain pass and there appeared to be little Turkish activity. In the early hours the Arabs captured an unsuspecting Turkish sentry who was given a gold sovereign to return to his officers with a warning that the Arabs would kill every Turk unless they surrendered. The Turkish garrison was of equal strength to the Arabs but the Turks incorrectly thought they were heavily outnumbered. The reply came back that they would like to make a token resistance for two days, a request that was refused. They then agreed to surrender by the following mid morning just as another 300 Howeitat riders came into sight. The Howeitat Arabs were unaware of the negotiations and prepared to charge the Turkish line; both sides opened fire on each other. Lawrence and the Arab leaders were able to race between the lines to restore control and the Turks then gratefully surrendered.

Lawrence had achieved the impossible; he and his Arabs rushed through the shattered remains of Aqaba and ran joyfully into the cooling sea. Aqaba had been taken.

7

Lawrence Goes to Cairo:
July–October 1917

Lawrence found that nothing had changed in Aqaba since his earlier visit in 1913. The small port was still home to a number of Arab dhows and the few residents lived in tiny stone houses around the old fort. Now, however, Aqaba was smashed beyond recognition. Regular bombardments of the Turkish occupiers by visiting French and British warships had taken their inevitable toll. The ancient fort lay in ruins and the harbour wall was seriously damaged. Most of the local people's houses had been damaged or destroyed. The area that had been the tented village to the Turkish occupiers had been completely flattened when Lawrence's charging Arabs took the port. The Arabs were disgusted with what was left of the town. There were no buildings or shops left standing and so there was nothing left to loot; few of them could understand the logic of all the pain borne from their two-month long and hazardous desert crossing. Worse, Lawrence was not in a position to pay them their promised gold, for he had none. Without the market there was no food and Lawrence now had over 2,000 tetchy Arabs to feed and in due course the 600 or so Turkish prisoners he had collected along the way and at Aqaba would also need feeding.

By sunset the euphoria of taking Aqaba had begun to fade and Lawrence's priority returned to defending the vulnerable port. He sent Auda back to Guweira to establish a defensive ring around Aqaba. To Lawrence, there was only one way to obtain stores quickly – he had to ride to Cairo by camel and break the astonishing news that Aqaba, the Turks' vital port on the Red Sea, had been taken from them by a small independent Arab army. But he was already seriously tired, as were the Arabs' camels, and now faced a 170-mile ride across the near waterless desert in order to reach the British line. Undaunted, he selected a dozen reliable Howeitat tribesmen as his escort and, as the evening began to cool, the small party set off towards the distant hills that would take him to Suez. Provisions for the journey were few; the men would have to rely on a bag each of dates and cooked but tough camel meat. As the weary group climbed the track that led from Aqaba into the stony hills their progress slowed to little more than a hobbled walk. The long winding track was rocky and steep and the ridge heading to the high plateau was only reached after midnight. The camels were exhausted from the climb and the party slept for two hours before resuming their journey towards the village of Themed, where water could be found.

The group continued on into the Sinai desert. Hour after hour of incessant desert and heat had to be endured; even the camels appeared to understand there was no stopping except to give up and die. As they approached the distant Suez Canal they saw an array of army huts, long since deserted by the British who were now fighting far to the north. There seemed no way across the canal until Lawrence discovered a telephone still connected to the British canal head-quarters somewhere on the far bank. He managed to raise an officious clerk who clearly didn't believe who Lawrence claimed to be. For-tunately, the telephone operator was listening in to the conversation and was able to connect the stranded Lawrence with the embarkation officer at Suez town. This officer had heard of Lawrence and realizing the importance of the call, sent his own launch to collect him. Lawrence's escort was directed to a nearby camel park where they could be fed and watered and await his return. Lawrence was ferried across the canal and taken to one of the British-controlled hotels.

He strode in, in full Arab attire, sunburnt, ragged and unrecognizable, and booked a room in the name of Lieutenant Lawrence of the Sherif of Mecca's army. He then drank a succession of iced lemonades before taking himself off for a well-earned bath. His appearance shocked the officers present, whom he ignored. It was a moment of high psychological drama repeated most effectively in David Lean's magnificent film *Lawrence of Arabia;* in reality, Lawrence would have enjoyed every moment of his brother officers' discomfort and indignation to the full.

Lawrence took the train for Cairo and was repeatedly challenged along the way. Military personnel in uniform could travel free and Lawrence continued bluffing his way through by claiming he was from Feisal's army. While waiting for an onward train at Ismailia, he was questioned by an intelligence officer who had been alerted to this possible impostor. While being questioned, he watched as a sturdy general officer, deep in thought and oblivious to his attentive staff officers, paced up and down the station platform. Lawrence learned that this general was none other than General Allenby, who had recently arrived from France. Lawrence was then directed to a naval officer who understood the implication of Aqaba and the information was telegraphed on to Cairo. On arriving at his hotel in Cairo, Lawrence immediately went to see Clayton and poured out his news and plans, which were for the British to concentrate on Feisal and move the Arabs north; the cost was to be minimal, perhaps 200,000 gold sovereigns to bribe the Arab tribal leaders, a fortune in gold but small money compared with the overall cost of the war.

Clayton pacified the excited Lawrence and realizing the phenomenal importance of Lawrence's achievement, he went straight to brief General Allenby. Allenby was also astonished that this insignificant captain had been able to execute a military coup of staggering value to his own forthcoming plans. The following day Lawrence was summoned to Allenby's office. Lawrence was still wearing his ragged, but now washed, Arab costume complete with gold dagger and without further thought went straight in to see Allenby.[1] It is known that Allenby was fully briefed by Clayton about Lawrence and was keen to meet him, but the general was certainly puzzled by Lawrence's striking appearance. Once Lawrence began to explain the success of the Arab Revolt and the strategic importance of Aqaba to the Allies, Allenby was fully attentive. All the general's questions were answered to his satisfaction. Lawrence then gave Allenby a string of urgent requests: artillery, machine guns, rifles, sufficient ammunition and a regular supply of gold sovereigns for payment to the Arab tribes. Lawrence had freely written promissory notes during the mission that now required redemption and an adequate supply of food was urgently needed for the Arab troops and Turkish prisoners hungrily waiting at Aqaba.

Lawrence also wanted a free hand in his dealings with Feisal and he requested that he be answerable only to Allenby. Allenby agreed. Newcombe was to be left to try and pacify the Grand Sherif Hussein at Mecca, and Colonel Joyce, whom Lawrence approved of, was to control the new base at Aqaba. The other British officers who had rendered such valiant service, Davenport and Wilson, were effectively sidelined to allow Lawrence his free hand. Allenby agreed to all Lawrence's requests; he recognized the young man's brilliance and fervour – and his achievements. Lawrence was promoted on the spot to the field rank of major and authorized to send all the necessary stores and gold on the first available ship. No one else could have achieved the successes and victory with which Allenby had been presented. Now, with the possibility of having a friendly Arab army advancing in parallel with the proposed Allied advance northwards through Palestine, it would be tactically invaluable to have the Arabs

---

1 Lawrence wrote in his Article 18 that he wore 'Arab kit' in order to acquire the trust of and intimacy with the Arabs that would not be possible by wearing British uniform. He may have been correct but his extroversion meant that he also wore it at British headquarters in Cairo and later at the Paris Peace Conference. There can be little doubt that he primarily wore it to show off.

protect Allenby's dangerously vulnerable right flank. An Arab army loose in the desert and able to strike at will would constantly occupy the attention of the Turkish Army and the Turks would no longer be able to focus their attention on the Allies. Allenby directed Lawrence to brief the Arab Bureau, responsible for advising Allenby, to bring them up to date with the Arabs' progress and, more importantly, their potential and military needs. The Allies, forthcoming advance on Turkey was gradually appearing less hazardous.

The staff officers were still suffering shell-shock following the arrival of the dynamic Allenby. The wily general swiftly saw through their inefficiency and began by marching through their offices and dumping the outstanding contents of their social in-trays into rubbish bins. Each senior staff officer had to personally justify his job to Allenby and any officer who failed the 'worthwhile test' was returned to his unit. The remaining headquarters staff was then given notice to transfer into the desert to be nearer the front line. Allenby's own advisers were introduced to Lawrence with instructions to deal with all his urgent demands and to cooperate with his main objectives, already agreed with Allenby, including having them halt all military action south of Aqaba.

Following his success in taking Aqaba, Lawrence was not only promoted to the field rank of major but also gazetted a Companion of the Bath. He was also recommended for the Victoria Cross by the High Commissioner of Egypt, Sir Reginald Wingate. Little is known about this gallantry nomination but in a telegram to the War Office, Wingate pointed out that the Turks had already placed a £5,000 reward on Lawrence's head and in consequence, this 'considerably enhanced the gallantry of his exploit.' The final line of the telegram reads: 'I strongly recommend him for an immediate award of the Victoria Cross, and submit that this recommendation is amply justified by his skill, pluck and endurance.' Wingate felt so strongly about the award that he also wrote seeking support for his nomination to Sir Mark Sykes. A letter from the Director of Military Intelligence comments: 'The DMI sends you his account of Lawrence's wonderful journey. Was ever a VC better earned?'

Lawrence claimed to have been relieved when he heard that the award of the VC had been vetoed, on the official grounds that his exploits had 'not been witnessed by another officer'. If this explanation is correct, then the reason given is invalid. VCs had been awarded in such circumstances, albeit rarely, since the Anglo–Zulu War of 1879. Lawrence's coup in taking Aqaba had taken the French by complete surprise and although astonished and taken aback by the secrecy, success and audacity of his raid, they nevertheless swallowed their pride by awarding him the coveted Croix de Guerre.

The Turks were now trapped in the far south. Without regular supplies and totally unable to exert any influence in the region they would be quickly rendered *hors de combat*. As a military force they would become impotent and Lawrence suggested they should be left to starve until after the war. Lawrence also advocated giving more political power to Feisal; this was part of Lawrence's master plan, to make Feisal the new Arab leader following the war. Feisal's father, Sherif Hussein of Mecca, was already old and unable fully to comprehend matters beyond his present base at Jeddah. The plan met with overall approval and Colonel Wilson, accompanied by Lawrence, was sent to sweet-talk the old Arab leader. Having been earlier briefed by Lawrence about his master plan, Feisal was then requested to close his operations at Wejh and move to Aqaba. His best camel troops went by the coastal route while the stores and foot soldiers went courtesy of the Royal Navy; the whole move took less than one month during which time a new landing ground for the delivery of supplies from the sea was built thirty-five miles from Aqaba.

While Lawrence was waiting for Wilson to placate the old king, he received the worst news possible from his friends in Army Intelligence in Cairo; Auda and his Howeitat tribe guarding Guweira to the north of Aqaba were conducting secret negotiations with the Turks. Lawrence was furious. He immediately rushed to get on board a warship bound for Aqaba. Three days later he arrived at the port and, taking Nasir's best camel, immediately set off for Auda's camp at Guweira. He arrived at dawn to find Auda taking breakfast with his top chiefs; all were stunned by Lawrence's unexpected arrival. Lawrence refrained from saying anything about his purpose as he wanted to assess the situation for himself and ensure that he would be able to escape if the intelligence report was correct. By midday he felt sufficiently confident to take Auda to one side and confront him with the report. Auda thought the whole episode was highly amusing and claimed that his chief, Mohammed, had played a confidence trick on the Turks offering support in exchange for gold. The Turks had taken the bait and sent Mohammed a supply of gold, which Auda had ambushed. It was a plausible story and Lawrence admired its ring of truth – but he thought that there might be more to the incident than Auda was admitting. Not wishing to prolong Auda's unease, Lawrence changed the subject and informed him that Feisal was now at Aqaba and that the whole Arab army was about to advance, collecting Auda's force as they passed through Guweira. This information let Auda know Feisal's force was growing by the day. Lawrence also advised him that Feisal was well armed with artillery and high explosives and further, that senior Arab leaders would be rewarded with much gold. Auda understood the implied threat and loudly professed his loyalty to Lawrence and Feisal. Auda never found out how Lawrence had discovered his secret liaison with the Turks and so Auda's loyalty was secured, for the time being.

Auda's deception had seriously shaken Lawrence and reminded him that his European concept of Arab loyalty and unity were little more than a wishful figment of his imagination. The incident made Lawrence consider the problems he and Feisal now faced. In reality, the Arab war against Turkey was over. The Turks to the south were trapped and with Allenby's Allied force ready to advance northwards, there was nothing to stop the Allies sweeping through Palestine and on into Turkey – the Turks were going to be defeated regardless of the Arab contribution. For Lawrence to achieve his aim of Arab freedom, all that the Arabs now had to do was hold together and advance in tandem with Allenby, and then jump ahead to seize Damascus. Only by achieving this bold move would the Arabs have any influence in their post-war future. But there were still serious problems to overcome; the Arab tribes persisted in maintaining their disunity, each jealous of the other, and inter-tribal feuding was an unwritten seething custom. The coastal Arabs were more used to European ways and culture; these were people with developing liberal outlooks and more sophisticated expectations, whereas the majority of inland Arab tribes were effectively nomadic desert Bedouins who rarely had contact with their coastal cousins. The final route to Damascus would involve moving through numerous regions, many separated by hills, mountains or deserts, each with different loyalties, jealousies, infrastructures and customs. The only common denominator among these diverse people was the Arab language and Lawrence fully understood the point made long ago by Socrates, that a disorderly mob is no more of an army than a heap of bricks is a house. Lawrence pondered whether and how they could be united for the final push to Damascus, for without Arab unity there would be no Arab capture of Damascus and without Damascus there could be never be a viable independent Arab nation.

There was only one solution that stood any chance of success. Lawrence realized it might be possible to repeat the tactic used in his recent advance on Aqaba, which started with a small loyal band and recruited its followers as they progressed. Lawrence proposed to Feisal that this tactic could possibly work again for the proposed Arab advance north. As Feisal's Arab fighters advanced northwards through the desert, Lawrence felt certain that Feisal would have the authority to coerce local tribes they met along the route, allowing them free passage and also supplying Feisal with armed tribesmen in support of his growing army. Lawrence had already been warned by Auda that none of the northern tribes would independently rise against the Turks so it would have to be left to the gathering Howeitat to start the chain reaction and recruit as they advanced from Aqaba. Feisal approved the plan.

By the beginning of September 1917 the coastline at Aqaba was seething with military personnel busy supervising the unloading of ships; there were huge crates of stores containing long-range guns, motorcycles and armoured cars. Dashing to and fro were chains of Egyptian workers engaged in rebuilding the town's defences and battered port. Feisal was responsible for manning the mountain pass to Guweira and detailing the scouts that ensured the Turks kept their distance. Lawrence had not anticipated having to defend Aqaba but the timescale to advance Feisal's army northwards was inexorably extending; it had taken Feisal longer than expected to move his army from Wejh to Aqaba, which had given the Turks time to reorganize. Their senior German commander, General Falkenhayn, had meanwhile taken control and unexpectedly moved a division of experienced troops to Maan. He was a sound tactician and Lawrence realized he could effectively block any advance by the Arabs on Maan. Then came worse news. The Turks appeared to be mobilizing at Maan for a full attack on Aqaba, no doubt with the intention of retaking the port; they were also preparing an area outside Maan to land aircraft. They had increased their infantry strength by some 6,000 troops and a full regiment of cavalry and additional artillery were on their way from Turkey. The Turks were also busy strengthening the defences at Aba el Lissan and rebuilding the blockhouses along the railway. Lawrence was galvanized into action.

Feisal's desert raiders began to attack isolated groups of Turks and their supply lines. Lawrence knew that not knowing where the wide-ranging Arabs would strike next would occupy a disproportionate number of the Maan garrison on widespread defensive duties. Lawrence then arranged for the RAF to bomb the Turks from their air base at El Arish in the British occupied zone. By their accuracy, such bombings were highly effective and especially demoralizing for the

Turks; Lawrence arranged for the two available aircraft to be refuelled after each sortie at a secret flat desert strip near Aqaba that had been specially cleared for the purpose. The RAF bombings from this strip added to the frustrations of the Turks; they knew the main RAF airfield was several hours' flying time distant yet, somehow, the two same planes could complete a bombing mission and then return within the hour to repeat the process. Such was the pilots' ability to accurately bomb the Turks that the Maan garrison commander had to spend valuable time constructing defences instead of preparing to attack Aqaba.

Until Allenby gave the word for Feisal to advance his growing army northwards, the Turks had to be deterred from even considering a move on Aqaba. Lawrence turned his attention to the sport he loved best, blowing up Turkish trains. Towards the end of September attacking the Hejaz Railway nearest to Aqaba was too close to Maan for comfort; heavily armed Turkish troops could be seen constantly patrolling along the line either side of the town so Lawrence focused his attention on their main railhead to the south at Mudowwara, considered by the Turks to be impregnable. This heavily fortified station was about eighty-five miles equidistant from Aqaba and Maan and was the key water-tank station for the trains supplying the Turks' garrisons at Medina and Mecca. There was no direct route to the station from Aqaba, other than across vast waterless wastes of desert, which added to the Turks' confidence. Having proved his endurance by crossing even greater distances to reach Aqaba, Lawrence believed that a sizeable Arab force could secretly reach Mudowwara and destroy the station, together with its water tanks and rail line, before the Turks at Maan even learned of the attack. The Turks would then be forced to re-establish the railhead and extend their defensive patrol line all the way from Maan to Mudowwara, which would occupy at least 500 extra Turkish troops. Conscious of the Turks' ability rapidly to patrol the line, Lawrence knew he had to be able to 'hit-and-run' otherwise the Arabs would take serious casualties. The Turks' trains were now properly armoured and, having got used to the Arabs dynamiting their trains, they had devised a system of placing trucks of Arab civilians or empty wagons in front of the locomotives to take the initial blast. The problem had been discussed with the Royal Navy engineers in Egypt who suggested the use of new electrically detonated mines, which could be safely detonated from a distance and at the right moment to cause maximum destruction, rather than have the first carriage detonate the explosives. Knowing the trains were now accompanied by armoured wagons and experienced Turkish troops, Lawrence also called for better artillery and more machine guns – all of which were provided from Egypt. The explosives and guns duly arrived along with two non-Arabic-speaking sergeant instructors, who ably relied on hand signals to train their non-English-speaking Arab pupils. The sergeants were named by everyone after their preferred gun type, and so 'Stoke' and 'Lewis' soon became part of Lawrence's team and were detailed to accompany the Mudowwara raid.

To ensure its success, the raid on Mudowwara station was planned with at least a hundred well-armed Arab raiders mounted on fleet-of-foot camels and supported by small field guns. Lawrence had already assembled his explosives team and intended to collect most of the fighting men from Auda's tribe, reputedly keen for another fight and now guarding Guweira. Lawrence and his escort, accompanied by the nominal leader for the raid, a Harith sheikh, and Stokes and Lewis, set off to Guweira on the far side of the head of the Aqaba pass. As they wound round the high pass they were spotted by a Turkish plane on its daily raid on Guweira; the aircraft never ventured to Aqaba where the artillery would have shot it down, but instead of causing its daily confusion at Guweira, the lone plane bombed Lawrence's caravan. The bombs all missed their target and the plane flew off back to Maan. The caravan plodded on to Guweira to find the camp in turmoil. Auda was, as usual, the cause of the problem. Knowing he was vital to Feisal's plan for the Arab march on Damascus, he had begun lording it over the lesser tribes and was demanding their loyalty. Unused to coercion, especially by a rival tribal leader, they were on the verge of leaving the camp and returning to the desert. Lawrence needed these men who were all experienced desert fighters and set about trying to resolve the problem. Auda saw reason and leaving him with firm orders to resolve the problem with the arguing Arabs, Lawrence and his small party continued on towards the abundant springs at Wadi Rumm, the renowned site of many epigraphical finds and archaeological remains. The weather was unbearably hot and the glare of the white sand affected everyone.

The approach to Rumm was one of Lawrence's favourite locations. The soft sand was interrupted by huge volcanic thrusts of red sandstone that soared a thousand feet into the deep blue sky. Rumm itself extended for over seventy miles and there were many secret places hidden among the sandstone cliffs. One of these was the spring that flowed from a fissure in the rock some 300 feet above the desert floor. As the water trickled down the hot sandstone it evaporated and could not be seen from below. This was to be their campsite for the night. That evening, while waiting for news from Auda, the Harith sheikh crept to Lawrence and cried that he had gone blind from the glare of the sun. Lawrence took pity on the man and had him escorted to a neighbouring friendly tribe who would return the luckless sheikh to his own people; the incident reminded Lawrence of the danger crossing the desert in summer, but he also knew the Turks would never expect him to ride to Mudowwara in the ferocious heat.

That evening a party of headmen arrived, representing several of the Arab clans in dispute with Auda. All were adamant they would not serve under Auda and a lengthy argument ensued; by dawn most of the leaders had reconciled themselves to remaining loyal to Feisal, except one particularly important Arab, Gasim Abu Dumeik. The stalemate continued until Zaal, an Auda lieutenant, arrived. Within minutes a heated exchange began between Zaal and Gasim. The argument degenerated into blows and wild swings before the pair were dragged apart; this was no way to commence a serious desert ride. Lawrence realized he needed moral support from Feisal and rode off alone back to Aqaba leaving the squabbling Arab leaders stranded. Perhaps without thinking, Lawrence took a direct route across the mountains and luckily came out directly above Aqaba; Feisal was astonished to see Lawrence return and dismayed by his account of the expedition leaders' disharmony. Feisal nominated one of his family members to accompany Lawrence back to the expedition and without pause, the pair rode back into the hills.

At the camp little had changed but the arrival of Feisal's representative restored sufficient peace for Gasim to calm down and half of his men agreed to ride under Feisal's banner. With relative peace restored the group set off. They were without a formal Arab leader, but all were prepared to accept Lawrence's orders. After an hour into the journey Lawrence noticed riders gaining on his party from the direction of their overnight camp. The Arabs loyal to Gasim had finally decided that their duty lay in supporting Feisal and had ridden hard to catch up. They also knew by remaining behind they would miss looting the Turkish station.

Lawrence now had the hundred or so men he needed but he was still left with the responsibility of planning and executing the march, agreeing halts, feeding and issuing orders for the proposed attack. Nevertheless, the marchers finally seemed to be working well together. The next day continued with unending desert and blasting heat and the party made for a sheltered valley just three miles from Mudowwara station where Zaal was certain water could be found. He assured Lawrence that the location was unknown to the Turks though the group approached the well with extra caution. The Turks had indeed found the well and although it was unguarded, they had made the water undrinkable by leaving a dead camel and some rotting sheep to pollute the water. The Arabs had no choice but to remove the dead animals and draw buckets of the foul-smelling slime from the well to fill their water bottles. The only alternative was to die of thirst.

That evening, Lawrence and Zaal took Lewis and Stokes to reconnoitre the Turkish position; they waited for darkness to fall and crawled to a ridge about a quarter of a mile from the station. They could see that the Turkish defensive trench was unoccupied and crept closer but Lawrence and his two sergeants agreed the station was now so well built that even their explosives would do little damage. They returned safely to their camp. Lawrence decided that an Arab attack on Mudowwara was unlikely to succeed and he was reluctant to consider putting any of his men at risk. By now both Stokes and Lewis were suffering from the polluted water and became uncomfortably ill with raging diarrhoea. This convinced Lawrence to change his plan and instead of attacking the Turks' stronghold he instructed the party to move three miles further south to where he knew the railway passed over a bridge, which would be a suitable alternative target. The following morning they approached the railway and made for a low range of broken hills leading almost to the rail track. From here they could work on the track unobserved by the Turks and then, if the attack was successful, they could open fire on the train wreckage from the safety of the hills before making their escape.

During the day Lawrence supervised the laying of the electrically fired mine. Due to the proximity of the Turks, scouts were posted on a neighbouring rise to warn of any unwelcome approach. Lawrence took great care moving the explosives to the point where the bridge met the line and set about scraping away the loose sand to hide the bulk of the mine, always conscious that he would never have more than five minutes warning of approaching Turks. None came. Each scoop of sand had to be carefully removed and dumped where it would be unseen by passing Turks and this he did by putting it in his cloak and having it carried away. After the laying of the mine came the drums of electrical wire that ran from the mine to the person charged with detonating the device. This aspect had, however, not been rehearsed and Lawrence found that as he uncoiled the wire, it sprang back naturally into loops that kept popping up through the sand. Stones had to be hurriedly collected and then, with the wires eventually covered, sand had to be poured over the stones to hide the tell-tale lines through the sand to the detonator. With the job done and no sign of any Turks, Lawrence caused great mirth among the Arabs by producing an old pair of fire bellows; he proceeded to gently puff the sand around the mine and line to remove any trace of footprints or human activity. When satisfied, the mine-laying party returned towards the main group behind the hillock. Meanwhile, bored with little to do, the main attacking force of Arabs had climbed the ridge to watch Lawrence's mine-laying. As the hours passed, the sun moved round until the figures became unwittingly silhouetted against the darkening skyline. Suddenly rifle fire came from the direction of the station, the Turks had seen the exposed figures, although at a distance of over three miles, but none dared to venture out and investigate. Lawrence deduced that they would suspect the figures to be passing Arab nomads and would probably visit the site next day. Lawrence decided to see what the following morning brought. They ate and slept well, rising about an hour before dawn on 19 September, in case the Turks were on the move in their direction but nothing stirred at Mudowwara.

An hour later, considerable activity was seen at Mudowwara station when the Turks assembled a patrol that then set off along the line towards the detonation point. Lawrence was confident his men had not been detected but with the Turks in open formation he guessed they were sweeping the area rather than investigating the railway line. With the Turkish party outnumbered by Lawrence's force, his Arabs were in no real danger but any action would immediately bring all Turkish rail traffic to a halt. Lawrence quickly sought Zaal's cooperation and within minutes a small force of his Arabs slipped away and rapidly moved out of sight of the Turks to a position nearer the station. They let the Turks go past and then began sniping at them from their rear. The Turks clearly believed this was the same small group of Arabs seen the day before and about-turned to face their fire. The Arabs let the Turks see them and once the Turks turned towards their party they mounted their camels and rode off into the desert. Satisfied they had repulsed the raiders, the Turks returned to the station.

By now the Arabs were in a considerable state of anticipation and eager for any action. They then noticed a second small line-patrol approaching from the station and all settled down behind the ridge so as not to give their position away. To their relief the Turks walked over the mine and carried on. Within minutes another much larger Turkish force was seen marching out from the station, this group consisting of an equal number to Lawrence's waiting Arabs, which prompted Lawrence to withdraw further into the desert with the intention of returning later. At that very moment train smoke could be seen approaching from the south so Lawrence quickly reverted to train-attacking mode – the train would arrive in ten to fifteen minutes and it would take the marching Turks another hour to reach his position, putting them out of the equation.

The Arabs moved off to their allocated positions nearer the bridge, including the seriously ailing Stokes and Lewis who nevertheless prepared their guns for firing from the nearby ridge. The train was approaching at speed and Lawrence saw that the Turks had protected the train by using two steam engines at the front so that any mine would strike the first engine allowing the second to reverse and pull the train out of danger. Lawrence was pleased he was using an electrical mine whereby he could control the explosion to a split second; he decided to detonate the mine under the second engine, which would leave the first in peril on the bridge with the second unable to move. The train continued at high speed and as it approached the position where the Arabs had been seen the evening before, the Turkish train guard opened fire on the now abandoned ridge, which indicated the Turks' communications were still effective. There were ten wagons full of soldiers and two machine-gun carriages that all joined in firing at the empty ridge, clearly oblivious they were rapidly approaching the mined bridge. Lawrence raised his hand in readiness and the Arab selected to press the plunger was sweating with excitement – if the attack was successful, his reputation among his tribesmen would rise inexorably – with his eyes locked on Lawrence's raised hand. As the first engine touched the bridge Lawrence dropped his hand. The Arab plunged the detonator and there was an instant and massive explosion from the bridge. The force was enormous and completely obliterated the train from view. All the Arabs could see was a huge cloud of sand, smoke and parts of the train, which could be seen rising a hundred feet into the air before hanging and then falling majestically back into the cloud of dust. After the deafening shock wave of the blast everything went silent as the dust began to settle.

The Arabs opened fire as soon as they could see the wrecked carriages. The surviving Turks were well trained for the event and those uninjured in the following carriages were seen clambering from the wrecked carriages and onto the roofs to get a better firing position from which to return fire. At that moment, however, Lewis opened fire with his machine gun and swept each carriage roof clear of Turks. He then opened fire into the carriages themselves. Stokes was dropping mortar bombs in quick succession onto the train and after less than a minute the surviving Turks were forced to run for their lives into the desert before turning towards the distant station and the approaching Turkish column. Lawrence returned his gaze to the train and saw the Arabs had already reached the carriages; as usual, slaughter of the Turkish survivors was the Arabs first priority and then they would commence looting. With the marching Turks now only about two miles away and briskly advancing towards the wrecked bridge and train, Lawrence gave his men about half an hour to finish loading their loot.

Lawrence ran forward to inspect the bridge and was well satisfied with its destruction. The first engine was hanging off the track and appeared in reasonable condition whereas the second had been completely blown apart. He took a charge of dynamite and fuse cord from his haversack and placed it against the first engine's boiler, anticipating the fuse would burn for about twenty minutes and explode as the Turkish relief column arrived. He then moved back to the first carriage and saw it contained sick Turkish soldiers. The Arabs had ignored it as most of the wagon's sick Turks were now dead from the blast and there was nothing left to loot. One dying Turk, perhaps believing Lawrence was a colleague, muttered the word 'typhus' whereupon Lawrence rapidly withdrew.

The train had carried a sizeable force of troops but two carriages at the rear of the train carried their families and another carriage contained the wives of Turkish officers. The cacophony of noise around the wrecked train was almost overpowering; the Arabs were shouting, firing wildly and looting with abandon while most of the women screamed in wild terror. There were several Austrian officers accompanying the train who were advisers to the Turks and on realizing who Lawrence was, went to him and politely pleaded for mercy for the Turkish women and wounded; Lawrence assured them they would not be harmed. One officer asked for a doctor but during his brief conversation with Lawrence another Austrian officer took out his pistol and deliberately shot at an Arab; within seconds the only Austrian left alive was the one lucky enough to be talking to Lawrence. Also on the train were half a dozen Egyptian prisoners being taken by the Turks for interrogation. They were relieved to be released and Lawrence gave them the task of rounding up the few able-bodied survivors and marching them off towards the return route to Aqaba. Stokes came down to see the effect of his mortar fire on the last carriage and was promptly sick at the sight of his work: there had been no survivors.

Lawrence suddenly realized the relief column of Turks had made good progress and were fast approaching the bridge. His Arabs had now all departed, urgently pushing their loot-laden camels back into the desert. Lawrence was relieved when Zaal returned with three camels, onto which they loaded their guns and mortars and made off for the safety of the ridge. Once secure, Lawrence gathered the remainder of the explosives and stores and placed a detonator with a short fuse under the pile. As they rode off the pile exploded making the Turks think there was still a sizeable force of Arabs behind the ridge. At the same time, Lawrence's dynamite charge on the first engine exploded; the destruction of the two engines had been ach-ieved. Lawrence's stragglers joined the rest of the retreating Arabs and headed back to the safety of the heat-blasted desert. As they moved onto the bleak sands Lawrence checked to see if any of his men had been wounded. A number of camels had minor shrapnel wounds; otherwise his force seemed intact, apart from one Arab known to have been killed in the rush on the train. Lawrence was relieved that his force had escaped relatively unscathed. By necessity, the Arabs always killed their own seriously wounded lest they were captured by the Turks. A favourite sport for the Turks was to slowly roast captured or wounded Arabs on an open fire. Lawrence then learned an Arab youth, Salim, was missing. Lawrence was annoyed that he had not been informed earlier and so, with Zaal and ten of his men, they raced back towards the scene hoping to find Salim. Coming in sight of the wrecked train they saw it swarming with Turks; knowing the fate of captured Arabs, Lawrence and his men turned back into the desert. As they approached their retreating caravan they saw the bloodied form of Salim hanging onto the back of a camel. He had somehow been overlooked in the initial search and in due course made a good recovery from his wounds.

The party's route back to Aqaba was easy to follow as they had their own footprints to trace. After two days of incessant heat and slow walking with nearly 100 Turkish prisoners and some Arab women refugees from the train, the party wearily arrived back in

Aqaba. The euphoria of their success was infectious and there was much celebrating to be done. In the warm afterglow of his triumph, Lawrence wrote a full report and extolled the virtue of using electrical detonations in future attacks on the Turkish railway. Stokes and Lewis needed to recuperate from their lingering dysentery so Lawrence sent them back to Egypt where they received a heroic welcome by their units and a medal each from Allenby for their endeavours.

There were still no orders from Allenby so Lawrence settled on using the time to continue wrecking the Turkish rail line. Feisal was keen to maintain the raids on the Turks as it occupied his men and kept the Turks from turning their attention on Aqaba. Lawrence decided that, in order to keep Gasim's Arabs on side while waiting at Rumm, he would use them on the next raid. He rode to Rumm where he collected a force of nearly 200 riders and set off in the direction of Maan. Lawrence intended to take the Turks by surprise by attacking the line north of Maan where they least expected an attack. They rode north keeping clear of Turkish patrols until they found where the rail line ran through a ravine and onto a small bridge. They settled half a mile from the line behind the safety of a long sandy ridge and prepared the charge of dynamite. A French officer, Captain Pisani, accompanied the raid and Lawrence allowed him to lay the charge under the bridge. Work commenced after dark and was completed within two hours; they settled down to await the dawn and the first Turkish train. See Appendix B for further details of French activities.

The call came at about 11 a.m. when an approaching train was seen; all waited expectantly for the explosion, which never came. The train passed on its way only for the Arabs to see it was a water train. It was to their relief that it had passed unscathed as there would have been no loot. Lawrence waited for the heat of the day, when Turkish scouts would be sleeping, and crept forward to re-fuse the mine. The switch had failed so Lawrence laid a new electrical mine over the existing charge and resited the guns covering the ambush site. As at Mudowwara he intended to totally destroy the train to minimize Arab losses.

The following morning, 25 September, the smoke of a train could be seen approaching the bridge from Maan. At the same time a party of Turks could be seen marching along the line towards the bridge. Lawrence hoped both would meet at the same time. The train approached steadily; it had twelve carriages and from its sounds the Arabs guessed it was heavily laden, Lawrence hoped not with too many troops. As the engine reached midway over the bridge Lawrence dropped his arm and the bridge exploded in a massive cloud of dust and debris. The engine disappeared from sight into the low ravine and immediately his machine-gunners opened fire. Mortar bombs plopped down onto the remaining carriages, their explosions ripping the carriages and track apart. Led by Captain Pisani, the Arabs poured down off the ridge and onto the train. The surviving Turks offered no resistance and stood in groups with their hands held high and were relieved to be taken alive as prisoners. The Arabs had learned of their prisoners' enthusiasm to talk under questioning and were now keen to discover the Turks' dispositions. With the train successfully destroyed and looted, the Arabs abandoned the wounded Turks to their fate and marched their prisoners off; four days later, they reached Aqaba.

At the beginning of October Lawrence was recuperating at Aqaba when he received orders to travel to Egypt to meet with Allenby. Meanwhile, the more enthusiastic Arabs had been divided into demolition groups and were being taught how to destroy trains successfully using the new electrical detonators. After Lawrence left for Cairo the Arabs, with Pisani, put their training to good use and over the following six weeks undertook a number of missions against the Turks' railway system and destroyed some twenty Turkish trains causing much panic and confusion in the Turkish High Command.

It was at this point that Lawrence discovered the full significance of the previously secret Sykes–Picot agreement. The Russians had somehow obtained a copy of the agreement and sent it to the Turks, who passed it to the Arabs to show the duplicity of the British and French.[2] The Turkish commander-in-chief in Syria, Jemal Pasha, thought that the disclosure of the secret treaty to the Arabs could stop the Arab Revolt in its tracks and turn them against the Allies, and especially against the British. When Feisal heard rumours of the treaty he contacted his father for details and clarification. Hussein assured Feisal that all was well and Feisal later recalled the event as follows: 'King Hussein communicated to London and the British Government assured him that the sensational news reported by the Turks was merely an intrigue on their part, and that England had no intention other than that of the liberation of all the Arabs.'

And so the myth that Britain would support the Arabs would be continued by both the British and Lawrence. Knowing the outcome of the war would be highly unsatisfactory for the Arabs, Lawrence's *Seven Pillars of Wisdom* clearly reflects his deep concern and embarrassment caused by the deliberate leaking of the Sykes–Picot agreement. His loyalty to his country was further shaken by the revelation that Britain's word to the Arabs would be broken at the cessation of hostilities and it can be no surprise that Lawrence felt his unswerving loyalty to his country had been sorely abused. It is at this point that Lawrence turned his allegiance to the Arab cause and focused on getting the Arabs to Damascus ahead of the British.

---

2 The original purpose of the treaty was for France and Britain to agree the disposal of Turkish provinces once Turkey was defeated and by definition, this included Arabia as a former part of the Ottoman Empire. After the war the treaty was never ratified but the most injurious sections for Arabia were taken into the subsequent San Remo Pact, which divided the area under consideration into five segments under British, French and Russian control. The two diplomats responsible for the treaty, Sir Mark Sykes and M. Georges Picot actually went to Jeddah in May 1917 specifically to explain the terms of the treaty to Emir Hussein. It may well be that the wily old king, as ever ferociously jealous of his son Feisal, kept the terms of the treaty from Feisal and, as a consequence, from Lawrence. The treaty was described by the Arab historian, George Antonius, as being a 'shocking document, greed at its worst and a startling piece of double-dealing.'

8

Stalemate: Winter 1917

With the Turks now on the defensive, Allenby spent the winter of 1917 planning the first stage of his 1918 attack on the well-defended Turkish positions across Palestine. Of utmost priority to the British commander was the need to understand the extent of Arab support for his right flank, which would otherwise be exposed to possible Turkish attacks from the open desert. Allenby had also received disquieting information that the Turks were still planning to recover Aqaba from their two bases at Aba el Lissan and Maan, which would place them immediately behind and on the flank of his army's advance northwards. Lawrence was already aware of the problem and his correspondence with Allenby was reassuring. His Arabs were constantly on the move, which meant that they could protect the Allies' desert flank and in so doing, were occupying many thousands of Turkish troops. Allenby accepted the wisdom of Lawrence's tactics; the Turks had no idea of Arab dispositions whereas Lawrence knew exactly where the Turks were. Lawrence intimated to Allenby that, rather than fear a Turkish attack against Aqaba, he would actually welcome the move so that the Arabs could trap the Turks in the high mountainous passes that led to the port. Allenby was satisfied with the report. Meanwhile, Lawrence proposed to continue harassing the Turks by organizing additional on-going raids against their rail supply lines.

Further north, the main British advance had previously made two attempts to take the Turkish front line near Beersheba and had been repulsed. But now Allenby was in charge and he ordered massive troop and artillery reinforcements for his own pre-emptive attack, which he would need to have successfully completed by the following month before the rains were due. Allenby needed to occupy the forward ground so that his armies could move forward during the winter and have their supply lines established by the coming spring. Allenby's agents had let the Turks believe the main British thrust would come at Gaza, whereas Allenby intended to repeat the earlier unsuccessful strike against the Turks at Beersheba and, if possible, take both Jerusalem and the port of Haifa, which he could profitably use as the supply port for his forward line. Lawrence assured Allenby that once the main Allied attack was underway he could muster sufficient Arabs to protect and support the Allied advance from the desert.

Lawrence did not want to commit the northern Arabs until British success was assured. He knew that another Allied defeat, especially one assisted by the Arabs, would result in the Turks exacting ferocious revenge on nearby Arab towns and villages. Instead, Lawrence proposed a serious raid, going even further north and behind Turkish lines, this time to the river Yarmuk, which flowed through a mountainous ravine. The Turk's main rail supply line followed this precipitous river gorge from the coast to Derra. Due to its strategic importance, the line had been built at great cost along the treacherous and steep-sided river and was vital to the Turks as it supplied their large force in Palestine with everything it needed from the main Turkish base at Derra. Allenby agreed with the planned operation; it would occupy and confuse the Turks behind their own line and any damage to the precarious viaducts and bridges that criss-crossed the river would greatly handicap the Turks' campaign. Such a successful raid would also cut the escape route for any retreating Turks attempting to rejoin their main army at Derra and make their relief a logistical nightmare. Apart from the Yarmuk raid, both Allenby and Lawrence agreed that the Arab Revolt, as such, should be delayed until the spring of the following year, when it could coincide with the final and main Allied attack through Palestine and on to Turkey itself.

Lawrence knew a successful Arab raid on the Yarmuk ravines would be a severe blow to Turkish military morale. They would never suspect a large Arab force to be capable of travelling so far north from Aqaba, especially with winter approaching. The mountain passes would soon be difficult to cross and with the first snow falls expected at high altitude, access would ordinarily become virtually impossible. The plan was swiftly prepared. Lawrence would detonate the viaduct and following the explosions a strong posse of Auda's Howeitat would lead the charge against any Turkish defenders, with their attack supported by Indian machine-gunners who were agitating for some action as they were still unproven in battle. A message came from Allenby that he wanted the bridges destroyed on or shortly after 5 November and Feisal agreed the plan. From Aqaba, the force would ride to Jefer and then on to Bair before resupplying itself at Azrak, a journey of almost 250 miles each way. The Arab force was to be led by Ali ibn el Hussein, a Harith chief who had considerable support in the north, especially with the Beni Sakhr tribe who occupied extensive territory through which the force would have to pass.

The Algerian tribal leader, Abd el Kader, together with several score of his followers was currently ensconced at Aqaba. Kader normally resided in the Yarmuk area and offered Lawrence his services as a guide. Just as the party set off, Lawrence received a message from the French liaison officer in Cairo, Colonel Brémond, that Abd el Kader was a spy in league with the Turks. Apparently the Turks were desperate to learn what was happening at Aqaba and had sent Kader to spy. Feisal was unsure of the strength of the warning so he nominated the suspect Algerian as Hussein's deputy in order that his loyalty could be put to the test. Lawrence was to be supported by Captain Wood, a Royal Engineers officer who had found himself at

Aqaba awaiting repatriation to England having received a bullet wound to his head. As a precaution against intrigue, Lawrence boosted his own bodyguard with the addition of some Syrian tribesmen, who had the bonus of knowing the Yarmuk gorge from their previous travels.

Lawrence's expedition split up to cross the desert in order to lessen the possibility of a Turkish ambush and the only party to be spotted and fired upon was Ali's group, accompanied by Abd el Kader, which further raised Lawrence's suspicions. The expedition met up at Jefer where Auda was in residence with some of his tribe. Auda was now content with life – the gold he had hitherto received ensured a comfortable life style and raiding the Yarmuk bridges, especially in winter, was definitely not part of his plan. Accordingly he elected not to accompany Lawrence. By 1 November Lawrence's group was well on its way to Bair when it was attacked by a group of Beni Sakhr Arabs. After much shouting, the Beni Sakhr ceased firing and rode up to apologize for the attack and sought to make amends by placating Lawrence's men with lavish hospitality. That night they could hear the distant sounds of Allenby's artillery as the Allies pressed the Turkish line, which invariably made the Arabs uneasy. After all, the Turks and Arabs were all Muslims and it was Christian guns that were pounding the Turkish positions. Lawrence understood their unease, which, when added to the earlier Beni Sakhr attacks, forcefully reminded him of the frailty of his mission for Arab unity.

Early on the following day, as they rode across the ridges of flowering saffron, Lawrence became aware that they were being shadowed by a large group of riders. The last thing he wanted was a fight, either with an Arab raiding party or the Turks. However, the group turned out to be friendly Arabs of the Serahin tribe wishing to join in the attack but uncertain of their reception from such a large fighting force. All were greeted by Lawrence but their news was not welcome. Being local to the target area along the Yarmuk, they had observed increased Turkish defences being built to protect the rail viaducts and hundreds of Turkish troops were now engaged in rebuilding and logging timber; all were billeted near the viaducts. Furthermore, the Serahin leader was alarmed that Lawrence was accompanied by Kader, whose people lived at the far end of the gorge and who were known to be friendly with the Turks; they mistrusted the man and suspected a trap. Another factor had already occurred to Lawrence: if the heavy rain continued the route into and away from the gorge would be difficult, it was well known for its mudslides and the tribesmen rarely went into the surrounding hills in winter. This meant Lawrence's men would have to traverse the area twice. Lawrence needed a show of success – without it Arab unity would suffer a serious blow, and worse, Lawrence would fail Allenby. So he and Ali ibn el Hussein gathered the Arabs together and appealed to their sense of loyalty over their judgement. Lawrence fortunately prevailed and preparations for the attack continued. Probably for the first time Lawrence realized the truth behind all his missions: he was lying to the people he loved and sought to unite, but his duty to Allenby was stronger. Lawrence desperately needed this attack to succeed as the alternative would be distress to both his masters, Allenby and Feisal.

With the Serahin Arabs accepted into the attack force, the whole party continued with the ride to Azrak where they would rest and feed the camels before moving on to complete their mission. It was as they approached Azrak that Lawrence learned that Kader had mysteriously disappeared; everyone now knew they had accommodated a traitor in their midst who was probably now on his way to inform the Turks of the Arabs' impending raid. A conference of leaders was called and the matter was discussed at length. Lawrence allowed the debate to run to-and-fro and was genuinely surprised at their decision – to continue with the raid. Their logic was based on the belief that the Turks would not believe Kader.

After resting the camels they set off for the last leg of the journey into the lightly wooded valleys; it was now 4 November and Lawrence was very conscious of the request from Allenby to have the viaducts destroyed on or just after the 5th. Shortness of time pressed Lawrence to make haste and by dawn on the 5th they reached the railway line, which was undefended but still some twenty miles from their viaduct objective. The terrain had been too soft for many of the now exhausted camels and the group's progress was getting slower; they were now in territory actively patrolled by the Turks and during daylight had to hide along the floor of a wooded valley, which Lawrence felt was too near the regularly patrolled rail line for comfort. At dusk he and Hussein decided to take a reduced force to complete the mission; they took just six Indian machine-gunners for support, as the remainder of the Indians' camels were too exhausted, and a party of Serahin was selected to guard the spare camels while the attack was pressed home. Lawrence had specially selected a group of Beni Sakhr to accompany him when he laid the charges. The attackers rode on towards their objective while the remainder of the party were sent back to await news at the village of Abu Sawana. It was a nightmare ride for the attackers; they met occasional travellers who were terrified of them and who had to be held hostage until the attack was over. A distant village raised the alarm at their passing and villagers opened fire into the night, other villagers avoided being caught and ran off into the night screaming, which, in turn, made the village dogs bark. Then it began to rain heavily. But for the seriousness of their mission, and worsening predicament, Lawrence would have been highly amused by the way the night's events were unfurling.

They finally reached the gorge at about 9 p.m; in the near distance they could just make out the viaduct of Tell el Shehab beneath the outline of Mount Hermon. Now protected by the noise of the river as it crashed through the ravine, the explosives were unpacked and issued to the Beni Sakhr who were to carry the charges onto the bridge. The machine-gunners set off to site their guns to cover the campsites of the inevitably sleeping Turkish defenders. The sides of the ravine were treacherous with mud and they slipped and fell repeatedly. As they progressed towards the viaduct they paused as a train crossed the bridge; Lawrence was nearest to the train and saw it was full of troops and drew the conclusion they were probably British prisoners; he was grateful the train missed the impending destruction of the viaduct. Then, as the attackers moved onto the viaduct, one of the group dropped his rifle; it fell through a gap in the wooden structure and then, unbelievably, bounced and clattered its way to the bottom of the bridge where the unexpected noise alerted the sole Turkish guard. The startled Turk looked up and clearly saw into the face of the Indian machine-gunner peering down after his falling weapon, now silhouetted against the light of the rising moon. As the Turk pondered the significance of the event he then saw the shapes of the remaining Arab demolition party stealthily moving along the railway lines and onto the viaduct.

The bemused Turk watched the Arabs for a full minute while trying to make sense of what he was seeing. He then began wildly firing into the air and screaming for help from the sleeping main guard. Within a matter of seconds the Turks were out of their tents and into their dugouts, and then they began firing in all directions. Thinking they were being fired on, the Beni Sakhr on the viaduct began to return fire thereby giving their positions away. The Indian machine-gunners were not yet in position and were unable to support Lawrence's group. With the Turks now clearly able to see the silhouetted figures running back across the bridge, shots began bouncing off the metalwork around the porters. Knowing that a single hit would detonate their explosives, they instinctively threw their explosive packs off the viaduct and into the ravine and then ran back across the viaduct to the safety of the camels. With one small mistake, Lawrence's mission was over; with the explosives now somewhere far below them and the Turks closing in, there was nothing to do but abandon the attack and chase after the fleeing group. Everyone swiftly ran from the viaduct, mounted their camels and abandoned the scene. By now the sound of gunfire was reverberating round the district and lanterns were being lit in all the surrounding villages. Shots were fired into the night, dogs barked incessantly and some brave villagers rode after Lawrence's men, though not daring to get too close. By dint of hard riding they eluded the furore behind them and dawn saw them safely back in the desert. Lawrence felt dismal; he had let down, or been let down, by his Arabs and worse, they could all hear the distant sounds of the British guns hammering at the Turkish line. The Turkish railway and viaduct was still intact: Lawrence had failed Allenby.

The cold rain continued all the way back to Abu Sawana where they were able to rejoin their recovering Indians and fires were lit. No one had eaten for nearly twenty-four hours and their hunger was accentuated by their failure. After a hot meal of rice and camel meat their spirits began to return; suggestions of action began to bubble to the surface from among the seated Arabs. Perhaps, they said, they could return to complete the raid, but there were no explosives in any quantity. Lawrence called for details of the remaining explosives and someone found a bag of gelignite to supplement an electrical mine. All faces turned to Lawrence as Hussein muttered that they had enough to blow up at least one train. But the Indian gunners were too downcast; they had eaten their rice but not touched their meat on religious grounds. All they wanted to do was return to sea-level Aqaba and regain their strength in the sun. Hussein pressed on with talk of a train and his Arabs' enthusiasm increased. Lawrence at last agreed and plans were made for the Indians to return to Aqaba while he and Hussein would return to the line to blow up a train.

Earlier in the year Lawrence had destroyed a small railway bridge near the village of Minifer; he suggested that he should guide the demolition party to the location and they could do the rest. They would not expect any Turkish resistance so the returning Indian gunners would not be missed. They set off at once and late that same afternoon reached the line. As expected, it was unguarded and

Lawrence led his party to a nearby gully where they could rest unseen by any casual Turks patrolling the line. They were gathering in the gully when a long train steamed by, but there was no time to take any action without revealing their hiding place. They settled down to wait for dusk before laying their charges; the incessant rain continued and in order to take their minds off their drenching, Lawrence posted guards and train spotters. When no activity could be seen along the length of line, Lawrence slipped down to the line and laid his charges. He ran out the wires from their hiding place to the track and disconsolately squatted down in the rain. Suddenly the long awaited call came in, a train was rapidly approaching and everyone scuttled to their allocated position. Due to the shortness of available electrical wire, the plunger had to be sited little more than fifty yards from the line, recklessly close, though the main force was some 200 yards further back behind some dunes. While there was still no sign of the train Lawrence dashed forward to wire the plunger. Then the train came into view; it was heavily laden, full of troops and struggling up the long incline. There was nothing Lawrence could do, it was too late to run back to the shelter of the dunes so he nonchalantly sat on the ground next to the detonator and waited while the train slowly approached. As the front engine's wheels went over the mine he pressed the ignition plunger – but nothing happened. He repeated the action but it was pointless, something had gone wrong. He looked up and saw the puzzled looks from the slowly passing troops sitting in their comfortable carriages; they stared at this forlorn Arab sitting next to a bush and must have wondered what he was doing. The train slowed to a crawl and Lawrence was conscious of the Turks in the rear carriages staring at him, the officers pointing at him and laughing. All Lawrence could do was lift his hand in a mock salute and calmly count the carriages as they crawled slowly past. The final carriage drew alongside him and after a further hundred yards the train finally came to a halt.

He gathered up the ignition plunger and jogged back to where his anxious Arabs were waiting for him. The group lay still but to their horror a group of curious Turkish officers alighted the train and slowly walked back down the line and over to the low bush where Lawrence had sat. They poked around for a few moments then walked back towards the train. The Arabs had to stay low for another hour before the engine had built up sufficient steam to continue on its journey. The Arabs on spotting duties had watched the whole episode in anticipation that they would all be caught and killed and once the train departed they rushed back to the group to find out what had gone wrong. The Serahin, who believed in matters mysterious, claimed the expedition was doomed to failure as an 'evil eye' was on the group. This was scoffed at by the Beni Sakhr and a fight between the two groups nearly erupted, until Hussein claimed that, in the name of the Prophet, their luck would now change. This pronouncement calmed matters and agreement was made to try again. While the Arabs were arguing, Lawrence had dismantled the plunger and discovered that one of the connections was faulty; he repaired the offending parts and with the device reassembled he pressed the plunger. The two wires leading from the apparatus sparked together and, with relief, Lawrence placed it inside his clothing to keep it dry.

An injured camel was killed for its meat but their tinder was wet and so no fire could be lit. The group huddled down for the night and all the while the heavy rain continued to fall on the sorry figures. Dawn brought some respite, it stopped raining and the scouts resumed their positions. The Arabs were determined to make a fire as they were all ravenous and Lawrence had begun to shave one of the sticks of explosive to make a firelighter when a cry of 'train' was heard from one of the scouts. All looked up and the scout was pointing north towards the faint rise of smoke that indicated an approaching train. They rushed to their positions and were quickly ready for action, which was just as well as the train was approaching at high speed. The train was long and was pulled by two engines; both were working together and Lawrence counted ten carriages, one bedecked with banners. He guessed the train was carrying a senior Turkish officer and wished he had insisted that the machine-gunners had accompanied him. As it was, he had some sixty Arabs armed with rifles but no substantial guns in support. Lawrence felt especially vulnerable so close to the mine.

The train rushed towards the bridge and Lawrence timed the explosion to hit the first engine, anticipating that, with the bridge destroyed, both engines would smash to the ground. He was right; there was a tremendous explosion and the two engines flew sideways off the bridge and the remainder of the train was then completely hidden by the smoke of the massive dust cloud. Parts of the train flew into the air and began crashing around the Arabs. Lawrence picked himself up, dazed from the explosion, only to be struck by a piece of flying metal. Then there was a thud in the sand in front of him; the mangled body of one of the train crew impacted into the ground, splashing Lawrence with the man's blood and entrails. The Turks in the rear carriages were mostly unharmed and quickly rallied to defend the train just as some of the Beni Sakhr rushed forward to loot, regardless of being hopelessly outnumbered. Their attention had been especially drawn to four locked boxes lying beside the track, having been blown from the front wrecked carriage. Regardless of their safety, the Arabs smashed the boxes open only to find they contained a case of Turkish rifles and boxed medals, which they grabbed at and stuffed into their pockets. Within moments the Turks were organized; they climbed onto the tops of the carriages and began firing at close range into the plundering Arabs while other Turks began firing at the Arabs, shooting at them from the safety of the dunes. The Beni Sakhr looters were rapidly forced to retreat but, because of their greed, left some fifteen of their number lying dead in the wet sand.

Under a wild fire from the Turks, the remainder of the Beni Sakhr rushed back to the protection afforded by the dunes. A group of Arabs had seen Lawrence fall; they rushed to him and gathered him up, pulling him back to safety behind the dunes. In the process seven more Arabs were hit by Turkish fire before they reached safety. Lawrence had a bleeding gash from the shrapnel and five minor bullet wounds – and had lost a total of twenty-two men. He had never lost so many men and was distraught. With the Turks' riflemen finding their range, a platoon of Turkish soldiers cautiously prepared to move towards the dunes and it was imperative the Arabs got away as quickly as possible. They mounted their camels and raced off into the safety of desert. For many hours it was a forlorn ride, all had lost friends and little was discussed between them until they saw a distant caravan of camels. The strangers were already preparing their tented camp for the coming night and were thankfully friendly, offering their fires to warm Lawrence's party. Several of his men had packed away camel meat from their aborted fire the previous evening and these delicacies were brought forward and cooked. They ate well and dried off their damp clothes. Assured they were in friendly company they all caught up on their sleep and at dawn the following day rode on towards their winter base. By the time they reached Azrak their spirits were once again high, the weather had improved and there was much showing off of booty and exaggerated claims of destruction of Turkish trains.

9

The Derra Incident: 21-22 November 1917

By November 1917, Allenby's army had made the expected advance towards the Turkish front line and began to settle in for the winter. The time would now be well spent with training and bringing up supplies for the renewed offensive scheduled to take place in the coming spring. Although Palestine enjoyed a Mediterranean climate, much of the hinterland and its mountains were at an altitude of 4,000 feet and the winter weather in the hills and mountains was cruelly cold and often wet. These adverse weather conditions were not conducive for an on-going military operation due to the difficulties of maintaining and moving supplies. For Lawrence, nearby Azrak was the perfect base; it was unlikely the Turks would find him and the location appealed to his fine sense of history having been used as a fortress by the Byzantines, the Franks and Arabs. Renault de Chatillon had also used it as a hideaway during the Crusades. The location was well positioned to give Lawrence a golden opportunity to preach the word to the northern tribes: in the spring, he and Feisal would be leading an unstoppable and growing force of Arabs to the site of Lawrence's dream, the city of Damascus and the beginning of Arab unity.

Perhaps due to his isolation, Lawrence began to suffer from severe doubts. His last expedition to the Yarmuk viaduct at Tell el Shehab had been a sorry misadventure and the more he brooded on his misfortune, the worse he felt. The truth was worryingly simple: he had failed. He had not been able to raise enough Arabs willing to accompany him to destroy the important Yarmuk viaduct, and the objective had been the one and only objective ever specifically requested by Allenby. Lawrence had not even been able to destroy his alternative target: had the destruction of the train carrying the Turkish commander, Jemel Kouchkouk, been a success, the bonuses to Lawrence and Allenby would have been considerable. As it was, the Turks were unscathed and the overall effect of the raid had been negligible.

Lawrence was relieved to learn that Allenby had, meanwhile, achieved his objective of capturing the Turkish position at Beersheba before moving on towards Jerusalem. Allenby had inflicted terrible losses on the Turks. He also learned that, like Lawrence, Newcombe had been requested by Allenby to mount a similar operation. Newcombe was to take some eighty men and block the Turks' supply road, and possible line of retreat, between Beersheba and Hebron. Such was the fury with which Newcombe's men fought that the Turks believed they faced a superior and well-defended force, which threw them into confusion. The Turks repeatedly attacked Newcombe's position, which drew off disproportionate numbers of Turks from other objectives in order to clear this blocking force. Newcombe had fought a raging battle for over two days and only surrendered when he had lost half his men and exhausted his ammunition. He was taken prisoner by the Turks and spent the next year as a prisoner of war. In Cairo the talk was of Newcombe, not Lawrence. Lawrence's bitterness began to get the better of him and it was while in this black mood that he began to make a plan to reconnoitre Derra.

As the days went by more Arab chiefs came to swear their allegiance to Feisal and it was evident to Lawrence that, come the spring, many would wholeheartedly support the revolt. Lawrence knew that for Feisal's force to succeed, he would need to reconnoitre the area from Derra towards Damascus – his earlier sleuthing on his own had been cursory and given him insufficient intelligence to plan such an advance and support Allenby at the same time. Getting bored with the daily ritual of meeting Arab leaders, he decided to go and inspect Derra and check the Turk's defences. One of the Arab leaders, who earlier came to support the cause, Talal el Hareidhin, came from a Hauran village and knowing the area well had already offered to escort Lawrence into Derra.

Derra was vital to all concerned. It was home to a large Turkish garrison and the hub for all their troop movements, supplies and road and rail links. Without control of the town the Turks faced certain defeat. For Allenby's Allied force and Lawrence's Arabs, neither could advance until Derra was neutralized. Perhaps as a distraction from his woes, he sought out Talal el Hareidhin and the two made a plan to visit Derra. Lawrence liked the Arab leader; he was known to be wanted by the Turks for killing a number of Turkish soldiers and now lived the life of an outlaw, but enjoyed the secret support of his tribe. Part of the plan was for the two to enter Derra disguised as beggars; Lawrence would then sketch the principal routes through the town and confirm the location of the Turkish barracks. He also intended to visit the rail junction with a view to sabotaging the rail network prior to Allenby's attack. It was while he was investigating these positions that Lawrence was apparently arrested by a Turkish patrol. The alleged event actually mirrors an almost identical incident in 1912 when, as a student, Lawrence was exploring Syria. On this first occasion he claimed to have been arrested during a visit to Urfa, beaten and then kept in a cell. He frequently mentioned this to his friends and capitalized on the story; the similarity with Derra cannot be ignored, and in any event, the incident was about to be repeated, with some remarkable parallels.

In *Seven Pillars of Wisdom* Lawrence wrote movingly of his tragic experience while in the hands of the Turks. Other authors muddled the facts of his arrest and then went on to write in considerable detail, describing his alleged torture and male rape by the Turkish guards.

Others orientated their books to a consideration of the effects of the 'incident' on Lawrence's psyche. Lawrence claims he eventually escaped the Turks' custody after a number of hours of torture but no one actually knows what really happened. The answer is simple: no one is ever likely to know, which is exactly what Lawrence intended. The whole alleged incident appears to be little more than a fabrication. The deeper one investigates his story the more unlikely it becomes. Lawrence appears not to have spoken to anyone about his capture, certainly not for more than twelve months following the incident and furthermore, each time he subsequently amended *Seven Pillars of Wisdom* or his notes about his experience the story appears to have been embellished, possibly to shock and dramatize his reputation among his friends. Perhaps his initial intention was to elicit their sympathy either after his aborted raid on the Yarmuk viaduct or, more likely, to offset the glory that Newcombe achieved following his recent success. The account was later to ensure his friends' sympathy when he left the army.

In any event, Lawrence claimed in *Seven Pillars of Wisdom* that he had already spied on the railway station at Derra before being arrested by a Syrian soldier at the nearby airfield; this is far from the usual portrayal of him sneaking along an alleyway in Derra and being arrested by a Turkish patrol. If he had been arrested by Syrians, he could probably have talked his way out of the situation as the majority of Syrians in the Turkish Army were increasingly unsympathetic to the Turks. In his earliest writings of *Seven Pillars of Wisdom* Lawrence claims he was initially taken to a Turkish guardroom, probably at the airfield, where he was questioned. Lawrence then states he was first whipped, as a prelude to being enrolled in the Turkish Army, then he was marched by three soldiers through the town to the Bey's headquarters. This is odd as Lawrence's capture would have been known to his bodyguards who would, surely, have awaited an opportunity to rescue him. They did not, and neither did Lawrence attempt to escape.

It is distinctly puzzling that Lawrence didn't mention his capture and ill-treatment until long after the event, and even following his own timescale for the incident, his accounts pose serious questions of credibility. For an officer to have been captured and tortured by the enemy, and to have then escaped and not informed his superiors is simply not credible. There is no evidence of him having written of the incident until nearly two years later when he wrote to his friend Colonel Stirling at Cairo to confirm that Kader, who warned the Turks of the Yarmuk raid, had been a traitor.[1] When many years later investigators sought out the identity of the Turkish guard commander, who had since died, they found nothing to support Lawrence's story. The Turk in question, Hacim Bey, had been a normal heterosexual male and a family man, and no allegations of homosexuality were ever levelled at his character, even by those with a grudge to bear against him. And then there is the question of Lawrence being taken prisoner; there was no record of his arrest and the Turks had offered an enormous reward for his capture or killing. Lawrence was a legend among Turkish troops and his arrest would have brought fame and fortune to his lucky capturer.[2] Given that Lawrence was white and blond-haired, even the dimmest of Turks should have suspected that their prisoner was not what he appeared to be, and Hacim Bey was known to be a respected and experienced officer.

Lawrence had only recently tried to destroy the Turks' vital viaduct at Yarmuk and so there was considerable anger and tension throughout the Turkish garrison at Derra. Lawrence acknowledges that when he was captured his blond hair and fair-skinned appearance made nonsense of him trying to pass himself off as an Arab, and it would have been obvious to the Turks that he was still limping from a

---

1 Lawrence was later able to take his revenge when, in November 1918, Kader was shot dead by Arab police on the orders of Feisal.
2 The ever increasing reward money always amused Lawrence who stated the Turkish reward was better than a medal or knighthood from the King.

broken toe and bearing the scars of his shrapnel and five recent bullet wounds. But Lawrence maintained throughout that the Turks' sole wish was to beat then sodomize him. Having been seriously beaten, Lawrence claimed he found some clothes, escaped through a conveniently unlocked door and having somehow obtained a camel, he then set off to ride several hundred miles to Rumm before, finally, he reached Aqaba, but now on horseback. On his arrival Lawrence behaved normally, appeared in good health and told no one of his experience.

In *Seven Pillars of Wisdom* Lawrence described the torture in vivid terms – the lashing lasting up to ten minutes and causing cuts, weals and bleeding 'from face to toe', with the torture working up 'to an intolerable height'. The most common method of Turkish torture during the First World War was bastinado, where a prisoner is beaten on the soles of his feet, an excruciatingly painful punishment that rendered the victim unable to walk for at least a week. If Lawrence had been taken prisoner, the very least he could have expected was to be bastinadoed. Lawrence never mentioned this as part of his experience and he was able to walk normally. His medical records that were completed when he re-enlisted after the war under a false name were detailed and made no mention of any injuries other than noting some minor scars on both buttocks. The tale of his capture and torture is a story that tests any reader's credulity.

The early drafts of *Seven Pillars of Wisdom* confirm that, post-Derra, Lawrence rode a camel the whole 250 miles, arriving at Aqaba on 26 November. For a man who was still recovering the effects of shrapnel and bullet wounds, a severe beating, whipping and rape, not to mention a broken toe, he did remarkably well. It was also a medical miracle as the clothes he wore were, depending on which version one reads, either filthy Arab robes or old European clothes. In any event, his open wounds would have probably become septic during the heat of the desert crossing and Lawrence was not displaying any wounds or treated for any ailment on arriving at Aqaba.

No one at Aqaba noticed anything untoward about Lawrence or his appearance; this is strange.

In order to complete the deception, or add to it, Lawrence removed the relevant pages, 21–22 November 1917, from his personal diary and these were the only pages known to receive this treatment. Subsequent scientific analysis of the diary shows that Lawrence left these pages blank, which, given the momentous experience he claims he had been put through, would have been a highly unusual omission for someone who meticulously kept a diary. Lawrence had actually returned to Aqaba by 21 November and it is known he accompanied Colonel Joyce on this very date on a motor reconnaissance through Wadi Itm. Motor vehicles were new to Aqaba and had only arrived at the port on the SS *Ozarda* from Egypt the day before; Lawrence wanted to prove the vehicles could manage the steep incline to the pass and so took Joyce for a reconnaissance drive.[3] According to the log of the ship guarding the Aqaba port, HMS *Humber*, the SS *Ozarda* reached Aqaba at 7.25 a.m. on 20 November and began unloading at once. One must presume this is a reliable contemporary source, it being unlikely that an official ship's record would be incorrect. Clearly, Lawrence could not have been at both Aqaba and Derra on the same dates.

Lawrence's first reference to Derra was not made until the end of June 1920 when he mentioned his 'capture' in a letter to the deputy chief political officer in Damascus, his former friend, Colonel Stirling. He had also been friendly with Colonel Richard Meinertzhagen and in July of the same year he sought out his friend while at the Paris Peace Conference. Lawrence admitted he had been captured and flogged but while Lawrence was using their communal bathroom, Meinertzhagen noticed several fresh weals around Lawrence's ribs. When asked about the wounds, Lawrence confirmed they were

3 James, Lawrence *The Golden Warrior – The Life and Legend of Lawrence of Arabia* London 1995.

from an incident when he fell on some barbed wire at Azrak. Meinertzhagen later confirmed that at their Paris meeting he saw no actual scars on Lawrence's body. After Lawrence's death, Meinertzhagen was so concerned about the account of the Derra incident gaining credibility that he wrote that Lawrence's story of Derra was false. Lawrence later admitted to his friend, George Bernard Shaw, that the story of Derra was not true.

By 1922 the first drafts of *Seven Pillars of Wisdom* were being circulated among Lawrence's friends and with each new draft, the Derra story received fresh embellishment. Sensible questions could not be answered: for example, why had Lawrence needed to enter Derra when there were up-to-date aerial photographs and accurate maps readily available? Later drafts of *Seven Pillars of Wisdom* omitted the fact that Lawrence claimed the Turkish commander, Hacim Bey, had recognized him, and Bey's name was given as Nahi, which was false; Lawrence may well have realizd that by giving the Turk a false name, the change would prevent his identity becoming known to researchers.

The final comment on Derra should go to Lawrence's biographer, Michael Yardley, who recorded in an interview with Channel 4 TV in 2004 that 'my gut reaction is that it didn't happen.'

10

Lawrence Returns to Aqaba

*N*ow promoted to major, Lawrence had only been back at Aqaba a few days when he was urgently recalled to another meeting with Allenby in Cairo. A plane was sent for him and he joined Allenby on 9 December 1917. Allenby was in high spirits after defeating the Turks at Jaffa and then taking Jerusalem. Buoyed up by his progress, Allenby appeared to be indifferent to Lawrence's failure to take the Yarmuk viaduct, to the extent that Lawrence was invited to accompany Allenby at the victory parade in Jerusalem. Lawrence borrowed a suitable uniform and clearly enjoyed the spectacle. For the man who modelled his life on the Crusades, marching into Jerusalem behind Allenby at the head of a Christian army, and freeing it from the Muslim Ottomans, would have been a crowning moment in his life. His friends in Jerusalem commented that Lawrence looked very fit and well and there was no mention by Lawrence to anyone of his alleged recent capture and maltreatment by the Turks.

During his visit to Jerusalem, Lawrence was made privy to Allenby's plans for the following year of 1918. The advance was to resume in February with an attack on Jericho, which lay just to the north of the Dead Sea. Lawrence agreed to move his force from Aqaba to the desert adjacent to Jericho, which would tactically place him ready to right-flank Allenby's next push northwards towards Damascus. With Lawrence's Arabs at Jericho, they could also strangle the Turkish supply line from the coast via the Dead Sea to all Turkish-held positions north of Jericho.

With the plans agreed, Lawrence returned to Aqaba to mobilize Feisal's Arab army in preparation for the long march north. At Aqaba he delegated the complicated administrative responsibilities and turned his mind to testing the use of the newly arrived armoured cars by again attacking the Turkish station at Mudowwara. The engineers had recently created a rough road from Aqaba to the top of the pass and from there the terrain was firm sand and easy going for the vehicles; an attack with armoured cars would be much quicker and their firepower that much greater than camel-mounted machine guns. In a French proposal Lawrence had been requested to consider attacking Medina where the Turks were still under siege from Feisal's brothers, Abdullah and Ali. But Lawrence saw no point in risking his Arabs' lives; the Turks there were trapped and consequently totally ineffective. If the Arabs were to take Medina they would incur considerable losses and then have to care for several thousand hungry Turkish prisoners. Lawrence ignored the request and left the Turks to fester in Medina until the end of the war.

Enthusiasm at Aqaba for the Mudowwara raid was enormous; the expedition was to consist of three new Ford armoured cars specially equipped with machine guns, a half-battery of ten-pound guns mounted on three Talbot armoured cars and an open Rolls-Royce for Lawrence's use when scouting. The vehicles had an enormous carrying capacity compared with that of camels and so, for the first time, adequate food and blankets could be taken along to bring unexpected comfort to the mission. It was to be the first attack by Lawrence on a Turkish position without a single Arab or camel present. The vehicles roared off with their crews in high spirits, the climb out of Aqaba took less than thirty minutes and then they were off at high speed across the flat desert. Three hours later and within sight of the unsuspecting Turks at Mudowwara, the expedition's mounted guns opened up on the station, which scattered the startled

Turks and sent them running for their trenches. The Fords' machine guns then hosed down the sheltering Turks but, without a force of mounted Arabs to charge in, there was no one to physically seize the Turkish line. They ceased firing, cut the telephone lines and then moved off towards Guweira, capturing a small Turkish outpost on the way home.

With the time approaching for the Arab move north, Lawrence decided that Aqaba could now be abandoned. Until they reached Jericho they would still have to continue being supplied from the port, then all supplies would be delivered directly by the British as they advanced northwards. Perhaps because Lawrence had experienced such suspicion and antagonism between the northern Arab tribes and the treachery of the Arab traitor, Kader, he now collected around him fifty or so ferocious-looking bodyguards. He employed two separate commanders: Abdullah, who was noted for his successful career as a robber and murderer, and Abdullah el Gaazi, who was more the 'officer' type. Both ensured that at all times Lawrence was shadowed by a number of his bodyguards; they received extra pay as well as having the prestige of forming such an elite group.

It was decided to soften the Turks defending the southern area of the Dead Sea so on 11 January 1918 an Arab raid, led by Nasir, attacked the main Turkish railway station at Jurf. This time the raid was carried out with no European presence and was a great success. The Arabs initially opened fire with guns and machine guns to force the Turks into their trenches and then charged down on them. The battle was over in a matter of minutes and as the stunned Turkish survivors were being gathered together, Nasir supervised the destruction of the station – two trains were destroyed and then the vital rail junction itself. The Arabs gleefully looted the rail wagons and found them full of food supplies destined for the Turks in the south. With the wagons looted, the Arabs marched their prisoners off leaving the wounded to the mercy of the weather and the attention of the local Bedouin people.

By now the main Arab force was making steady progress north-wards and to keep the momentum going, Lawrence decided to use some of his Arab raiders to take the Turkish held town of Tafileh, which was situated high on a mountain plateau at an altitude of 4,000 feet, making it bitterly cold in the deepest part of winter. Lawrence took Auda and most of his Howeitat men for the attack. They approached the town from the protection of a hilly ridge that led down from steep cliffs that overlooked the village. Auda called down on the Arab villagers to support them. His call was met with rifle shots; clearly the villagers were more intimidated by the Turks than by Auda. This infuriated the Arab leader, who strode down towards the village; seeing this great man approaching them the villagers ceased firing and rapidly persuaded the Turks to surrender in order to save all their lives. The grateful prisoners were sent back to Aqaba while Lawrence and the Arabs moved into Tafileh to await the remainder of their force coming up from Aqaba.

On 24 January Lawrence received disturbing news; the Turks under Hamid Fakhri Pasha were marching in force to retake Tafileh from their northern strong point at Kerak. Lawrence's scouts reported about 1,000 infantry supported by some thirty machine guns and two field guns making a determined approach on Tafileh, all supported by Turkish cavalry. It was a disproportionately huge force, which perplexed Lawrence. Tafileh was of no strategic use whatsoever to the Turks, who needed all their men to defend the Turkish line along the river Jordan, now under increasing threat from Allenby. Lawrence discovered the approaching Turks were led by the Turkish com-mander of the Amman garrison and presumed that the Turks wanted a quick victory, perhaps for propaganda purposes. Lawrence was unaware that the force was also under the mentorship of his German equivalent, Colonel Neidermayer, who was shortly to be taken as a prisoner of war.

At a rapidly called meeting to discuss tactics, Zeid and Lawrence inevitably disagreed. Zeid sought to abandon the protective cliffs and surrender the town before, in turn, attacking the Turks from the safety of the flanking hills. Lawrence argued in favour of holding the cliffs and then with the Turks stalled, attacking them from the protection of the cliffs with accompanying attacks from the flanks. Zeid gave way and preparations were made for the coming battle; it was mutually agreed that Sherif Nasir would be in command, with Zeid as his deputy. It was to be the first battle fought by Lawrence using vaguely recognizable British Army tactics. He organized the Arabs into defensive positions along the ridges that commanded the Turkish approach across the desert from the direction of the gorge at Wadi Hesa. It was the only exit route out of the position and effectively cut Tafileh off from the nearest town at Kerak. As dusk fell the advancing Turkish cavalry began forcing the Arab scouts to retreat back to the protection of Tafileh. Unwilling to fight in the dark, both sides settled down for the night.

The local population were shaken with terror at the prospect of the Turks preparing to attack and possibly retake Tafileh, especially as the townsmen had largely rallied to the rearguard of Lawrence's men or disappeared. Their women were left busy trying to remove their few valuables and children and making a terrible wailing noise while so doing.

By dawn the defenders were chilled to the bone from the freezing wind. As the sun rose the Arabs could make out the Turks resuming their slow but methodical approach; half an hour later Turkish artillery was close enough to commence a bombardment of the approach ridges concealing Lawrence's men. The Turks' attitude annoyed Lawrence who decided, instead of retreating and leaving the Turks stranded in Tafileh, to make a determined stand and fight back, and to quote Lawrence 'kill them all'. The Turkish bombardment continued throughout the morning with the Turks slowly making ground and forcing the Arabs back, ridge by ridge, but not causing any Arab casualties. Lawrence knew that he was coming under pressure but also knew that he could duly expect reinforcements from his bodyguard, armed with automatic weapons, and an approaching large force of Ageyl tribesmen. He also needed to rest his men; he deployed a small number of snipers to discourage the Turks from moving closer and deployed the remainder of his men along the narrow Motalga Ridge overlooking the Turkish approach; they could rest until the arrival of their reinforcements, who began to bolster their line half an hour later.

Lawrence took time to notice that the edge of the ridge was peppered with Byzantine foundations, possible evidence that the position had been used before for similar purposes. He also took time to study the layout of the ground over which the Turks must advance; the plain itself was no more than two miles across and was flanked by a series of ridges. From Tafileh, a rough roadway led across the plain in the direction of Kerak and it was along this roadway that the centre of the Turks' advance was focused. Sheikh Gasim was then despatched to lead a camel charge on the extended line of advancing Turks, but with a novel tactical difference. Lawrence instructed Gasim to ride his men to the Turks' extreme flank and then attack the Turks along their extended line, taking out the Turkish soldiers one by one. It was a brilliant tactic; the attacking Arabs were not intimidated by the enormous line of advancing Turks and the Turks could not fire back at the Arabs as they cut and shot their way steadily along the line.

At the same time most of the male villagers, including several hundred Armenian refugees armed with pitch forks and long knives, arrived to offer Lawrence their support. Lawrence was now commanding a most motley army. He ordered a group of Arabs to seize the Turks' right-hand ridge and, being armed with a Hotchkiss gun, they easily took the ridge and then commenced firing into the Turks from their left flank. Lawrence then ordered all his guns to open a sustained fire on the Turks which, combined with Gasim working his way along their line cutting down the Turks in clusters, slowed the Turkish advance to a halt as widespread panic set in. By dusk the

Turkish force was seriously weakened and disillusioned, the officers had been recalled to the general for a tactical discussion and in their absence some Turkish units began to withdraw independently. Such a movement on the part of the Turks sparked the inevitable Arab preparations for a camelry charge. Regardless of the danger or the size of the opposing force, the Arabs began to gather ready to charge, which set the leaderless Turks fleeing in all directions. As panic spread through the Turkish ranks the Arabs closed with them. In immediate pursuit behind the Arabs were several hundred Armenian men, refugees from the Turkish massacres of the Armenian people over recent years; they were armed with swords and makeshift weapons. It was time for retribution. Lawrence and Zeid watched as their wild force closed with the horde of fleeing Turks.

The Turks offered little resistance and many attempted to surrender to the approaching mob of screaming Arabs and Armenians. But there was no quarter: the Turks were systematically and literally cut to pieces. Those at the far side stood and watched in sheer horror as the Arabs cut their way through the once proud force of Turkey's best soldiers. Some managed to dump their equipment and began running in sheer panic into the desert, only to be cut down by camel outriders or vengeful villagers; by the end of the day, barely forty Turks managed to escape to tell the tale. As darkness fell the Arabs recovered some twenty-five of their own dead and began to administer to their wounded; wounded Turks were of no interest to the Arabs who left them to the mercy of the villagers and Armenians. With dusk came the bitter night-time temperatures, snow began to fall and by midnight a blizzard was raging. None of the Turkish wounded survived.

On the positive side, the Arabs had saved their day and much valuable equipment had been captured; there were artillery pieces and nearly thirty new machine guns and crates of ammunition to be gathered in. Lawrence was now forced to ride out the heavy snow storm and try to regroup his Arabs. The following day, and until the weather improved, Lawrence's time was spent writing a report, a rare occurrence for him, but the report was unintentionally impressive and well received at British headquarters in Cairo. Lawrence had intended the report to be a parody, a joke into which he wove wild unconventional Arabs into conventional tactics easily recognizable to conventional staff officers. The result of the report was the immediate award of the military Distinguished Service Order, which Lawrence later countered with his own recommendation that he receive instead the naval DSO. Even in severe adversity, Lawrence delighted in confusing Cairo's staff officers. Unbeknown to them, Lawrence had also interrupted Turkish supply lines across the Dead Sea. He had arranged with some local Beersheba Bedouin to attack Turkish supply ships at anchor in the small harbour of Kerak. With a combination of cavalry and camelry, Lawrence's Arabs attacked the Turkish sailors as they slept on the beach. The action was over in moments; the Arabs then destroyed the moored vessels and storehouse and captured the entire Turkish force of sixty sailors, without a single casualty to themselves. They returned to Tafileh, which was still strewn with the drying frozen corpses of the Turks, but without adequate shelter it was too cold, even for Lawrence. He left the Arabs to guard the town and at the beginning of February started back to Guweira to collect sufficient gold to pay his men and for inducements to local Arab leaders when they eventually moved north.

Tafileh was undoubtedly Lawrence's greatest battle and must rank equally with his taking of Aqaba. It was fought against vastly superior forces by using conventional tactics supported by Lawrence's own flair to adapt to swiftly changing events on the battlefield. Perhaps because of his conventional approach to the battle, Lawrence played down this notable success; he much preferred the use of intrigue, sudden strikes and heroic long marches, themes that matched his personality.

It often comes as a surprise to winter visitors to Jordan that weather in the high desert and hills equals the worst that can be experienced in Europe. Lawrence now faced leaving balmy sea-level Aqaba for the high mountain snow-covered passes that would take him back to Tafileh. He knew he faced snow storms and deep snow and there were few Arabs willing to accompany him. Six eventually agreed to undertake the journey and, on 4 February, with their supplies packed and each camel carrying a twenty-pound bag full of sovereigns to pay the northern Arab leaders, the small group set off. After no more than ten miles the Arabs found the going too difficult. In typical style, Lawrence collected their money bags, loaded his own camel and set off alone. On his final snow-swept approach to Tafileh the route was obliterated by deep snow and he had great difficulty pushing his camel forwards. When the camel refused to continue, Lawrence was obliged to pull then push her, all the time testing the depth of snow with his riding stick and eventually forcing her to run at snow drifts in order to make progress. Lawrence writes of finally seeing the lights of Tafileh many thousands of feet below him and sliding down the snow-covered scree towards the village below, much to the mirth of Zeid's men who were alerted by their guards of the stranger's bold approach.

The next day Lawrence went forward to explore the terrain for the forthcoming Arab advance. The Turks still held Jericho but with reduced numbers and it was obvious that they were in the process of scaling down their presence in the town. This pleased Lawrence who returned to discuss the advance with Zeid; but Zeid was disconsolate about the prospects for the advance. There had been too many false starts and it would be difficult for the Arabs to rise against the Turks until they were certain of British success. This placed Lawrence in an impossible situation; he knew Allenby was counting on his right flank being protected by a well-intentioned Arab force. Lawrence decided to go to Allenby and admit his failure.

That same afternoon Lawrence took a small bodyguard and set off to Allenby's headquarters at Beersheba. Although not a great distance, the party first had to descend some 5,000 feet, cross the plain and then climb back up to an altitude of 3,000 feet to Beersheba in Palestine. By the time Lawrence reached Beersheba, he was exhausted and becoming even more depressed. He sought out his old friend, Hogarth, who struggled to restore Lawrence's spirit. Lawrence rightly pointed out that he had been wet, tired, cold, exhausted, hungry and thirsty for too long to be able to continue. He had also been wounded on several occasions and truly felt he could go no further. But more important to Hogarth was the pursuit of Allenby's march north to engage the Turks and so Lawrence was pressured to change his mind, the meeting culminating in Lawrence being ordered to supervise the Arab army's advance.

When Lawrence later met with Allenby it was made crystal clear to him that he must ensure the Arab army was in place to coincide with the Allied advance. Lawrence agreed, subject to the British making adequate supplies available and neutralizing the Turkish hub of Maan, which was holding up the Arab army's advance. Allenby concurred and in turn Lawrence agreed that he would move the Arabs beyond Maan when the way was clear.

Lawrence returned to Aqaba on 4 March in order to brief Feisal with the news that Maan would shortly be taken by the British and the promise of a gift to Feisal of 2,000 riding camels, Feisal's enthusiasm returned and preparations were made for the Arab march northwards to begin.

II

Spring 1918

With the war in Europe not going the way of the Allies – Ludendorff's offensive on the Western Front had pushed the Allies back to Amiens – it was decided by the Grand Interallied War Council to make a concerted push against Turkey with the intention of neutralizing the Alliance and thus weakening Germany in Europe. The agreed plan that was passed from London to Allenby for execution required that his force undertake an all-out offensive to push the Turks all the way back from Palestine to Turkey. In theory it was possible, indeed probable, that this objective could be quickly achieved but the Turks still had sufficient troops opposing Allenby to frustrate the Allied plan. The Turks were strongly defending two lines with several armies; their Seventh (7,000 strong) and Eighth armies (10,000 strong) were occupying the region between Jaffa to the north of the Dead Sea while the Fourth Army, based at Amman, was spread out along the Jordan Valley (6,000 infantry and 2,000 cavalry). To unsettle the Turks, Allenby had nearly 60,000 infantry, 12,000 mounted troops and superior artillery firepower with over 500 guns.

Allenby's plan was to use Feisal's Arab army to inconvenience the Turks by destroying their rail network wherever and whenever they could, and to protect Allenby's right flank from the desert. It was of overall importance to Allenby that the execution of the plan was conducted as efficiently and swiftly as possible, while avoiding unnecessary casualties. To this effect, Allenby had stiffened Feisal's

Arab army by allocating sufficient British staff officers to both Feisal's staff and to administer the port of Aqaba. Additional British advisers and supplies now poured into Aqaba including technicians, engineers and instructors in everything military. There were also additional British heavy guns to back up the French artillery contingent of Captain Pisani and his Algerian gunners. Newly appointed British officers at Aqaba began to copy Lawrence's style by accompanying raids against the Turkish rail line, some even took to wearing Arab dress, and a number achieved spectacular successes in such raids. None, though, had Lawrence's reputation, or possessed his access to discuss matters with Allenby and Feisal as and when he chose – and no one other than Lawrence had a fiercely loyal and flamboyant bodyguard who accompanied him everywhere.

By April the task of guarding Aqaba had been taken over by the Egyptian forces, which freed up Feisal's Arabs for the move north. The Egyptians despised the Arabs and both sides had to be kept separate to prevent local squabbles from escalating. Feisal's Arabs were allocated three British officers to oversee the main tasks: Colonel Joyce aided by Jaffar, Maulud and Nuri Said were to concentrate on destabilizing the Turks at Maan; Colonel Dawnay was to focus on destroying the Turk's rail line to Medina thereby isolating that garrison; and Lawrence was to continue raising the Arab and Bedouin tribes proximate to Amman. Lawrence's task was particularly important as, once Allenby's advance was under way, he was to harass the retreating Turks from their unprotected rear and so prevent them from falling back to re-equip themselves or to bolster other Turkish units.

Lawrence's force consisted of Sheikh Mirzuk and his personal bodyguard of several hundred riders, with some 2,000 pack camels. The caravan contained sufficient gold, British rifles and ammunition to buy off the dithering Beni Sakhr leaders. Lawrence arrived at Atara and made camp; he anticipated shortly hearing of early Allied success and settled down to wait for the call. Instead, whispered rumours soon began to circulate among the Arabs that the British had been repulsed to the east of Amman. This was serious news as Lawrence knew that, if true, the uncommitted northern Arabs were most likely to change sides and, in order to protect themselves, confirm their allegiance to the Turks. Curious why the British should be rebuffed, Lawrence decided to undertake a rather dangerous mission; he would enter Amman in disguise to see for himself how well defended the city was. He went disguised as an Arab woman and was accompanied by three other women and his servant, Farraj. He quickly realized that the Turks were in serious strength and that the city was too well defended for his Arabs to attack. Lawrence claimed that his small group attracted the attention of some Turkish soldiers and in order to escape their attention, all had to run away.

Being so far north, Lawrence was exposed to the vagaries of Arab loyalty and so retired on the main Arab camp near Maan where he learned that the Turks had indeed repulsed the British advance on Amman. The causes were cumulative; bad weather had slowed the British advance, the Turks were well dug in and resisted furiously, and worse, local Arabs were often hostile to the British. Having lost over 1,500 men, Allenby ordered a cessation of hostilities and withdrew his men back to the safety of the river Jordan. As Lawrence had correctly anticipated, a number of the northern Arabs had united against the Allies and collectively sworn allegiance to the Turks. Worse news was to come; Zeid's Arabs had been pushed out of Tafileh by a combined attack from several Turkish divisions and the harassment of Maan by Joyce had failed due to the Arabs insisting on a full frontal attack, which faltered before reaching its objective and suffered significant Arab losses. To get a better overall picture of the confused situation, Lawrence went to Maan and conducted a number of local reconnaissance trips. It was when returning from one of these that he paused to attack a small Turkish rail station and dynamited a section of the Turks' rail line. The attack was a pointless exercise but during the exchange of shots his loyal servant, Farraj, was severely wounded by a stray Turkish bullet, which severed a section of the boy's spinal cord rendering him partially paralysed and screaming with pain. With the Turks collecting themselves together to pursue Lawrence's group and with Farraj unable to move, Lawrence was not prepared to leave him to the mercy of vengeful Turkish soldiers with their penchant for torturing captured Arab wounded. Lawrence took out his pistol and cradling Farraj's head, fired one fatal shot into his writhing body. The incident shook Lawrence, who realized no one was immune from Turkish rifle fire, however random.

The sole success went to Colonel Dawnay who, with Lawrence present as his interpreter, had succeeded in destroying the rail station at Tell Shahm and severely handicapping Turkish rail movements between Maan and Medina. Lawrence had enjoyed raiding with Dawnay; the whole venture had been planned with meticulous efficiency with conventional military orders given to all concerned, unlike Lawrence's attacks. Everyone involved knew who was to fire at what and when. Lawrence later wryly commented that the raid had failed as the Turks surrendered ten minutes earlier than anticipated. With the Turks' surrender came the usual Arab looting; this time Lawrence took a memento, the station bell. For the Arabs, the spoils were enormous; there were new machine guns, boxes of ammunition, food stores and other goods of great fascination to the Arabs.

By now Lawrence was coming under severe pressure from two sources. Some senior officers in the British High Command were becoming more confident in attacking Lawrence as a maverick officer. They cited his apparent failure to produce the promised 'Arab Revolt' and openly discussed his inability to unite the Arabs and, indeed, this was proving to be increasingly impossible. Also, Emir Saud of the Nejd region, ruler of the Wahabite people living across half of Arabia, still declined to support Lawrence's ideal and openly attacked

Sherif Hussein for supporting the Allies. In one incident, Wahabite tribesmen attacked and massacred a troop of Lawrence's friendly Arabs. Lawrence began to spend more time with Feisal dealing with political issues than fighting Turks, which frustrated him. Meanwhile, and unbeknown to Lawrence, the Arab units supporting Allenby's main army were being squandered in full frontal attacks against Turkish positions. They took terrible losses; their officers had been trained in British and French tactics more suited to the Western Front, which Lawrence had ably proved to be wasteful against well dug-in Turkish positions.

Then, on 19 March, the British troops attempted to advance north-east through the Moab Mountains and on towards the town of Salt with a view to establishing an advanced stronghold. It was to be a showcase advance and was watched by HRH the Duke of Connaught who was on a morale-boosting visit to British troops in Palestine. They attacked against well-fortified Turkish positions and took a terrible beating before withdrawing, but because the British took 3,000 prisoners, they considered the venture more of a success than a defeat. The British retreat was hampered by many of the Arab population of Salt who had, unwisely, welcomed the British and now feared Turkish retribution. It was widely rumoured by loyal Arabs that the British had suffered a major defeat and that some of the Beni Sakhr had assisted the Turks to repulse the British advance; Lawrence's dream of a united Arab nation marching on Damascus was rapidly becoming a nightmare.

Lawrence then rode to Maan to observe how the Arabs were managing against the beleaguered Turks. They had performed some spectacular feats that included cutting the Turks' rail link to the north of the city and destroying a huge stock of spare rail lines. To the south his old friend, Nuri Said, had similar luck: he had totally destroyed a Turkish station and a similar amount of track. Within hours, Auda's Abu Tayi captured two Turkish positions and followed up with an assault on the main railway station. They succeeded in reaching the station but were beaten back when the Arab artillery ceased firing having run out of ammunition. Meanwhile, to the south, Dawnay was making plans for another concerted attack on the main Turkish link with Medina at Mudowwara. The attack on 21 April was to be against the Mudowwara outposts and on a scale totally unexpected by the Turks, who were initially bombed by two RAF planes, then attacked with raking machine-gun fire from armoured vehicles. The attack was followed up by a devastating charge by Egyptian and Arab mounted troops, Lawrence arriving in time to see the attack pressed home; the Turks guarding the two furthest outposts defended their position until they saw the charging Arabs and then rushed from their buildings and trenches with their hands held high. As ever, the Arabs rushed in to loot.

Those still able to ride on accompanied Lawrence and Dawnay towards Mudowwara main station; they were part of a major force of some 2,000 riders and everyone anticipated success, but unfortunately a troop train had just arrived from the south, complete with two long-range artillery pieces, and the Arab force was subjected to intense machine-gun fire. It was too dangerous to subject the camelry to such sustained fire so Lawrence aborted the raid but, as a consolation prize, rode round the station from a safe distance and totally destroyed the viaduct to the south, thus trapping the Turks at both Medina and Mudowwara for two weeks. Following their success the Arabs, under the command of Muhammad el Dheilan and his Abu Tayi, moved unmolested northwards towards Maan destroying five stations and a number of bridges and culverts as they journeyed along the line. The damage caused by this raid finally destroyed the efficacy of the Turks' rail line to Medina and isolated many thousands of Turkish troops from the coming Allied push to Damascus. Mudowwara eventually fell in early August following an overwhelming assault by the British Imperial Camel Corps.

In the meantime, Allied and Arab pressure on Maan had to be maintained. Any relaxation of effort to keep the Turks on full alert would have encouraged them to retaliate towards Aqaba, the Arabs' main supply line. The Turks constantly sought to maintain Maan and to this effect despatched a further large force from Turkey to Amman prior to strengthening Maan. Lawrence was already teaching his Arabs to dynamite railway track and, at his suggestion, Nasir and his men were requested to destroy a number of bridges at Hesa, equidistant between Maan and Amman. In consequence, the Turks remained tightly contained within Maan town limits.

With events now turning in favour of the Arab offensive, Lawrence flew to Palestine to discuss tactics with Allenby. To his horror he discovered that Allenby's army chief of staff, General Shea, had ordered a further combined British and Arab assault through the Moab hills against the strongly Turkish-held town of Salt. Without consulting Lawrence, who knew the Beni Sakhr Arabs involved were prone to treachery, the attack was ill-conceived and failed miserably, causing serious casualties to both British and Arab participants. The Turks had anticipated a renewed British attack against Salt and had reinforced their positions; Turkish cavalry also lay in wait ready to ambush the unwary British as they advanced through the difficult hills, only to become bogged down and heavily outnumbered. The result could have been a major disaster for the British but for a bungled order that caused the advancing Turks to counter-march away from the battle. On 3 May Allenby realized the task was hopeless and gave the order to retreat, which enabled Shea's men to make good their escape. Shea reported losses of 'only' 1,350 casualties and although beaten back, claimed a great success. Lawrence made the point strongly that he should have been invited to voice his opinion, adding that, had he been consulted, there would have been no casualties. As it was, the British had probably fallen for a scam to obtain gold and attacked the Turks on a false promise of Arab support; indeed, it was later believed that elements of the Beni Sakhr deliberately colluded with the Turks.

Confirmation of a major British failure did not sit well with Feisal, who was becoming more wary of the widespread belief among Arabs that the British were invincible. Lawrence used Allenby's embarrassment to obtain over 2,000 camels from the British quartermaster overseeing the army's supplies. This was a huge coup for Lawrence and he returned to Aqaba with the good news; it easily offset Feisal's disappointment with the British defeat at Salt. Such a large number of camels would give Feisal complete freedom to move his whole army northwards towards Damascus.

While planning a number of diversionary raids against the Turks, mainly against Amman and Derra, Lawrence received a call to attend a meeting of senior officers in Cairo. Allenby had completed his plan for the summer offensive and required all senior participants to be present. Events in Europe were now going well for the Allies: the feared German advance across France had been held and with reinforcements now pouring into France, the Germans appeared to be unable to maintain any further offensive. Allenby was instructed to finish the Turks to further demoralize the German High Command, and to this effect, many of the troops earlier withdrawn from Palestine to support the Allies in France were now being returned to Allenby. With retraining and logistics now well under way, Allenby planned for his final push to begin in early September.

His plan was remarkably similar to that of the previous advance; feints by Lawrence from the desert and the dissemination of false information were intended to mislead the Turks into believing the main Allied thrust would come from the east, with Allenby advancing up the Jordan Valley and Lawrence at the head of the Arabs sweeping in from the desert to attack Maan and Derra. The intention of this feint would force the Turks to reinforce these two towns but instead, Allenby would attack in force along the coast, his weight of numbers should suffice to smash his way through and then maintain the impetus to rout the Turks and force them in disarray back towards Maan. To prevent the Turks reinforcing their armies, Lawrence was required to maintain a constant run of attacks against the railway line to the north of Derra, thus depriving this garrison of reserves or supplies.

Allenby's plan was bold and, in theory, it would result in the destruction of the Turkish Army in Palestine.

12

The Advance on Damascus: June–September 1918

With nearly one-third of the Turkish forces in Palestine effectively besieged by the Arabs at Maan, the main Arab supply line and caravan route from Aqaba to the north was now secure. Any Turkish plans to foil the Arab advance hinged on the Turks retaking Aba el Lissan, but the combined Arab siege of Maan and the threat of the British advance, which would cut their supply line to the coast, further hindered any such excursion. Lawrence and Feisal now allocated their forces to achieve maximum support for Allenby's advance. Over 1,000 camelry were selected for an attack on Derra and another 3,000 Arab infantry were despatched to join Allenby for his attack on Jericho, with the remainder held back to join the final attack against Maan. Feisal and Lawrence were aware that there was still a large Arab force besieging Medina and it was decided that, with the Medina Turks now in a pitiful state of hunger and disease, there was no further need to maintain such a large Arab force to guard them. But Sherif Hussein would not agree to their release; he gave no reason but as the nominal commander-in-chief of the Arabs, he did not need to lend his support. Sherif Hussein stuck to his refusal, which Lawrence put down to his jealousy of his son Feisal. In an attempt to resolve the stalemate, Lawrence flew down to Jeddah to discuss the matter with the sherif who promptly took himself off to Mecca and out of Lawrence's reach. Lawrence attempted to telephone him but as soon as he made contact the telephone line, unsurprisingly, went dead. With time running out Lawrence returned empty-handed to Feisal. They agreed they would have to leave the Medina Arabs where they were.

All administrative arrangements for the Arab advance were coordinated by a number of skilled British officers working under Colonel Dawnay as Allenby's chief of staff at Aqaba. Colonel Joyce, Allenby's adviser to Feisal, was still nominally Lawrence's superior officer. It was to Lawrence's credit that he never disputed the other officers' roles. Aqaba was now a hive of industry with ships unloading stores by the day and British officers supervising the preparations for the Arab advance. Ever the masters of deception, Allenby and Lawrence hatched a skilful hoax to mislead the Turks as to British intentions. Lawrence arranged for Captain Buxton, on loan from the Sudan Civil Service, to lead a large decoy force of 350 men from the Imperial Camel Corps at Suez on a march across the desert to attack Derra and then retreat back into the desert. After all his exertions, Lawrence was now content to accompany Buxton as an observer on his forthcoming Derra raid. The scheme was ingenious. The force was to depart from Suez on 23 July and news of its route and probable target would soon get back to the Turks via their system of spies. The column would then travel across the Sinai desert resupplying at Aqaba before moving through the wastes of Rumm to raid Mudowwara, where it would destroy the water tower, rendering the station all but useless to the Turks. The force would then turn north and follow the ancient caravan route via Bair to Kisser where it would attempt to destroy the main viaduct before moving on towards Maan, but would then retreat back into the desert to deliberately confuse the Turks into believing it was heading even further north. In reality, the group would detour back to join up with Allenby's main army at Beersheba to arrive in time for the main British attack.

As if a desert journey of nearly 700 miles was not daunting enough, permission would need to be obtained from the Arab leaders through whose territory the men passed. This force consisted of many British soldiers and, being Christians, they would all, theoretically, be the sworn enemies of a number of local Bedouin tribes. In fact, few problems arose; some pot-shots were taken at the force but there were no casualties and permissions were readily given. Lawrence accompanied the group for part of the way and he found it a unique experience to be serving again with British soldiers, many of whom were initially suspicious of this legendary officer sweeping around them in flowing white Arab dress. In typical Lawrence style he sat them all down and briefed them, in clear soldiers' language, of what they could expect: thirst, hunger and even death in the desert. After the boredom of earlier inactivity, this was music to their ears and morale soared. Buxton continued on to attack Mudowwara while Lawrence returned to Aqaba where he collected his bodyguard. On 8 August Buxton and his force attacked Mudowwara and this time the attack was pushed through – although Buxton lost a dozen men in the attack, he took over 150 Turkish prisoners and totally destroyed the station and many hundreds of rail tracks. Having sent the prisoners off under escort to Aqaba, Buxton headed north towards Amman where he was joined, en route, by Lawrence. Their journey was not without incident – stores specially dropped off for them were raided by Bedouins and in consequence, the party had to travel lighter until they reached Bair. With little time for rest they moved on to Maaggar, just south of Amman, where they intended to destroy the Turks' rail line to the south. As they approached the line they realized that it was now heavily defended and that nearby villages were coincidentally being subjected to their annual tax assessments. Worse, the Turkish officials were all heavily guarded. The ruse had worked well – too well in fact, as the whole rail network around Amman was virtually impregnable. This was good news for Allenby, who was relying on the Turks taking the Lawrence bait and reinforcing the area to the east of the Dead Sea and their force at Amman. Many of Lawrence's men wanted to attack the line regardless of the danger but they were to be disappointed. Lawrence knew that if the

Turks retaliated, unlike the Bedouin, these town Arabs would be easy prey in the desert; further, by maintaining his presence and unexpectedly appearing from the desert to conduct pin-prick raids, he could cause a vast number of Turkish troops to be deployed far from Allenby's main advance. To deceive the Turks' patrols into believing they had evidence of a large Arab force somewhere nearby, Lawrence's men deposited their litter in obvious places and his soldiers used his single vehicle to make numerous tracks in the sand. With the deception in place, Lawrence moved his force back into the desert and after a sufficient rest, he headed for Aqaba; his Arabs moved on to join Allenby's main force at Beersheba.

With many Arab leaders still slow to support Feisal, and Arab tribesmen generally reluctant to support his various long-distance attacks, Lawrence was only too aware that his dream of uniting the Arabs to take Damascus as the prelude to forming their own nation was becoming little more than a hazy desert mirage. He had managed to confuse the Turks into believing they would be attacked by Allenby coming through Jordan, but the raid had not been conducted by Arabs but by Christian troops and the realization disturbed him. Looked at the cold light of day, Lawrence's exploits were certainly the stuff of romantic adventure, though he now realized full well that he was unable to raise the army of nomadic Arabs necessary to achieve his aim of Arab unity. The Arabs would occasionally assist his ventures but their support was perfunctory and short lived; each operation required the same renewed effort to raise sufficient loyal support, which sometimes only amounted to 150 Arabs. Post-operations, this support always evaporated. Once the Arabs had killed any captured or wounded Turks and completed their looting, they would invariably return to their homes.

All was not well either with the senior echelon of Arab leaders; many of Feisal's officers at Aqaba were in open revolt following a fit of pique and a *diktat* from Sherif Hussein that their ranks and honours were invalid. By using the telegraph line to contact Sherif

Hussein at his Mecca palace, Lawrence was able to persuade the sherif to ameliorate his *diktat*, which he did, though not to Lawrence's complete satisfaction. Lawrence resolved the problem by deliberately omitting the negative aspects of the *diktat* and reprinting only the section that was acceptable; Feisal was delighted though quietly suspicious that his father could so rapidly change his mind.

With Feisal's officers confirmed in their ranks and a semblance of unity restored, Lawrence now had to turn his attention to the disgruntled Arab soldiery. Their pay was long overdue, they resented strong discipline and were still suffering low morale after a number of botched skirmishes. They were also becoming influenced by subtle Turkish propaganda that assured them of the inevitable British defeat and the painful consequences of having sided with the Allies. The situation became serious when a number of Arab gunners effectively mutinied and trained their guns on the officers' quarters. The Arab officers abandoned their tents and fled, leaving Lawrence to go among the mutineers and pacify them with promises, promises that he knew he might not be able to fulfil. Having calmed them down, he requested Feisal to make a personal show to the troops rather than remain distant and aloof from them. This he did, which restored calm and order. Seizing the moment, Lawrence and Feisal ordered the advance to commence. The disputes had taken two days to resolve and not a moment could be lost as Allenby's main attack was scheduled for 19 August.

The composition of the expeditionary force makes for interesting reading. Lawrence had intended it to be an Arab army led by Feisal. The master plan was for Feisal and his Arabs to take Derra, move on to occupy Damascus and then a united Arab nation could be proclaimed. But the reality was already very different; the main Arab column was nominally commanded by Nuri Said as Feisal's representative, but he was to take orders from Lawrence. So many Arabs had 'gone home' or declined to accompany the expedition that the fighting column now consisted of just 400 Arab fighters commanded by Nuri Said with another 200 of his men remaining behind at Aqaba as a rearguard. Captain Peake was in command of thirty-five Egyptian sappers supported by a similar number of Gurkhas under the command of Captain Scott-Higgins. The five armoured cars carrying the heavy machine guns and small artillery pieces were crewed by some forty Englishmen. The most effective force after the armoured cars was the French contingent under the command of Captain Pisani and his deputy, Lieutenant Leimbacher; they had 150 fighting men (North Africans), a battery of artillery made up of four guns supported up by a platoon of machine gunners.

The expedition was instructed to spread out during its desert crossing and then converge on Azrak some 200 miles distant where Sherif Nasir and Auda would join the force and endeavour to recruit local Arabs for the final push on Damascus. The whole force naturally divided into two rough columns that took twelve days to complete the desert crossing. In support were two fighter aircraft from the RAF that were to be based on a specially cleared desert airstrip at Azrak. Lawrence now knew his dream of Arab unity was failing; all he could see were two loosely connected columns of Arab ruffians and peasants being assisted by French and British troops. This was not his dream of a united Arabia. His vision was one of well-equipped Arabs on fine camels dashing in and out of glorious attacks and forcing the Turks to hurriedly depart Arabia. He also knew that if Allenby's advance were to fail, these loyal Arabs would be massacred to the last man.

Just before the column containing Peake's men reached Azrak, Peake found his allocated stores had been commandeered by Auda – who would only release them on payment of £10,000 in gold. Lawrence had to intervene personally and to Peake's chagrin, Lawrence paid the ransom. It was money ill-spent as Peake's Bedouin then mutinied; Lawrence again intervened and some order was restored. These two incidents were serious and threatened the whole Arab advance, yet Lawrence never mentioned either incident in *Seven*

Pillars of Wisdom. At the time, any admission from Lawrence of Arab disunity would have seriously undermined his position with Allenby.

Better news awaited Lawrence at Azrak where he learned that the Turks were putting up a spirited defence and were slowly and inexplicably advancing southwards on both Tafileh and Maan. This news alarmed the Arabs and it took a calm Lawrence to restore equanimity through Arab ranks; he pointed out that, with the Arab advance northwards now under way, the Turks were welcome to move south as they would be placing themselves even more at the mercy of the Arabs. Each Turk so engaged in moving south was one less Turk to face on the final push; the logic appealed to the Arabs whose morale was promptly restored. Lawrence actually ratcheted up the deception by sending out reliable Arabs to purchase corn in the southern areas, which further misled the Turks into thinking that these purchases were for the approaching British main force. Now the Arab march north gained momentum; Lawrence's spirits were raised when Feisal arrived with over 1,000 camelry followed by Nuri with his Ruwalla, Auda and the Abu Tayi and Fahad with the Beni Sakhr. As these camelry troops swept into Azrak, they were followed by numerous weary Arabs on foot, all determined to play their part, and take their loot, in the coming battle.

Lawrence and Feisal received the anticipated confirmation that Allenby's attack would commence on the night of 19 September and the Arabs were tasked with taking Derra to block the Turkish retreat. Lawrence was aware that his force was seriously outnumbered by the Turks and requested a heavy bombardment of Derra prior to his Arabs sweeping in from the desert. Allenby agreed but, in order to maintain secrecy of Allied plans, he instructed the bombardment to commence nearer the time of the Allied advance. At dawn on 16 September, 144 Squadron attacked Derra by dropping three tons of high explosive bombs on the town, seriously damaging its central rail network and Turkish communications. Lawrence's Arabs went to work with added enthusiasm: Lawrence personally led the attack on the rail line at Umtaiye while other groups caused havoc and destruction at nearby Samakh. Ever ready to take risks, Lawrence ran forward with Joyce to place their explosives under an apparently undefended bridge while their second armoured car held the Turks back within the nearby station. As the pair ran up to the bridge they were surprised to discover a cluster of Turks on guard, who promptly surrendered to Lawrence. With the charges laid, they spotted a large force of Turks approaching from the other direction; they exploded the charge and sheltered while the debris fell around them, then set off back to their vehicle. With gusto the two armoured-car crews set off but Lawrence's vehicle struck a rock and bogged down in a patch of soft sand. One of the springs had snapped and the driver, known as Rolls, suggested using a plank of wood bound with wire to act as a makeshift spring. The group lacked a saw to cut the wood, but two short bursts from the vehicle's machine gun rendered the plank to the required size and within minutes a suitable repair was made; it would last all the way to Damascus.

They then set off to Tell Arar, which lay just to the north of Derra; within minutes the telephone lines were cut and a long stretch of rail line exploded in a huge cloud of dust. Supported by one of the armoured cars, the Arabs moved on to attack the railway station, only to meet stiff resistance. Captain Pisani's guns opened fire and blasted the station, which was then looted by the Arabs. Meanwhile, Peake's group were led on a false trail by their Beni Sakhr guides, who were evidently still loyal to their Turkish paymasters. Perhaps to erase the memory of his earlier failure to destroy the Yarmuk viaduct at Tell el Shehab, Lawrence set off to complete the earlier mission. But it was not to be, the Turks were guarding the viaduct in strength so, instead, he moved along the steep-sided ravine and demolished a stretch of inaccessible track which, due to its isolated location, would be impossible for the Turks to repair.

The Turks were in far greater strength along the line than expected but Lawrence's use of armoured cars gave the Arab teams great speed and mobility enabling them to take isolated groups of Turks by complete surprise. The sudden burst of Arab activity confirmed the suspicion of the German commander in Syria, von Sanders, that something was seriously amiss at Derra. He despatched his deputy, Major Willmer, to take command of the town and supplied him with eight aircraft to improve their defence and reconnaissance. With the Turks regaining air supremacy, the Arabs' movements were no longer a secret and they began to suffer regular aerial bombing and strafing. Lawrence had recently lost both his aircraft due to enemy action and with the Arabs in imminent danger of being routed, Lawrence urgently requested RAF support. Three RAF fighters arrived and within two days most of the Turkish aircraft had been shot down; control of the air returned and this likewise gave control on the ground back to Lawrence. Meanwhile, the Arab force moved to Nesib, which lay just ten miles to the south of Derra. Pisani's guns blasted the Turks hiding in the railway station but it was the destruction of the long bridge just to the north of the station that was Lawrence's immediate objective.

Lawrence and his Arab dynamite carriers made their way towards the bridge but the level of fear was too much for the inexperienced town Arabs; they dropped their packs and ran off and Lawrence had to call upon his bodyguard to move the 700 pounds of explosives into position. The bridge was tall and long, even by normal circumstances, and its pillars were six feet thick and at least twenty-five feet tall. The explosion shattered the bridge; it was the last one that Lawrence would destroy. He later recalled it was his seventy-ninth bridge. He then decided to go to Azrak and requested a plane to take him to see Allenby in order to learn how the advance was going. The Arabs were especially impressed when a Handley Page bomber arrived full of urgently needed stores; such an aircraft had never been seen by the Arabs, who wondered at its size. With the aircraft crew came news that Allenby's advance had been a great success and the Turks were now retreating in total disarray. Lawrence seized the opportunity of the bomber's arrival and arranged with the crew for the aircraft to bomb Derra and nearby Mafraq, which it did on 23 September. He immediately sent word to Feisal and headed off to see Allenby.

Lawrence learned from Allenby that the Allies were now advancing and attacking in three columns: the New Zealanders were advancing on Amman, the Indians on Derra and the Australians on Kuneitra. Allenby appointed Lawrence as his political liaison officer to General Sir Harry Chauval, who commanded the Australian Division, and it was to be with Chauval that Lawrence was eventually instructed to enter Damascus. Allenby requested Lawrence to assist all three columns and asked him not to advance on Damascus until the Allies were ready to take the city. A special interim request was made by Allenby for Lawrence to use his Arab army to harass the Turkish Fourth Army on its retreat north. With the Turkish Army in disarray and retreating towards Derra, Lawrence knew they would be forced to surrender once they came up against the Arab army blocking their path, but Lawrence was now determined to move the Arabs as quickly as possible to take Damascus. Without the Arabs in Damascus, there would be no honourable peace settlement for them; the French would take Syria and Lebanon while the British would take Mesopotamia leaving the Arabs with little more than the desert wastes. While he pondered his dilemma – loyalty to Allenby as a serving British officer or loyalty to Feisal – the routed Turkish Army approached Derra, now little more than a massive disorganized rabble being ferociously harried by the following Arabs. It was only when the Australian advance guard reached Mafraq railway station that the fury of the Arabs was seen.

The Arabs had beaten the Australians to the station and had left a scene more reminiscent of Hades than a conventional battlefield. The Australians found trains that had been stranded by the Allied attacks; the carriages had contained the bodies of Turkish wounded, but all had been systematically slaughtered by the Arabs. Worse was to follow: as news of the Turkish rout spread through the Arab ranks and villages, Arab mobs moved on the retreating and unsuspecting Turkish Army as it slowly retreated northwards. The Arabs began by picking off wounded stragglers and then, finding little resistance from the demoralized and thirst-crazed troops, began attacking them at random by cutting off groups of Turks and then falling on them with their swords until all were slain. Hearing of easy pickings, the Beni Sakhr sped to the attack just as the Turkish commander frantically sought to surrender. His plea was accepted by the Australians, who deployed between the Turks and the approaching Beni Sakhr. The Australians had been so appalled by what they had seen they allowed the Turks to retain their arms until they reached the safety of captivity. But the Arabs, seeing the opportunity for revenge, were now in a bloodthirsty mood and even British troops came under occasional fire in the mistaken belief they were supporting the Turks. Lawrence, meanwhile, gave the marauding Arabs free reign to mop up Turkish stragglers. Some prisoners were believed to have been taken in minor skirmishes but there is little evidence that this was the case. Most Arab leaders were not interested in prisoners, though they claimed to have given a number of captives to Arab villagers to be put to work in the fields. Despite pleas from a number of Allied officers for Lawrence to intervene to curtail the Arabs' wanton revenge, he declined, believing the Arabs were entitled to exact their revenge on the Turks for all the barbarities inflicted on the Arab people during the long Turkish occupation.

The overall situation for the desperately retreating Turks then took a serious turn for the worse. Two large Turkish columns were slowly moving across the desert north-west of Derra – one column consisted of over 2,000 soldiers from Mezerib and the other 6,000 from Derra. The Arab force first set off in pursuit of the smaller column that had just passed through the villages of Tura and Tafas. For reasons best known to the Turks, they had gathered the villagers, raped the women then watched as the elite Governor of Syria's Lancers massacred the remaining terrified and screaming villagers. There was no mercy given to anyone and there were no survivors. Lawrence and his Arabs recoiled at the first reports of the civilians' massacre. The Arab leader of the Tafas village, Tallal, was beside himself with despair and fury. Lawrence arranged for the Arabs to close in on the fleeing Turks and set an ambush for them from the protection of a hillside. The waiting Arabs were surprisingly calm as they overlooked the remnants of the Turks marching away from the shattered, burning villages. Although beaten, the Turks marched out in reasonable military order. Lawrence noted that the column was led by horse-mounted Lancers with the remainder of the column made up of marching soldiers flanked by horse-drawn field artillery.

Lawrence deployed his machine guns along the ridge facing the Turks and held his main force back, hidden from the Turks' view by the rising ground, and gave orders to the machine gunners to await his signal. As the last of the troops were clearing the burning buildings the Arabs opened fire on the Turks, who quickly rounded on the hill and returned fire with their field guns; firing in a hurry, their fuses were incorrectly set and no casualties were inflicted on the gathering Arab force. Pisani returned fire with his mountain guns as more Arabs, having learned of the massacre of the villagers, rushed to join in the firing at the massed ranks of retreating Turkish soldiers. Tallal was all for entering his shattered village alone but agreed to wait to be accompanied by Lawrence and Sheikh Abd el Aziz; Lawrence wanted high-ranking witnesses of the Turks' massacre. They led their camels back behind the dunes and scouted around the rear of Tafas and cautiously entered the outskirts of the village. Bodies were heaped everywhere and all the buildings were burning or smouldering; the only sounds came from the cracking of still burning timbers. Lawrence later wrote how Tallal saw a small barefooted girl aged about four years old stagger from a burning building and then collapse in a pool of blood: she held out her hand and as Tallal rushed to her she died in front of him. Leaving the girl where

Lawrence's spring at Wadi Rumm.

Above Three of Lawrence's fellow officers attached to the Arab armies: from left to right, Major Davenport, Colonel Pierce Joyce (who commanded at Aqaba) and Colonel Cyril Wilson (in charge of the mission at Jeddah). *Below* Desert raiders: Colonel Stewart Newcombe (second left in Arab dress), Lieutenant Hornby (far right in British uniform), Major al Mizri (second right in Arab dress) with Arab irregulars, 1917.

Train on Damascus–Medina railway, guarded by German troops 1918.

Damaged station and wagons, Ghadir al Haj, 1918, a picture possibly taken by Lawrence after a raid.

In Wadi Itm, while discussing terms of Turkish surrender, 5 July 1917.

Turkish prisoners at Tafileh.

Lawrence's armoured car and mounted gun section.

The viaduct at Yarmuk.

Above Lawrence with Gertrude Bell and others at Amman, 1921.

Opposite page Allenby with his staff (including Lawrence) entering Jerusalem on 11 December 1917.

The Arabian commission to the Peace Conference in Paris, 1919: Prince Feisal (front) with Mohammed Rustem Bey Haider, Brigadier-General Nouri Pasha Said, Captain Pisani, Colonel Lawrence, and Captain Tahsin Bey Qadri.

Lawrence on his beloved motorcycle.

she lay he leapt back onto his mare and without a word to Lawrence rode down the steep dune and onto the flat desert towards the retreating Turks, whose rear ranks were now less than 400 yards away. Lawrence saw him draw his sword as he gained speed. For a moment both armies stopped firing at each other and watched, as if mesmerized by the charging figure. As the Arab chief bore down on them the Turks waited until he was less than thirty yards from their position then fired a volley of shots at him; Tallal and his mare crashed into the sand and lay motionless, riddled by the concentrated fire. Silence then hung over both armies, but only for a moment. A ferocious buzz quickly built up among the Arabs and Auda took charge; within moments the Arabs began their massed attack on the retreating Turks.

Lawrence wrote in *Seven Pillars of Wisdom* that he gave the order 'No prisoners' and commanded, 'The best of you brings me the most Turkish dead.' It is an extraordinary statement for a British officer to claim to have made; again, like so many of Lawrence's statements, its weight lies in the shock effect of the words, less than the actual implication of what was said. There is every likelihood that most of the Arabs would not, in any event, have either expected or performed otherwise, given what they had witnessed. Auda's men charged the Turks and in their desperation to flee, the unwieldy body of stumbling soldiers, now nearly one mile long, split into three main protective groups. Auda's men set about the nearest group who were desperately attempting to make a defensive stand while Lawrence led a camelry charge after the two other groups of Turks still attempting to run further into the desert in a forlorn attempt to flee the mass of screaming Arabs bearing down on them. Even the Arab infantry joined in; within minutes they had collected Turkish pistols and rifles abandoned by the fleeing Turks and enthusiastically joined the mass execution, shooting at stragglers and chasing individual Turks who tried to hide or run off. The Arabs would shoot at them in ragged volleys and then charge the Turks down, hacking at them with their swords until their victims lay motionless. It took the Arabs two hours to account for the whole column and then Lawrence and Auda returned to their agreed assembly point.

The only group of prisoners to be taken would not survive long. When Lawrence arrived at the assembly point he found 200 Turkish, German and Austrian troops staring defiantly at him. Lawrence enquired why prisoners had been taken; he may well have been prepared to spare their lives but they had already inadvertently sealed their own fate. While Lawrence was pondering the situation, the prisoners stood calmly together although they were fully aware of the earlier fate of their colleagues. Lawrence's attention was then drawn to a dying Arab who had just been brought in; the wounded Arab had earlier been caught by the prisoners before the Arabs launched their retributive attack. Though severely injured and barely alive, the man's previously uninjured shoulder and leg had been firmly pegged into the ground with two German bayonets. The dying Arab had been found and rescued by some of Auda's men; he was still conscious and angrily jabbed in the direction of the group of prisoners. Within moments a machine gun was trained on the prisoners, and despite pleadingly anguished looks the Arabs opened fire into the group. There were no survivors.

Another small group of motorized German officers and soldiers had managed to avoid the main column's slaughter; they sped off to the safety of the north in their machine-gun equipped vehicles but were continuously harried at each turn by Arab camelry. When cornered they would calmly defend themselves and then move off, each time abandoning their wounded in the forlorn hope they could slow the relentlessly pursuing Arabs. Only their commander and his staff eventually escaped.

The larger retreating Turkish column of 6,000 initially made better progress; they managed to hold together until nightfall, their size being their best protection. After dark everything changed. The Turks were exhausted, they were without food and water and their chain of command began to fail. The Ruwalla and Anazeh Bedouin under Nasir continued to harass them with camelry charges and finally succeeded in driving through the main body, which caused the Turks to break off into uncoordinated splinter groups. The whole area was now seething with sword-wielding Arabs and panicking Turks. Most of the chasing Arabs were mounted on camels or horses while others acted independently in clusters of stabbing foot soldiers who relentlessly pursued stragglers and the wounded, putting them to the sword. Of the six complete Turkish regiments that had departed Derra at dawn on 27 September, only a few traumatized soldiers were able to reach Damascus.

That night Lawrence was able to reassemble a sizeable number of his Arabs and moved them off towards Derra with a view to taking the town that had so long held out. Nasir led his Ruwalla in a charge into the town but there was no resistance. During the previous evening hundreds of Bedouin and Arab peasants had slipped away and entered the town; finding no organized resistance they set about murdering every Turk they could find before turning their attention to looting. Most Turkish troops had already fled northwards in the hope of reaching Damascus before the Arabs caught up with them. The town was in chaos when Lawrence arrived; not content with murdering captured Turks, the rabble had rounded up and mercilessly slaughtered any Arab civilians who had assisted the occupying Turks, and many sympathizers had their throats slit. Lawrence overlooks the matter in *Seven Pillars of Wisdom*. With a strangely poised detachment, he only mentions watching Turkish police officers from Derra being marched off for execution by Arabs wielding whips and swords:

> They were driving them mercilessly, the bruising of their urging blue across their ivory backs; but I left them to it, for these were Turks of the police battalion of Derra, beneath whose iniquities the peasant-faces of the neighbourhood had run with tears and blood, innumerable times.

In the midst of all the chaos and confusion the Australian general, Sir George Barrow, arrived in Derra at the head of his Indian cavalry; he was both horrified and infuriated by what he saw. Nasir had installed himself in the town hall and declared that Derra was now under the control of the sherif's army. Young, Winterton and Pisani arrived with the French artillery at the head of a thousand Turks who had surrendered to Pisani and the European officers had great difficulty preventing the Arab mob massacring the Turkish prisoners where they stood. Barrow called for Lawrence and at first requested, then ordered, Lawrence to remove the Arabs. Lawrence declined, stating that it was the Arab way of fighting, at which the infuriated Barrow over-rode Lawrence and gave orders for the Arabs to be removed. Lawrence threatened Arab retaliation but Barrow disregarded him and gave the order. There was no Arab retaliation.

Derra convinced the British officers under Barrow that the Arabs were little more than murderers and plunderers; sadly the sight of Lawrence and his bloodied officers, unshaven and in unrecognizable uniforms covered by Arab robes, did little to maintain their reputation as leaders of a fine Arab army. Barrow was indignant that he had to request Lawrence to supply his Indian cavalry with food and fodder. He was further annoyed when he rode to the town hall to meet with Nasir; Nasir had hung his pendant from the flag pole and when Lawrence suggested that Barrow should salute it, he grudgingly obliged to the delight of the Arabs. He duly complained to Allenby that he had felt humiliated by Lawrence; Allenby's response was that Lawrence had acted correctly. Lawrence later sought his own retribution in *Seven Pillars of Wisdom* by diminishing Barrow's role in taking Derra and maligning the general and his troops.

To exert his own authority, and to prevent rival Arab tribes claiming possession of captured towns and villages, Allenby gave an order that the only flag to be flown in Palestine was to be the Union Flag.

13

Damascus

*A*llenby's main Allied force had spent the summer months retraining and amassing stores and equipment ready for the coming offensive. Having witnessed the efficacy of the Arab camelry, the Indian cavalry were re-equipped with lances rather than carbine rifles. The Australian mounted infantry kept their firearms but added swords to their equipment, while the regiments of inexperienced infantry had to be completely retrained when it was discovered that most had never fired a shot. Nevertheless, the backbone of Allenby's troops remained the British Army.

The whole force was effectively divided into three main columns: the desert Mounted Corps under General Chauvel, the XX Corps under General Chetwode and the XXI Corps under General Bulfin. The army consisted of regiments from Australia, Britain, France, Egypt, India, Hong Kong, Italy, South Africa, New Zealand and the West Indies. It totalled nearly half a million men, with 175,000 from Britain, 93,000 from India and the remainder from Britain's colonies. The multi-national and multilingual force was difficult to coordinate; for example, since the Indian troops spoke little English and their British officers spoke no Hindustani, hand signals became of paramount importance. Three battalions of Jewish troops, the 38th, 39th and 40th Royal Fusiliers joined the Allies; one of their officers was David Ben Gurion who later became Prime Minister of Israel.

The Allies faced three Turkish armies. The Eighth was 10,000-

strong supported by three German battalions under Djemal Pasha and held the line between Arsuf and Furkhah. Poised in the hills of Judea was the Seventh Army under Mustafa Kemal and the Jordan Valley across to Amman was defended by the Fourth Army under Jemal. The overall German commander, Liman von Sanders, who had just taken over from Falkenhayn, had his headquarters at Nazareth with a full division held in reserve. Some 7,000 Turkish troops were still occupied holding the Hejaz Railway.

The Allied army was now in the best possible shape to commence advancing against the dug-in Turkish positions. Allenby had nearly 60,000 troops under his command plus 12,000 cavalry. He possessed awesome artillery firepower with nearly 600 guns and plentiful ammunition; a fifth of the guns were for medium- to long-range bombardments. Not content with superiority of numbers, Allenby ordered a clever pattern of systematic deceptions to mislead the Turks – not an easy undertaking as there were still many Arab spies sympathetic to the Turks. Under the control of generals Bartholomew and Dawnay, enormous dummy camps had been constructed to the front and left of the Turkish line along the Jordan Valley and many thousand dummy horses, made of canvas and wire, were set out in neat cavalry style. Troops were marched across the desert into fake positions during the day and then secretly withdrawn under the cover of darkness; the deception was then repeated daily over several days. Decoy bridges were constructed across watercourses and a dummy HQ was laid out within sight of and opposite one Turkish position. Fake telephone lines were installed and sand sleds were towed by vehicles through soft sand to create vast dust clouds that, from a distance, appeared to indicate large Allied troop movements. The overall consequence was that the Turks fell for the deception and concentrated their troops to the east of the front whereas Allenby was preparing his troops to attack the coastal positions in the west. Allenby's plan was to then launch a full scale infantry attack on the Turkish right flank, which would be immediately followed up by cavalry riding inland and then swinging east, cutting Turkish communications as they went, and trapping the Turks. At the same time a small Allied force would strike the Turkish left flank, aided by part of Lawrence's Arab army; this force would be taking an enormous risk as it was hopelessly outnumbered and the inhospitable terrain was a barren and baking hot dust-bowl, being 1,000 feet below sea level and spread out for the whole ten miles to Amman.

Allenby reckoned on the Turks believing a massive attack was coming and either surrendering or retreating. To assist their decision-making process, Allenby ordered massive leaflet drops by the RAF instructing the Turks to surrender or be killed. Many Turks 'jumped the gun' and began surrendering in advance of the Allied attack, and were only too keen to be questioned in exchange for food or cigarettes. The Allies quickly built up a picture of demoralized and uninterested Turkish troops who were ill-led, lacking rations and inefficient. They also learned that the German troops were currently suffering from an unknown serious illness. This subsequently turned out to be the 'Spanish' influenza that, within the year, would spread worldwide and kill many millions – three times more soldiers on both sides than had been lost in hostilities during the whole of the First World War.

Allenby's awaited order went out to his top commanders on 9 September. It was confidently headed with the words 'the Commander-in-Chief intends to take the offensive' and confirmed that the pre-attack barrage of artillery would open fire at 4.30 a.m. on 19 September. Allenby retired early on the night of the 18th having instructed his personal staff officers to awake him at 4 a.m. The following morning found the group standing in the cold dark of the early morning looking north; Allenby looked at his watch and made a comment, but it was unheard because there was a majestic explosion of artillery fire along the whole length of the Allied front and then the skyline in front of the Turkish positions erupted in fire and spiralling dust clouds. The Royal Navy, now less than a mile from the coastline, joined the barrage and shelled Turkish positions along the coastal road. At the agreed signal, Allied infantry began their measured advance under the cover of the artillery's creeping barrage; as dawn broke so did the Turks' resolve to defend their line. The RAF bombed the various Turkish headquarters, which destroyed their communications with the front line, and British fighter aircraft deterred their aerial reconnaissance and any retaliation. The RAF went on to attack a three-mile column of Turkish troops trying to escape to Nablus through the Wadi Fara. The pilots successfully bombed the head of the column which blocked the Turks' forward movement; the whole column shortly surrendered to British cavalry who were hard on their heels. The first inkling of trouble for the German commander at Nazareth was the arrival of a British cavalry brigade outside his headquarters. Liman von Sanders was still in bed and made an undignified and hasty exit; he came within a few minutes of being captured and escaped only due to the mistaken belief of the British troops that his HQ was at the appropriately named Germania Hotel 200 yards away.

By 10 a.m. the Turkish front line was overrun; the infantry poured through and began their move northwards along the coast while the British cavalry, for the second time in history, drove the Turks back towards Haifa.[1] The 4th Cavalry Division advanced through to the ancient fortress at Megiddo, the scene of numerous major battles that dated back to biblical times. So rapid was the Allied advance that by nightfall on 20 September, the retreat of the Turkish Seventh and Eighth armies had been blocked off; they were relentlessly attacked and only a small contingent managed to escape across the Jordan Valley. The towns of Haifa and Acre were taken on 23 September, Haifa by a gallant cavalry charge supported by the 15th Field Troop Royal Engineers who, in the absence of orders to the

---

1 In 1191 Richard Coeur de Lion drove Saladin's force of Turks back from the coastal plain and across the very same terrain Allenby's army was now advancing over.

contrary, joined in, having previously gathered a sufficient number of Turkish lances and sword trophies along the route, which were now put to good use. Amman was finally taken on the 25 September and by the 26th Palestine was completely in Allenby's hands. He had over 50,000 Turkish prisoners, many suffering the effects of malaria and influenza. The remnants of the Turkish Fourth, Seventh and Eighth armies were now being picked off in the blistering heat of the desert by Lawrence's Arabs.

With Allied troops arriving and taking up position outside Derra, some semblance of order returned to the town, which began to calm the excitable Arab forces. With peace eventually restored, clusters of frightened Turks came out of hiding to surrender while others were brought in by the Allied troops. Most were duly sent back to Egypt but, with the Allies overwhelmed by the numbers and wishing to press on with the advance, over 2,000 were set to work in the fields of nearby Arab villages. According to Brian Gardner's biography, Allenby wrote home to his wife that he suspected they 'would have their throats slit'. On 29 September Feisal arrived at Derra in his green staff car, followed majestically by the Arabs' armoured cars. Allenby requested that Lawrence and Feisal were to right-flank the final Allied advance to Damascus, which suited both Feisal and Lawrence as they could gather in the Ruwalla tribesmen who were still doggedly tearing away at the survivors of the Turkish column. Without further delay the combined Allied and Arab march on Damascus commenced.

The following day there was little to see or do at Derra that required his attention so Lawrence took time to wander off alone into the desert and ponder his future plan. His moment of truth was now rapidly approaching and he was fully aware of his obligation to support Allenby, yet his personal ambition remained the same – the installation of the Arab leadership in Damascus before the Allies could arrive. His dream of Arab unity could only be fulfilled with Feisal in control of the city. Lawrence was now a man truly torn by his loyalties but there could only be one decision; Allenby would come second to Feisal. The next day Lawrence set off in his Rolls-Royce armoured car to catch the huge Allied column and, finding his way blocked by slow-moving troop columns, he skirted round the troops by driving across the open desert. He regained the front of the column to find himself called to see Barrow. Lawrence was asked what he was doing and where he was stopping that night, only for Barrow to be told 'At Damascus'. Relations between the two men were already severely strained following Barrow's arrival and indignation with the Arabs' undisciplined brutality at Derra. The British general, with all his European values and ingrained military discipline, saw Lawrence as an odd-ball and inwardly fumed at his lackadaisical approach to military matters; yet he had to tread carefully, knowing only too well that Lawrence had Allenby's ear.

Lawrence knew that Barrow had been put in his place by Allenby for querying Lawrence's actions and so he ignored him and pressed on at speed: he urgently needed to recall the many groups of Arabs, still harassing the retreating Turks, for their triumphal entry into Damascus. Two hours later Lawrence could see distant columns of dust and he headed straight for them; the Arabs were tenaciously hanging on to the dwindling Turkish force, now spread out in clusters across the stony desert and desperately fighting to hold off their inevitable fate. Of the 6,000 Turks that had departed Derra in good order, less than 2,000 still survived. As Lawrence approached he could hear the occasional sound of Turkish gunfire; he then saw several Arabs on horseback riding towards him, led by Nasir and Nuri Said. Both were breathless with excitement as they had finally managed to halt the Turkish retreat. Auda was somewhere in the thick of the fighting and Nasir urged Lawrence to call forward extra troops as he needed urgent help to hold the Turks. Lawrence agreed, turned about and sped back to a column of Indian cavalry he had passed earlier. But the colonel leading the cavalry was cautious and inexperienced and had already halted on hearing the distant sound of gunfire. Lawrence's plea for a rapid advance to take the Turks fell on deaf ears and the colonel missed his chance of instant recognition. Dusk fell and the Turks banded together in the forlorn hope that they could protect each other. It was not to be. The wily Auda withdrew his force and set up an ambush between the Turks and their escape route to Damascus. As night fell, the Turks began to break up in the false hope that they could slip round the Arab positions; they abandoned their guns and other heavy equipment and headed off towards, as they thought, the safety of the nearby city. Auda allowed the Turks to move out onto the hard flat open desert and then unleashed his Arabs. They fell upon the scattered clumps of staggering Turks and by dawn little was left of the column, their bodies scattered over many miles of bleak desert.

The long drawn-out battle along the approach to Damascus had been totally successful for the Allies but terrible in cost to the Turks. It is impossible to look back on the events that led up to the taking of Damascus without reflecting on the massacre of thousands of Turkish soldiers. This act of mass slaughter has to be counterbalanced by the knowledge that this was also the Turkish way of fighting; the Turks had created the template for modern desert warfare and were hardly in a position to protest. Little was ever written about the Turks' appalling defeat and final days of their Fourth Army, and even official despatches tended to be restricted to pure military facts. The official British handbook *A Brief Record of the Advance of the Egyptian Expeditionary Force* merely commented:

The Fourth Mounted Division (General Barrow's force) coming up from the south with the Arab forces on its right entered Derra unopposed on September 28th, and the next day got in touch with the retreating Turks in the Dalli area. For two days the enemy was pressed and harassed, his columns were fired upon and broken up, and on September 30th the division got into touch with the other divisions of the Desert Mounted Corps and reached Zerakiye late that night.

With Damascus now only 100 miles away victory for Allenby was assured. By nightfall on 30 September all three Allied divisions were on the outskirts of Damascus. Three Turkish armies, the Fourth, Seventh and Eighth, had been destroyed. Of the estimated force of 150,000 Turkish troops in Palestine, Allenby's advance had already taken half as prisoners including 3,790 German officers and men. An estimated 10,000 had been killed by Lawrence and Feisal's Arabs and 17,000 escaped; the remainder had been killed in action. Allied losses amounted to 5,666 casualties of whom 850 were killed, 4,450 wounded and 388 missing. Lawrence gave his own figures for the war in his *Oriental Assembly* as: 'Thirty-five thousand prisoners, killed and wounded and worn out about as many, and occupied a hundred thousand square miles of the enemy's territory with little loss to ourselves.'

When Lawrence despatched messengers to gather his far-flung Arabs for their triumphal entry into Damascus, many of them were still engaged in their pursuit of remnants of the Turkish Army and looting the Turks' baggage trains. While this reorganization of the chaotic Arabs was under way, Lawrence made his way towards Kiswe, just five miles from Damascus, where he found the Australians waiting for General Barrow to take command for their own entry into Damascus under the overall commander, the Australian general, Sir Harry Chauvel. Lawrence wasted no time; he had just received a message from Allenby, dropped from an aircraft, that the Arabs should enter Damascus first to restore order throughout the city and to ensure the Turks had departed before the main British entry. Indeed the bulk of the Turks and their German advisers had departed that same day and left the city under the command of the Turkish deputy governor, Shukri Pasha, who awaited the arrival of the Arabs with some trepidation. In an attempt to appease them, he had already raised an Arab flag above the town hall.

A British Headquarters declaration dated June 1918 stated irrevocably: 'The Arabs will possess with all sovereignty whatever they conquer by force of arms.' This statement was the final key to Lawrence's aspirations for the Arab people. It was now imperative for him to give the world the impression that the Arab army was the saviour of the Syrian capital of Damascus. He wanted everyone to see that the Arab army had achieved the expulsion of the Turks, not only from Arabia but also from Syria. Lawrence and Feisal had long anticipated the Arabs taking administrative control of the areas they liberated, with the exception of Palestine. By the end of September, and with the end of the war in sight, the French were changing their minds and demanding French officials be placed in senior positions throughout Syria. Allenby acknowledged French interests but took no further action other than to allow the Arabs first entry into Damascus. Yet the sum total of Lawrence's force was minimal with just the Ruwalla still within his sphere of command; the bulk of the Arab force had now given up chasing the remnants of the retreating Turkish columns and began to head for Damascus. Lawrence also learned that Feisal would be with him the following day. To ensure the Turks and Germans had left the city, and to prevent civil unrest, Lawrence sent his 4,000 Ruwalla tribesmen into the city as a token force to represent the Arabs. His plan was to allow the remaining Arabs to enter Damascus the following morning, take control of the city administrative centre and then await the arrival of Feisal, who would formally accept the Turkish surrender. Such action should, thought Lawrence, be sufficient to block French interest in Syria.

Late on 30 September, while the main Australian force was surrounding Damascus, the Australian general, Wilson, was ordered to seize the city exit road to the north. Finding this difficult he took his force straight through the city centre and quickly reached the north side. With no Turkish opposition, the Damascenes poured onto the streets to welcome their Australian liberators. Students of *Seven Pillars of Wisdom* will find no reference to the Australians inadvertently liberating Damascus in advance of the Arabs or of the role of the Indian forces. Lawrence would ignore this important fact in favour of his misleading claim that his Arabs relieved the city. This was political tinkering of the first order, which was perpetuated in both Rattigan's *Ross* and Lean's *Lawrence of Arabia*. That night Lawrence was unaware that Damascus had been accidentally liberated by the Australians; he wrote that he slept well in the mistaken belief that he would have a sizeable force of Arabs in Damascus before Barrow's Allied troops arrived. However, there are others who claim that Lawrence was less than happy that night. Lawrence's entourage had now been joined by Colonel Stirling, recently appointed as chief of staff to Feisal, and he wrote that:

> T. E. was very despondent that night. Just before going to sleep I asked him why he was so depressed seeing we were on the eve of our entry into Damascus, and in sight of the final act which was to crown all his efforts with success. 'Ever since we took Derra', he replied, 'the end has been inevitable. Now the zest has gone and the interest.'[2]

That night the outskirts of Damascus were rocked by a long series of explosions. Lawrence deduced that the rearguard of German troops had placed charges to destroy the city following their departure but, instead, they had merely detonated their own ammunition dumps on the far side of the city to prevent them falling into Allied hands. At dawn, Lawrence, Nasir and Emir Nuri peered through the mists of the sunrise and all were relieved to see that the famous minarets and cupolas of the city were still intact; Damascus had been

---

2 Stirling wrote in his autobiography *Safety Last*: 'In my considered opinion, Lawrence was the greatest genius whom England has produced in the last two centuries, and I do not believe that there is anyone who had known him who will not agree with me. If ever a genius, a scholar, and artist and an imp of Shaitan were rolled into one, it was Lawrence.'

spared. In acknowledgement of Nasir's numerous battles against the Turks (Lawrence estimated there were some fifty in total that he had personally led), he gave Nasir the honour of leading the first formal Arab delegation into the city. Lawrence decided to give him an hour's head start and meanwhile he and his group sought out some water for an overdue wash and shave. All were mounted in Lawrence's Rolls-Royce and the group moved off in search of this elusive water, only to be halted by a contingent of Indian Lancers. Highly suspicious of Lawrence, and ignoring the significance of the Rolls-Royce, the Lancers detained Lawrence's party in the understandable belief that they were Turkish spies. Lawrence later claimed he was deliberately prevented from joining the first Arabs into Damascus in order to reduce his personal influence on those taking control. In any event, the party were taken under arrest to the Lancers' headquarters and then, with identities established, promptly released. As Lawrence's Rolls-Royce approached the city limits a Damascene rider approached, calling out 'Damascus salutes you' and carrying bunches of grapes for the party: it was a peace offering from the pro-Arab Turkish administrator of Damascus, Shukri Pasha. The welcome gift was graciously accepted by the party. As they entered the city the overwhelming impression was of quiet joy; crowds had gathered earlier that morning in anticipation of the main Arab arrival, which had been led by Nasir less than one hour earlier. The crowds quickly discovered that the car contained Lawrence and word of his arrival preceded him. Many cheerfully waved as he passed by.

At the town hall Lawrence was to receive a shock. Waiting for him were two of his former enemies, Abd el Kader, who had betrayed him to the Turks on the Yarmuk raid, and his assassin brother, Mohammed Said. Nasir and Emir Nuri sat silent and forlorn in the background. Kader and his brother, supported by their Algerian retainers, had earlier invaded the city halls and forcefully seized control from Shukri in the name of Hussein of Mecca; Shukri had been somewhat bewildered by the unexpected turn of events and decided to await the outcome. Shukri confirmed to Lawrence that the pair had been loyal supporters of the Turks until the day before. There followed a heated and bitter few hours until, finally, it was announced by Lawrence that Kader and his brother had been deposed in favour of Shukri as Acting Military Governor, pending Feisal's arrival. The announcement infuriated Kader who drew his dagger and lunged at Lawrence. Auda jumped between the two men and rained blows down on Kader until he was subdued. All eyes turned to Lawrence, who would dearly have liked to let Auda tear the traitor to pieces or lead him away to be shot. Such a remedy would have been perfectly appropriate in the desert but not in the chamber of the City Council. Instead, Lawrence ordered the Algerians to be taken to the city limits and released; he knew full well their richly deserved execution would have set a bad example on the very first day of the fledgling Arab government.

Within a few hours of the triumphal Arab entry into Damascus, Lawrence was faced with resolving the severe conflict between the Arab and Algerian delegations. He was painfully aware that he now faced the biggest challenge of all: to maintain law and order until Feisal could arrive from Derra. Lawrence left Shukri in temporary charge and provided selected Arab leaders such as Nuri Said and Emir Nuri to assist the deputy governor to bring control back to city life. There was much to be done, mainly by people who had no knowledge of running public utilities. The population was still cheering its salvation but within hours they would be demanding fresh water, street lighting, sanitation and other visible bodies such as a police and fire service, which would help bring a semblance of normality. However, the city water supply was clogged with the bodies of dead Turks, the streets were littered with the detritus of the departing Turkish Army, the police stations and prison cells were now empty and disease was rapidly spreading through the Turkish prisoners, most of whom appeared to be suffering from dysentery.

Towards the end of their first day in Damascus Lawrence and Shukri were nevertheless beginning to re-establish some form of civil order. The citizens were encouraged to surrender rifles and ammunition taken from fleeing Turks, houses near to burning buildings were dynamited to prevent the fires spreading and hospital staff were requested to return to work. The Arabs were ordered not to slaughter surrendering Turkish soldiers but to set them clearing away and removing the numerous bodies of slain Turks to outlying cemeteries. Others were detailed to open hitherto secret Turkish warehouses and begin distributing food to the starving. In order to bring in fresh supplies, the Arabs restored the railway system, telegraph operators were reappointed to run communications and a newspaper had to be prepared to keep the population informed. It then occurred to Lawrence that a currency was also needed; the Turkish currency was the only currency known to the Damascenes but this had been devalued to the point of worthlessness when a contingent of Australian troops seized a huge amount of Turkish currency and then threw it to the Arabs. A suitable printing press was found and a replacement currency was soon in preparation. The administration set up during those first days of liberation would last, in one form or another, for nearly two years.

Lawrence knew that time was running out before the Allies arrived; if the city was still in chaos then the Allies would, with total justification, take over Damascus and the Arab dream would quickly fade. By putting the Damascenes back to work and with order restored, at least there would be a façade of normality, and that was all that was required for Feisal to claim his Arabs' success.

Lawrence retired early that night, only to be awoken by his liaison officer, Lieutenant Kirkbride, with news that Kader had gathered his Algerians together and was stirring mutiny by telling the Damascenes and any Arab who would listen that Lawrence's actions were nothing more than an English ploy to seize the country. Kader had managed to recruit the Arab Druses to his cause, a people who had avoided supporting Feisal and who had preferred to subjugate themselves to Turkish rule. In the early hours reports reached Lawrence's HQ that the Druse were ransacking shops on the outer limits of the city. Lawrence and Nuri Said laid a trap; they allowed the Druse to believe they were unopposed while they were actually unwittingly moving towards strategically placed Arab strong points manned by Nuri Said's men, armed with machine guns. As dawn broke, so the rebels were subjected to a few well-aimed bursts of automatic fire. They fled back towards the outer city limit where Nuri Said's men were waiting. Kader fled and his brother was captured and imprisoned. The Druse were disarmed and ordered back to their own district where they would be unable to influence the greater part of the city. Lawrence had meanwhile called on General Chauvel, waiting outside the city, for support troops. They were readily sent but in the end they were not required and, by midday, Damascus was back to some normality. Allenby was still at Jerusalem and had been sent some scare messages about Arab massacres of Turks in Damascus. Lawrence received a stiff note requesting details of Turks killed or injured by the Arabs and Lawrence responded with a message that gave the names of five dead and twelve injured.

During the morning disturbing reports began to reach Lawrence of hospitals still overflowing with Turkish sick; he was visited by an Australian doctor who reported scenes of indescribable squalor and death at the city's Arab hospitals, but the worst scene was to be found at the main Turkish military hospital. The Arab hospitals were beginning to function although they were devoid of drugs and medicines. A request for drugs to General Chauvel had fallen on deaf ears, in part because none were spare. Mindful of the possibility of cholera and typhus spreading to the civilian population, Lawrence took Kirkbride to investigate the Turkish military hospital. They first had to negotiate with the Australian guards to gain entry and were shaken by what they saw. There were no doctors or medical orderlies in sight: they had apparently fled with the Turkish abandonment of

Damascus. There were dead and dying throughout the building and even the garden was littered with scores of bodies. The wards were similarly occupied; most beds contained a body and the officers were amazed to find that some patients were still alive, just. Lawrence then learned that there were some Turkish doctors hiding in an upstairs room. He and Kirkbride bounded up the stairs to find seven doctors sipping coffee and making toffee. Lawrence ordered them downstairs; they were slow to respond to his order so Kirkbride drew his revolver, which sent the men scurrying down to the wards. Lawrence left Kirkbride in charge and set off to find an Arab doctor to take control of the hospital. He also found some forty weak but able-bodied Turks who were put to work digging graves in the hospital garden. Once their work was done they were appointed as hospital orderlies to disinfect the wards and wash the patients. Kirkbride later reported nearly 1,000 patients at the hospital of whom 100 were recently dead, 200 dying and the remainder too sick to do anything but to remain where they were. A similar number were later found in other nearby Turkish military hospitals. Lawrence was thankful that there was no sign of typhus or cholera. With little more that he could do, he retired late that evening to his hotel and slept soundly until the following morning.

To his delight, the next day vindicated all the effort of the previous thirty-six hours. The city was continuing its steady return to normality. Even the trams were running again. Shops were opening and the markets were busy with traders and milling shoppers. The water supply had been restored and an enterprising official had even instructed the streets to be hosed down to lay the dust of two years' neglect. The final proof of normality was the sight of groups of unarmed British servicemen sightseeing around the city. Over his breakfast he learned that Arab troops had also taken Beirut; Lawrence finally accepted that, at last, the war was over.

Mindful of the appalling conditions at the nearby Turkish hospital, Lawrence made his way there and was pleased to see that some semblance of normality was evident; the orderlies were busy and the patients were receiving all possible care. Lawrence was discussing matters with Kirkbride when the recently arrived Australian Colonel Single from the Army Medical Corps strode up and asked who was in charge of the hospital. Lawrence, in his Arab clothes, admitted responsibility. The colonel had no idea who he was speaking to and exploded with rage and threatened to have Lawrence shot due to the conditions inside. Having done what he could during the previous twelve hours, and having been refused help from the approaching Allies, Lawrence broke out in a laughing fit and was promptly slapped by the indignant colonel. Lawrence continued to be amused by the colonel's indignation and set off back to his hotel; as he approached the building he saw Allenby's Rolls-Royce parked outside and ran in to find his commander, who made him most welcome.

Allenby was delighted to find Damascus intact and thriving and thanked Lawrence for his efforts, especially in setting up Arab governments at Derra and in Damascus. In fact, much of the rapid improvement was due to the Australian calming influence. Their troops maintained a presence throughout the city and the day before, 2 October, Damascenes had witnessed the Allies march into the city. The marching Australian, British, French and Indian troops had been a timely reminder to Lawrence that the defeat of the Turks was not only due to the Arabs. But now he was with Allenby and, bathing in reflected glory, Lawrence made a number of suggestions relating to the division of responsibilities that Allenby agreed with. The most important were split between Chauvel and Feisal, who was now on his way to Damascus. Lawrence learned that Allenby had advised the War Office that he would recognize Feisal and that consequently Feisal would have to follow the terms of the Sykes–Picot agreement under the eye of a French liaison officer. While Allenby and Lawrence were in discussion, they learned that Feisal had arrived at the railway station and was already on his way to join Allenby. Lawrence was requested to be the official interpreter; it was to be a unique moment for Lawrence, for the first time in two years he would be in the presence of both his masters.

To smooth the passage of the meeting, Allenby gave Lawrence a telegram that had arrived for Feisal from the British government recognizing 'to the Arabs their status as belligerents'. Neither Allenby nor Lawrence knew what it meant but Feisal was pleased to receive it. Their meeting lasted less than fifteen minutes. Feisal was too overwhelmed by his triumphal entry into the city to be much aware of the significance of his meeting with Allenby, though Allenby was fulsome in praise for Feisal. He later wrote:

> I had the honour of association with King Feisal in the Palestine and Syria Campaign during the war. His work in the Allied cause was very valuable to us; and to me specially. He was a brave and loyal ally; and we owe to him, his family, and his army, a deep debt of gratitude.

Feisal then departed the meeting leaving Lawrence alone with Allenby. Allenby began by thanking Lawrence for everything he had done. Lawrence sat and listened to the great general who soon noticed that Lawrence was not really taking any part in the conversation. Lawrence then dropped his bombshell; he requested his commander's leave to depart Arabia and go back to England. Allenby was astonished, having had no warning whatsoever that Lawrence would do anything other than remain, perhaps as Allenby's principal adviser. Allenby spent some minutes trying to dissuade Lawrence but on realizing his decision was made, he reluctantly agreed. Lawrence made only one request, to be promoted to the rank of colonel so that he could travel back to England with a first class rail ticket and have his own berth on the ship home. Allenby promoted him then and there. Lawrence was requested to remain in Damascus for the formal arrival of Feisal and the sherifs; this took place three days later on 4 October. Lawrence departed after the ceremony and headed straight to the railway station. He paused in Cairo to write an account to *The*

Times of his recent experiences with the Arabs, which included the assertion that the Arabs had liberated Damascus. The seeds of the Lawrence myth had been planted.

In a matter of two days, control of Damascus had swung from the Turks to the Arabs and finally to the British. Lawrence understood that his dream of Arabia for the Arabs was rapidly fading. He was exhausted, mentally drained and now wanted nothing more to do with the war. Then, suddenly, he was gone and his departure from Damascus went largely unnoticed. For most combatants, Lawrence was nothing more than a vague name, a myth, and nothing to do with them or the real war they had been fighting and would continue to fight against the German-led Turkish forces until they were finally defeated. With Derra and Damascus now taken, the Turks were routed. They lacked transport and supplies and were fleeing in total disarray back to Turkey. British intelligence guessed that there were less than 4,000 armed Turks between Damascus and the last Turkish-held town of Aleppo, and these troops were not expected to offer any resistance. The last hurdle for Allenby would, nevertheless, not be easy. The Allies were now stretched to their full limit; their advance had been spectacular and was undoubtedly the swiftest advance ever made by an army – but Aleppo had to be taken, regardless of difficulties. The urgency to eliminate Turkey from the war was enormous. With Turkey neutralized, Germany would have little option but to offer total surrender and the First World War would come to its inevitable close. The British government nevertheless ordered Allenby to continue with his advance and suggested a rapid deployment using his cavalry. Allenby made plans but these, too, were thwarted, this time by sickness spreading through his army. His soldiers were beginning to succumb to malaria and many were becoming sick with the same type of influenza that had infected the German troops – Spanish Flu. With the troops' repatriation to all parts of the globe, this deadly, virulent and highly contagious variation of influenza would soon spread worldwide.

Allenby was more than satisfied with the Allies' progress and decided to move northwards using his own tried and tested tactic of leapfrogging his forces forwards. With the Australians delegated to occupy Damascus, the remainder of his force moved steadily northwards. The Indians advanced along the coast towards Beirut only to find that French warships were already stationed off the coast and offshoots of Feisal's Arabs were in occupation of the town. There was a tense stand-off between the Allies and the Arabs that ended when Feisal was ordered to withdraw his men. The Allied advance continued, Aleppo was taken without opposition but the Allies were aware that the Turks were preparing one final last stand at Haritan, just north of Aleppo. The British commander, General Macandrew, boldly advanced on the Turkish positions and, though greatly outnumbered by the Turks, frightened them into abandoning the town and withdrawing for the final short journey back into Turkey. On 31 October the Allied armistice with Turkey was announced.

Allenby's advance had been truly brilliant. In five months, his army had fought well and had advanced 550 miles across some of the most inhospitable terrain in the world. It had suffered the broiling heat of summer before finally shattering the last vestige of the once powerful Ottoman Empire. Allenby's cavalry had been the star of the show: it had taken part in all the major battles and its exploits were beyond those ever before achieved. It was fitting that the cavalry's final action had taken place within sight of the great battlefield of Issus where in 333 BC Alexander had used his cavalry with skill equal to that shown by Allenby and his generals. The Germans and Turks had lost well over 100,000 men captured as prisoners with a similar number killed in action or from disease. Allenby's casualties, by comparison, amounted to a total of 5,000 men lost.

The war in the desert had taken four years to win but, for the Allies, it had been worth the wait. Brian Gardner records in *Allenby* that Lloyd George wrote: 'Had this operation been undertaken at an early stage of the war, and properly supported from home, the Turkish collapse would have come sooner, and the repercussions in Europe would have been shattering.'

14

End of the Arabian Road

*C*olonel Lawrence DSO, CB, arrived back in London on Armistice Day, 11 November 1918 and was immediately required to attend a number of official meetings at the War Office. There was also discussion throughout the War Office of probable decorations. Indeed, Lawrence had previously been nominated for the decoration of the Victoria Cross though the nomination had been perfunctorily rejected by the War Office who, it was widely believed, might now seek to make amends. Rumours abounded that a knighthood would be a formality, having been recommended by both Sir Mark Sykes and General Allenby, and Lawrence was advised it would soon be bestowed upon him. Within days he was informed that the king had expressed a wish for a private meeting with him, and it was anticipated by the Palace establishment that the king would decorate Lawrence. The meeting was not to run as smoothly as expected.

The earlier recommendation for the Victoria Cross, supported by the Director of Military Intelligence, had been made by the High Commissioner of Egypt, Sir Reginald Wingate, for Lawrence's lone reconnaissance journey into Syria, described by Wingate as 'little short of marvellous, I strongly recommend him for an immediate award of the Victoria Cross and submit that this recommendation is amply justified by his skill, pluck and endurance.' Wingate had subsequently and officially informed Lawrence that:

The Chief of the Imperial Staff has requested me to convey his congratulations on your recent exploit and I do so with the liveliest satisfaction. It was a very gallant and successful venture, which it has been my pleasant duty to bring to the notice of the higher authority for special recognition, and I sincerely trust this matter will not be long delayed.

The recommendation had been refused by the War Office. At the time, Lawrence wrote home that he was pleased the recommendation for the decoration had been refused; it is more than probable that he was expressing indifference to mask his enormous disappointment. After all, the recommendation was widely known about in Egypt and the rejection would have been viewed by many of Lawrence's colleagues as an official snub, which would have seriously embarrassed Lawrence. This official rejection by certain highly placed non-combatants, some from the developing anti-Lawrence clique, may well have resulted in his subsequent resentment of decorations and his associated practical joking. Later in the war, Lawrence nominated the French artillery officer, Captain Pisani, for the Military Cross – which was awarded, to the amusement of Lawrence and the bemusement of the little Frenchman. Lawrence did accept the French Croix de Guerre, but he used the decoration in Oxford as the collar for Hogarth's dog. When Lawrence was then recommended for the DSO, which was officially approved, he countered the approval by requesting instead the Naval DSO on the grounds that the raid in question had sunk Turkish ships in the Dead Sea and that, therefore, only the naval decoration was appropriate. The humour of Lawrence's request was totally lost on the War Office's senior officers, who rejected it. The whole question of decorations had, once again, raised a flurry of mixed emotions for Lawrence and his reaction would take everyone by surprise.

And so, on 30 November, Lawrence was invited to Buckingham Palace for a private audience with King George V. Much has been written that is untrue or misleading about this meeting; it was not a formal investiture but a private meeting with only His Majesty, his equerry and Lawrence present. Lawrence was still unknown in England and, had the occasion been formally to present Lawrence with his DSO and knighthood, it is probable that Lawrence would have been included in a forthcoming investiture along with numerous equally deserving recipients. And yet we know that the purpose of the meeting was to enable the king to make an award. It is possible that Lawrence might have been anticipating the belated bestowal of the Victoria Cross along with the promised knighthood, or perhaps he intended to use the occasion to further the Arab cause. No one knows exactly.

In any event, it is known that a decoration of some kind was to be bestowed. It is possible that because it was a private ceremony the king was about to decorate Lawrence with the Companionship of the Bath whereas Lawrence had anticipated a knighthood and the Victoria Cross. In any event and at some point in the meeting, wisely or unwisely, Lawrence declined to participate in whatever was about to happen and, instead, used the opportunity to bring the plight of the Arab cause to the attention of his bemused Majesty. The king later told Storrs that he 'had been left holding the box' until his equerry realized what was happening and stepped forward to relieve his perplexed monarch of the decoration. This regal confirmation that there was a box confirms the event, though what the box contained remains a mystery.

It is probable that Lawrence took this action on two counts. Raising the issue of the Arab cause was still his prime motive, but he also knew that his refusal would devalue similar awards to other equally deserving officers and men who had gallantly served their king and country. Indeed, when the matter became public knowledge Lawrence's refusal infuriated many, including Winston Churchill. Perhaps Lawrence's behaviour, albeit immature, enabled him to 'get his own back' for his earlier embarrassment when Wingate's recommendation for the Victoria Cross had been rejected by the War Office.

The matter was eventually clarified in part by Winston Churchill who was then Secretary for State. Churchill wrote, 'someone told me I should meet this wonderful young man, "his exploits are an epic" so he came to luncheon.' During the occasion the matter of Lawrence's meeting with the king came up and Churchill commented that any man might refuse a decoration but to choose the occasion when His Majesty was acting in pursuance of his constitutional duty was monstrous. He went on, 'as he was my guest, I could not say less. He accepted the rebuke with good humour.' Lawrence quietly told Churchill that it was the only way he could rouse the highest authority in the State to realize that the honour of Great Britain was at stake due to its unfaithful treatment and betrayal of the Arabs. Lawrence said that the king should be aware of what was happening in his name. Although he was annoyed by Lawrence's behaviour, Churchill was puzzled by the incident and, clearly impressed by Lawrence, conducted his own enquiry into Lawrence's reason for the rebuke. Churchill requested the reports on the subject and studied them carefully.

The king's private secretary, Lord Stamfordham, was later able partially to clarify the matter but in so doing we learn of 'decorations' intimating that there were to be at least two. Lord Stamfordham asked the king for his opinion of the matter. He wrote that the king's recollection was:

> In asking permission to decline the proffered decorations, Colonel Lawrence explained in a few words that he had made certain promises to King Feisal: that these promises had not been fulfilled, and consequently, it was quite possible that he might find himself fighting against the British Forces, in which case it would obviously be wrong to be wearing British decorations.

And there that particular matter rested.

*

On 4 November Lawrence was called to give evidence before the Eastern Committee of the Cabinet; in anticipation, Lawrence had prepared a lengthy paper that dealt with the whole Arab question from his personal perspective. It ranged from the opening stages of the Arab Revolt to the present time. The tone of the report, apart from being overtly pro-Arab, endorsed the notion of a Jewish State and firmly rebutted French claims to Syria. It has to be said that Lawrence knowingly and forcefully tapped into the vein of British mistrust of the French; the two countries had just fought themselves almost to a standstill against their common German enemy, only to have their mutual mistrust exposed again like a raw nerve. According to Robert Graves anti-French feelings were almost an obsession. The British press were quick to ferment these sentiments and most wrote that it was not in Britain's interest to surrender territory to the French that had just been liberated at such a high cost of British lives. France, at a stroke, went from being Britain's ally to her colonial rival. When the French High Commissioner duly arrived in Syria, Feisal ignored him; his rejection of the French diplomat was, without doubt, bolstered by support from his British liaison officers.

By now, Feisal had learned the full strength of the Sykes–Picot agreement and, not having been part of the making of the treaty, Feisal resolutely refused to remove his Arab troops from the territory reserved by the treaty for France. Feisal wrote:

The first deception occurred when Field Marshal Lord Allenby announced that Syria had been divided into three zones under the pretext that this arrangement was purely temporary and administrative. The second blow levelled against the Arabs' happiness was the confirmation of the Sykes–Picot treaty which had been denied in 1917. I have seen with my own eyes the map of the country under three colours, revealing the different fate of the three zones. Conflict again seemed inevitable.

Feisal contacted Lawrence to request his advice and assistance. Lawrence used his political contacts to bring Feisal to London for a meeting and within the week, Feisal was brought to Marseilles by a British warship for the onward journey by train. The French government was confused by his arrival and, being uncertain how they should treat him diplomatically they dithered. The confusion arose because French officials saw Sherif Hussein as the acknowledged Arab ruler whereas Feisal was merely one of his sons. The ball was passed to the Minister for Foreign Affairs who, having first contacted Colonel Brémond for his advice, rushed to Marseilles to meet Feisal. Brémond, who had been Lawrence's former adversary in Cairo, also set off for Marseilles, having advised his minister to exercise extreme caution in his dealings with Feisal, 'especially if Lawrence was present'. And indeed he was present. Brémond caught up with the official delegation at Lyons and Feisal was immediately advised that Lawrence was not welcome; Lawrence departed that evening but only after a long discussion with Feisal. For the next few days, the French politely hosted Feisal as the joint Arab-French delegation made its way north, first to Paris and then on to Boulogne. One can imagine Brémond's surprise when he took Feisal to board the British warship sent to take him to England; Lawrence was waiting, as ever in his Arab clothes, and stood at the bottom of the gangplank. As Feisal arrived, Lawrence gave Brémond one of his irritating half-smiles. Brémond instantly knew all his efforts to dissuade Feisal from maintaining his anti-French stance would soon be shattered. Lawrence asked Brémond if he would like to come to London to which Brémond replied, and later recorded in *Le Hedjaz dans la Guerre Mondial*, 'I cannot accept. My mission is at an end, I am returning to my post in Belgium.'

For the next few weeks Lawrence escorted Feisal on a grand tour of English cities during which time they made a number of official visits to Westminster and Buckingham Palace. As Feisal's interpreter, Lawrence insisted on wearing his white Arab clothes, even when accompanying Feisal to an audience with the king. A senior palace official viewed Lawrence's attire as a serious breach of etiquette and tried to intervene. When politely challenged, Lawrence replied, 'When one serves two masters, is it not right to wear the uniform of the least powerful of the two?' The official took too long to ponder the significance or otherwise of the reply and Lawrence walked on alongside Feisal and into the presence of the king; on this occasion the meeting went without a hitch. Feisal returned to Damascus and there then followed a number of high-level meetings at the Foreign Office in preparation for the forthcoming Paris Peace Conference. Lawrence was present and advocated the following divisions of Arabia, all to be supervised by the British in Egypt:

1. Mesopotamia be divided into two halves, north and south.
2. Syria to be ruled by Feisal using Damascus as his capital.
3. Lebanon to be ruled by the French.
4. Palestine to be ruled by the Arabs but permitting Jewish settlement.

The Paris Peace Conference began on 19 January 1919 and in the days leading up to the grand opening it was clear that Paris was never going to be the venue for a peaceful solution. France was determined to hold on to her Arabian gains and her reasons were well established. France had long since considered herself as the protector of the Christian faith in the Middle East and had fought to maintain that right. Since 1861 France had especially exerted strong political and economic control over the Lebanon with French missions, schools, hospitals and French culture and language permeating all aspects of Lebanese society. They ran the Lebanese railway system and a shuttle of ships between the two countries, known as the *Messageries Maritimes,* which ensured France monopolized this considerable trade. France now wanted to add Syria to her colonies.

In order to diminish the role of the Arabs, the French government initially refused to acknowledge Feisal as the rightful Arab delegation leader and tension grew. With Lawrence busy in the background, a solution was soon found. Sherif Hussein was persuaded to nominate Feisal as the official delegate, but only subject to him acting in his father's name, to which the Americans likewise agreed. French attention then focused on Lawrence in a blatant attempt to have him removed but as he was officially a member of the British delegation there was little they could do, so he remained.

At the grand opening Feisal was resplendent in his brilliant white robes and silk and diamond headdress. He was, as ever, the shrewd politician and this was his chance to impress the twenty-seven nations' delegates taking part. In this aspect he was a complete success and the American leader, Colonel House, described Feisal as a 'Christ who could have shown his worth in battle'. But Feisal and Lawrence had yet another insurmountable hurdle; there were so many pressing problems for the new European governments to solve and the Levant was insignificant when compared with the question of the Rhineland, the disarmament of Germany, reparations to the victors, Eastern Europe, oil and international debts. The conference would run for several months and all the time Feisal and Lawrence could do nothing to prevent France slowly weakening the Arabs' claims while strengthening theirs. France was determined to exert the same level of control over Syria as it enjoyed over Morocco and Tunisia. The French campaign was fierce, both at the conference, in open session and behind closed doors, and especially in the French press. However, Lawrence and Feisal obtained support from both the American delegation and Britain's prime minister, Lloyd George, who spoke from a position of considerable strength – it was, after all, Allenby's army that was still in control of the whole area. To break the stalemate, the Americans set up an independent enquiry that became known as the King–Crane Committee, which recommended that the USA should take the mandate for Syria and Great Britain that for Mesopotamia. The French were excluded as the

USA recognized their belligerent attitude towards the Arab cause. But the US president was ailing and the recommendations were ignored by Britain and France, who independently sought their own solution. Britain finally took unilateral action, which entailed pulling Allenby's troops out of Syria in favour of the French but with Britain remaining the occupying power in Palestine and Mesopotamia. Lawrence thought the arrangement was fair until Feisal arrived in London, furious at what he saw as a British betrayal. Feisal protested that the French intended to begin a military occupation of Syria and was told to discuss the matter with the French. Britain's decision was final. There was little that Feisal could now do, especially as his main personal ally, Lawrence, was effectively *persona non grata* in France. Feisal returned home in mid April having meanwhile been declared, by the General Syrian Congress, king of an independent Syria, which included Lebanon, Palestine and northern Mesopotamia. This enraged the French and irritated the British.

Unbeknown to Lawrence, Feisal had undertaken a number of secret meetings with Clemenceau and between the two, they made a pact. This left the Arabs in control of inland Syria, the French would have Beyrout and the Syrian coastline while the Jews would be permitted to have a homeland in Palestine, so long as Jewish territory was under British control. This private agreement was never part of the Paris Peace Conference and within months the new arrangement began to disintegrate. The death of Sykes from influenza coincided with his openly regretting his earlier Sykes–Picot findings.

With no resolution in sight for the future of Syria, Lawrence decided to return to Oxford. He effectively absented himself from all his duties and informed a startled War Office that he was now demobilized, news which equally startled the Foreign Office officials who believed he was still a member of their peace delegation. After three years in the limelight, Lawrence no longer held any formal position. Most officials were delighted that Lawrence had gone. His theatrical appearance, superior attitude and Francophobia had long since alienated him from those best able to support his cause. Officially, Britain still sought to assist Feisal but its forces were too stretched to be of real assistance. With the writing of *Seven Pillars of Wisdom* firmly in his mind, Lawrence decided to return to Cairo to collect his manuscripts, photographs and books. Like everything Lawrence involved himself with, his journey was eventful. He managed to obtain passage in an RAF Handley Page bomber that crashed near Rome killing the two pilots. Lawrence sustained injuries including three broken ribs and a collar bone, and numerous bruises. He eventually reached Cairo, collected his documents and returned to London.[1]

By mid 1919, thousands of British troops had still not been repatriated following the end of the war and many were still serving as far away as Russia, Germany, Arabia and along the North West Frontier of India. Matters came to a serious head when a number of British army mutinies occurred because of the unwillingness of the troops to have their service extended beyond the end of the war. The Australian troops in Palestine were becoming increasingly uncontrollable so Allenby ordered a full parade of Australian troops so that he could personally warn them of the consequences. The Australians listened to him in silence then, on a hidden signal, they began shouting in unison, 'One, Two, Three ...' and on the count of 'Ten' they shouted in unison, 'Out, Out, Out'. Clearly shaken by this mass display of open disrespect, Allenby ordered their immediate return to Australia. While Britain attempted to deal with these serious issues, matters in Arabia were left to resolve themselves and Lawrence took himself first to Barton Street in Westminster then back to Oxford where he worked full-time on *Seven Pillars of Wisdom*. Like Allenby, Lawrence was to realize his mission had not been a total

---

1 Flying in 1919 was dangerous. Fifty-one Handley Page bombers were sent to Egypt in response to an urgent request. Records reveal that only twenty-six ever arrived; fifteen were destroyed, written off or crashed. What happened to the remainder is unknown. It took Lawrence nearly three months to make the journey to Egypt by air.

success; with each day taken up with writing his book Lawrence would have realized the cause was long since lost and that he was writing about a dream that had gone sour. Even so, his writing persisted in being optimistic.

Meanwhile, and totally unexpectedly, Lawrence's fame was beginning to re-emerge from a most unlikely source – from an American, Professor Lowell Thomas, formerly of the Chicago Law School and Princeton University, now working on behalf of the American government under the guise of being a journalist. America was aware that the world would need reshaping following the years of conflict and destruction, and President Wilson had a strong Jewish community with even stronger views on the future of the Jewish people – views which accorded with his own – to emancipate those peoples and nations previously repressed. Lowell Thomas had been sent to Arabia to report on the war and in 1918 had made his way from Aqaba to Guweira where he was regaled by a number of officers and soldiers with lurid accounts of Lawrence's alleged feats, which the gullible Thomas took at face value. To enable Thomas to report his findings, he was accompanied by one of the foremost cameramen of the age, Harry Chase. There were a number of British officers in Arabia who had outshone Lawrence for deeds of bravery and action, but none of these were as flamboyant, extrovert, powerful, photogenic, regally connected or as available as Lawrence. Thomas quickly realized that Lawrence was also a rebel with a cause, and one with access to the most powerful figures on the Arabian stage. Being an intelligent operator, Thomas quickly saw the potential in isolating Lawrence and made him the focus for his filming. America needed propaganda and someone like Lawrence was a gift; Thomas built him up as a modern-day Richard the Lionheart and began grooming Lawrence for stardom. Thomas and Chase filmed Lawrence wherever they could, and Lawrence readily obliged them with poses and film opportunities. Little did Lawrence know that Thomas would produce a performance that would catapult him into the everyday lives of people worldwide. The story of Lawrence, as told by Thomas, was, by comparison with the horror of the trench warfare of Flanders, a refreshingly new perspective of war. There was excitement, gallantry and an intelligent handsome young blond hero wearing flowing white Arab dress at the head of the Arab army and going into battle, from victory to victory, on the back of a camel. It was an irresistible story with an audience hungry for excitement.

On their return to America, Chase converted his film footage into remarkable newsreels that were shown across America and then Europe. Due to their popularity, copies were requested from Australia, India and New Zealand. Thomas then collated his still photographs into a two-hour presentation that opened in New York to packed houses; he called it the 'most romantic story of the war'. With every evening sold out, it was only a matter of weeks before the London impresario, Percy Burton, persuaded Thomas to come to London. On 14 October the first lecture was presented at the Royal Opera House in Covent Garden under the title 'With Allenby in Palestine'. Within days the title was amended to 'With Allenby in Palestine and Lawrence in Arabia'. The production was engaged for a two-week run, the demand for tickets was enormous and a new, larger venue had to be found. The Royal Albert Hall was booked for one month, which was extended to three then six months. It was enormously popular and quickly became London's most famous production with more than a million enthusiastic customers. Lawrence was known to have attended a number of the shows and was reported to have been amused by being able to sit in the audience, unrecognized by those around him. Britain also needed an identifiable hero and Lawrence quickly became the role model for modern youth; his story spawned comics and books that, in turn, fed the growing 'Lawrence' mythology. Lowell's mission, apart from making money, was to further the Lawrence story, which Lawrence encouraged. When Lowell once checked a particular story with Lawrence, he retorted, 'Come, come, you must know that history does not consist of the truth.' One is left wondering to what extent this sentiment coloured his writing of *Seven Pillars of Wisdom*.

In due course, Thomas wrote a book with the evocative title *With Lawrence in Arabia* which was an immediate bestseller, as was Lawrence's *Revolt in the Desert*, an abbreviation of *Seven Pillars of Wisdom*. The latter was started in Paris in 1919 and Lawrence claimed the main manuscript was stolen from him at Reading railway station. It was never found and one is tempted, knowing Lawrence's tendency for the theatrical, to ask whether it was stolen, deliberately lost or destroyed. The 'loss' of the manuscript certainly elicited considerable sympathy from those who knew him. He wrote to Hogarth that he had 'lost the damn thing' and Hogarth insisted that Lawrence rewrite it; this second version was eventually finished in 1920. It is curious that Lawrence's earlier work, based on the seven cities of the Orient, and also titled *Seven Pillars of Wisdom*, was similarly 'lost' in 1914. Lawrence claimed at the time that he had deliberately destroyed the completed draft. He continued editing and rewriting it as version number two in London, though he bizarrely claimed also to have destroyed this version with a blow lamp in 1922. While the three losses may have been a coincidence, the copy-cat pattern is remarkably strong and statistically improbable. Version three was compiled in London and Jeddah and completed back in London during 1922; this resides in the Bodlean Library in Oxford. Lawrence commenced the final and fourth draft of *Seven Pillars of Wisdom* after enlisting in the army under the assumed name of Ross and by 1926 the manuscript had been rewritten no less than four times; it is the 1926 limited edition version that would later become so well known to the public. When complete, the various drafts had been written and worked upon in Amman, Jeddah, Oxford and London. Much was written while Lawrence was in the army (1923/4) and in the RAF (1925/6); during this time the text was reduced from 330,000 words to 280,000. Publication in the French language was required by Lawrence to bear the legend: 'The profits of this book will be devoted to a fund for the victims of French cruelty in Syria.' This clause held its validity until his death.

Seven Pillars of Wisdom was not published publicly until 1926 when it was issued as a limited edition of 100 books at £30 per copy. Despite the high price, demand was enormous but the public had to wait until after his death in 1935 for the book's general publication; the book has never since been out of print. It was and remains a masterpiece: Churchill wrote that *Seven Pillars of Wisdom* ranked with the finest books in the English language, a treasure of English literature, and eminent writers of the day queued to agree with him. Churchill wrote in his book *Great Contemporaries*:

> As a narrative of war and adventure, as a portrayal of all that the Arabs mean to the world, it is unsurpassed. It ranks with the greatest books ever written in the English language. If Lawrence had never done anything except write this book as a mere work of the imagination his fame would last – to quote Macaulay's hackneyed phrase – 'as long as the English language is spoken in any quarter of the globe.'

Yet Lawrence was always unsure and constantly worried about reaction to his work. He wrote, as quoted in David Garnett's *The Letters of T. E. Lawrence*: 'I've shot into it like a builder into his yard, all the odds and ends of ideas which came to me during those years.'

In 1922 he wrote to his friend V. W. Richards, 'the story I have to tell is one of the most splendid ever given man for writing.' And one must agree with him; Lawrence realized he was telling a story more than writing a narrative of the desert war. He continually added or altered passages until the continuity became disjointed, accounts were changed and the text drifted to and fro between romanticism and naturalism. He openly wrote about death and the raw brutality of war, he brought in passages that were openly homosexual and some that were tinged with sadism. This was a totally new style of writing and a style that was becoming increasingly popular at the time. He also exaggerated a number of ideas that had been omitted from the earlier drafts, the best example being the lurid and highly descriptive account of his arrest and assault by the Turks at Derra, later described by Colonel Meinertzhagen, his friend and former army colleague, as 'untrue'. The overall historical context of *Seven Pillars of Wisdom* is also dubious because there are few military documents to substantiate his accounts. Lawrence wrote: 'I began in my reports to conceal the true stories of things and to persuade the few Arabs who knew to an equal reticence. In this book also, for the last time I mean to be my own judge of what to say.'

There is no means of ever verifying the authenticity of many of the events written about in his book as no one but Lawrence was present at many of the incidents, although the overall framework certainly matches contemporary military records, apart from the Derra incident. The French author, Jean Beraud Villars wrote in *Le Colonel Lawrence ou la Recherche de l'Absolu*: 'One is compelled to realize that Lawrence, by the skilful use of emphasis, by altering perspectives, by exaggerations and often omissions, has managed to falsify the truth every time he has found it necessary to support his doctrines and support his prejudices.' And therein probably lies the key to the deeper meaning of *Seven Pillars of Wisdom,* and even to Lawrence himself. Lawrence was using the written word to prolong his fight for the Arab cause into the future minds of the press and general public, even though he knew the result of valiant fighting in the desert was long since lost at the negotiating tables in Europe.

Villars is also correct in his views of Lawrence's book, which unaccountably omits the one all-powerful dividing factor between Europeans and Arabs, that of religion. Lawrence knew exactly that religion was divisive; he had witnessed the enormous difficulties of taking European troops into Arabia, of mixing troops of different religions, of the distrust and developing enmity between the Arabs and Jews, yet he omits any discussion on the subject. Religion throughout Arabia was just as dangerous a powder keg to Lawrence as it is to the politics of the region in the twenty-first century. A further contradiction relates to Lawrence's dismissal of the enormous assistance rendered to the Arab cause by the French, the Egyptians and the Hindus, especially the Gurkhas, who accompanied his raids; but as Lawrence wrote: 'In these pages the history is not of the Arab Movement but of me in it.' *Seven Pillars of Wisdom* is indubitably a contradiction but the fact that it achieves masterpiece status is equally indisputable. On the other hand, it is interesting to record that when Lawrence later wrote articles under a nom de plume they were invariably rejected, which added to his growing self-doubts.

For Feisal, his world had suddenly turned upside-down; by July 1920 France had fully occupied Syria and when the Arabs opposed French troops by occupying Damascus, French military might, under their commander in Syria, General Gouraud, quickly smashed and dispersed the 2,000 Arab troops defending the city. The war was swift and brutal. It was the Arabs' first experience of being gassed and it lasted just five days before Damascus fell to the French. Feisal was unceremoniously taken to Damascus railway station and left alone to take a train into exile. No one can imagine how he felt; after all the battles, his struggles, hopes and expectations were now dashed. He crossed the Syrian border and sought refuge in Palestine. He was so confused when he arrived that he thought the waiting British guard of honour was there to arrest him.

Without further delay, the French substituted Syria's legal system, changed the official language from Turkish to French, took control of the press and arrested Arab nationalists. In the final analysis, Lawrence and Feisal had achieved nothing more than facilitate the substitution of Turkish rule by that of France. A bewildered Feisal took refuge with the British in Palestine. His brother, Abdullah, retaliated by marching his Hejaz army northwards and within two weeks had taken control of Maan. At the same time the Arabs in Mesopotamia rebelled. Arabs everywhere were now totally dis-illusioned by post-war events; they had fought to remove the Turks only to have them replaced by the French and British. The initial disquiet developed into unrest that quickly spread throughout the Arab world prompting Lawrence to write a number of scathing letters to the British press. Their publication awakened both politicians and readers to what was happening in their name and the Arab cause was again taken up by the British Parliament. On 22 July 1920 Lloyd George announced to a packed House of Commons that the new state of Iraq was to be formed and four days later the order was given for power to be restored to the Arabs. In late January 1921 Winston Churchill assumed the position of Secretary of State with special responsibility for the colonies and swiftly formed a sub-committee to be known as the Middle East Department.

At Churchill's request, Lawrence was offered a post within this department, which he immediately accepted. Without further delay Lawrence resumed his connections with Feisal to ascertain what exactly he would accept by way of a political compromise. Feisal wanted an Arab state encompassing the Jordan Valley, the strengthening of the Arab position in Iraq and British control over the powerful Saud family, who Feisal rightly guessed were intent on taking over central Arabia. In turn, Feisal would annul his father's claim to Palestine. Churchill convened a new conference, which met in Cairo in mid March. By the end of many wide-ranging meetings, it was agreed that Feisal would be crowned King of Iraq. The other serious Iraqi problem related to the large number of Kurds who occupied northern Iraq; Churchill and Lawrence wanted an independent Kurdish state to act as a physical buffer between Turkey and the Arabs. But there was little consensus for the plan, despite very strong views on the subject from both Churchill and Lawrence, and so the plan was never enacted. The Kurds were left as part of the Iraqi population, which was a decision that would lead ultimately to their genocide and an unsolvable situation for future generations of Western and Arab politicians to weep over. Lawrence strongly pushed Feisal's plan for an independent state of Jordan and it was eventually agreed to form a new state northwards from Aqaba extending to the east of the River Jordan; Abdullah would be the new king. When the Cairo Conference closed, most were highly satisfied.

Within months the fragile peace collapsed, Arabs began attacking Jewish settlements throughout Palestine and the area again became unsettled. Lawrence was sent to Jordan to assist Abdullah and remained there until Christmas 1921 by which time he had become thoroughly disillusioned by the weight of administration and the intractability of Arab leaders. Lawrence was now exhausted by championing the Arab cause and on returning to London he resigned from the Colonial Office, refusing Churchill's pleas to remain.

Palestine remained volatile and fifteen years later the country ran into a further crisis when Hitler began pursuing his anti-Jewish policies. Mass European Jewish immigration into Palestine commenced, which in turn led to the Arab Revolt in 1936. This involved Britain in a number of military actions against the Arabs, resulting in massive disruption and divisions across the Arab world. The legend of Lawrence now faded; he had sought to unify the Arab people and struggled valiantly to achieve his aim of taking the victorious Arab army to Damascus, only then to watch, impotently, as the Allies' promises of an Arab state melted away.

Thereafter the French had serious difficulties trying to control Syria. King Feisal remained an Anglophile and sent his son to Eton; Zeid became an undergraduate at Balliol College, Oxford, and developed a love of rowing. Prince Abdullah ruled Jordan in a kindly fashion and he and his people enjoyed British patronage and the associated commercial benefits. The Saud family, disregarded by the British at the outset of the Arab Revolt, began to exert their control over inner Arabia and Saud's police inflicted a strict religious and moral code on the population. Many Saudis became fanatics and in 1922 an army of them marched against Amman slaughtering villagers as they went. Unfortunately for this group of terrorists, they were caught by the Beni Sakhr and in true Arab tradition, and remembering the days of Lawrence, there were no survivors.

Lawrence's attitude to prisoners will always perplex following generations but it has to be remembered that Lawrence was always a realist. During Allenby's advance he took some Red Cross camels on a raid and, being lightly laden, he loaded the camels with extra explosives. The Senior Medical Officer in Palestine heard of the exploit and admonished Lawrence – who on his next raid left the Red Cross camels and doctor behind. This infuriated the SMO who cabled him enquiring what would befall the wounded in the absence of a medical officer. Lawrence replied, 'Will shoot all cases too hurt to ride off.' No further SMO messages were sent to Lawrence.

15

'His name will live in history'

The Lawrence legend will live on through his writing, especially his book *Seven Pillars of Wisdom*. It is not this author's task or intention to review the book; this has been performed expertly and repeatedly by numerous critics. However, there is one aspect of the book that is relevant here, because it typifies Lawrence's character. Lawrence opens *Seven Pillars of Wisdom* with a beautifully worded piece of poetry, dedicated to 'S. A.': if ever there was an unsolvable literary mystery, then the identity of S. A. has to rank with the best. Many writers, historians, biographers and philosophers have tried to guess who the dedicatee was and most surmise that it was his young Arab servant, Dahoume. I doubt this.

It was deeply ingrained in Lawrence's nature to enjoy both mocking his friends and shocking those around him. Ever unconventional but at the same time highly intellectual, he would have relished inserting a blatant tease at the very beginning of his book, a tease that would probably remain indecipherable for ever. Lawrence perfectly understood the philosophy that every theory very nearly stands on its own, but not quite. There are some clues, mainly to discount Dahoume, and this author agrees we will never unravel the identity of S. A. Lawrence was erudite and well knew that the mysterious 'W. H.' in Shakespeare's twentieth sonnet had never been conclusively identified and so, like Shakespeare, Lawrence leads his readers into one blind alley after another.

A comment from Lawrence on Shakespeare gives a strong clue behind the reason for his imitating him: 'There was a man who hid behind his works, with great pains and consistency. Ergo he had something to hide, some privy reason for hiding. He being an admirable fellow, I hope he hides successfully.' Furthermore, in a post war conversation with Liddell Hart, Lawrence stated that: 'The personal motive (for the Arab cause) was S. A. but S. A. croaked in 1918 ... of the two initials, one corresponds to a person, the other to a place.' Other clues can be found in Lawrence's subsequent letter to Buxton in September 1923: 'S. A. was a person, now dead, regard for whom lay beneath my labour for the Arabic people. I don't propose to go further into detail thereupon.'

Robert Graves was a close confidant of Lawrence and the pair collaborated on Graves' book, *Lawrence and the Arabs* published first in 1926. Lawrence delighted in teasing Graves and when Lawrence proof-read the book, he added by way of an author's comment: 'You have taken me too literally, S. A. still exists, but out of reach, because I have changed.'

One is tempted to believe the popular view that S. A. was Dahoume, though the above comments by Lawrence tend to negate this possibility. Yet Lawrence never denied that S. A. was Dahoume, which was the one true course of action Lawrence would have taken to throw enquirers off the real track. It has to be said that S. A. as a person may never have existed, or existed in the form of a number of people, depending on where Lawrence was, or his mood.

Lawrence's sexuality, or lack of it, has led some writers to speculate that he was a homosexual, although actual evidence of this does not exist. Certainly he didn't associate with Oxford University's young women but he had several female acquaintances, and even went as far as proposing marriage to Janet Lawrie, although neither party pursued the matter. He certainly had no opportunity to mix with European women in Syria where he worked as an archaeologist until the outbreak of war – simply because there were no young European women there. By having missed out on female company due to his work and then the war, as did many young men of his generation, Lawrence later left himself open to those disposed to make whispered hints and suggestions of possible homosexuality. During his lifetime, only two veiled suggestions were ever published and both were malicious gossip. The first public accusation did not arise until twenty years after his death, but even that was without definite evidence and was nothing more than an innuendo. Unfortunately for Lawrence, his writings occasionally observed such behaviour, possibly because it was an accepted practice among certain Arabs he met, and Lawrence occasionally commented on it for being so open. Later he fabricated the Derra incident where he suggested he had been the victim of a flogging and rape by a Turkish officer. Although this incident portrayed him as a victim, it inadvertently helped those interested in homosexuality to romanticize the alleged incident. Lawrence was certainly not being homophobic – it was all around him – but by commenting on it he gave others a basis for presuming he favoured the practice.

By weaving so many webs, Lawrence's life, like his writing, was complex. This has led many critics to ponder whether Lawrence achieved any meaningful result during his time with the Arabs. His military actions were indeed relatively insignificant compared with Allenby's advance against the Turks, but this is hardly surprising. Lawrence was still in his twenties and had not received any form of military training. Yet news of his deeds and actions spread through the Arab people and, for a brief period, brought a semblance of unity to widely spread and previously warring tribes. Lawrence's actions were a massive morale booster to the Arabs who supported Feisal, and they were justly proud of their feats. In this sense his achievement was more political than military. Likewise, his capture of Aqaba was just as politically significant as militarily. Towards the end of Allenby's advance, the presence of the Arabs on the Turks' left flank severely tried the Turks who were required to divert regiments of experienced Anatolian troops from the Gaza–Beersheba front to guard their empty desert flank – just in case the Arab army arrived. At the time it was estimated that the presence of Lawrence's Arabs, moving at will against the Turks, was 'worth an Army Corps to the British Army on the Palestine front'. If this was so, then the cost of the Arab Revolt, estimated by writer Robert Graves to be £10 million and a score or so of British casualties, was more economical than any other First World War campaign.

Critics have also pondered Lawrence's tactics, for they seem incomprehensible. The truth is that they were simple, and with simplicity came effectiveness. He knew the terrain and understood the Turkish enemy as well as the bravery and skill, or otherwise, of his Arab followers. It was understood by Lawrence's colleagues that an Arab force fighting an operation under Lawrence was very different from the same force without him. He fought many small actions and left scant details; he fought some fifty or so incidents using armoured cars yet only mentions a handful in his accounts. Due to the great success of these vehicles in action, there is plenty of scope for a detailed examination of his tactics using them, which eventually gave rise to the Long Range Desert Group of the Second World War. He certainly introduced the Arabs to the art of terrorism by stealth and explosives, a skill that now rebounds on Allied forces seeking to bring peace to Arab countries – and the rest of the world trying to protect its borders.

The immediate post-war period witnessed a severe on-going crisis for Lawrence; despite his Civil Service salary of £1,200 he claimed poverty, yet he was the most famous man in England. He chose to suffer hunger and cold, yet he was offered powerful positions within the British government that he refused, along with titles and honours. Psychologists and psychiatrists have written volumes to explain his actions but the truth may well be more clear-cut than complex. Lawrence was only thirty-two years of age at the end of the Great War; he was famous but he had also been severely shaken by the ferocity of desert warfare and the duplicity of world leaders whom he respected. Few young men have ever been required to face what Lawrence endured, living in such a hostile environment as Arabia, experiencing repeated hand-to-hand battles and artillery duels, and witnessing death and destruction of friend and foe on a massive scale. He witnessed the scene of mutilated women and children following torture by the Turks; he had to execute his own injured men to save them from capture and torture or to maintain order; he gave the order, several times, not to take prisoners; he witnessed the mass murder of European and Turkish prisoners in his charge; and he was forced to live a lie on behalf of his British masters to coerce his Arab friends to support Britain. He survived all these ordeals. One only has to consider the incidence of post-traumatic stress disorder on modern-day well-trained professional soldiers fighting in an identical desert environment to realize that few, if any, would be expected to endure Lawrence's trials and tribulations, even for just a few days, let alone two years.

J. M. Keynes knew Lawrence throughout the 1919 Paris Peace Conference and later wrote that Lawrence appeared to be fully in control of himself and 'as normal as most of us in his reactions to the world'. He considered that Lawrence only later became disillusioned following the disappointment of the Peace Conference and his partial disablement resulting from his aircraft crash, which left him with a troublesome lung injury – which Lawrence did his best to hide. Following Paris, it is no wonder that he could not face public and political adoration; he needed to clear his mind and escape to a new life, and this he did in 1922 by enlisting in the Royal Air Force, in the lowest rank, as Airman John Ross. According to a number of men who served with him during his first period of service with the RAF Lawrence participated in a parade where troops were instructed to wear their medals – Lawrence ignored the order. The CO reached Lawrence and asked where his medals were. Lawrence replied that he had not bothered with them and was ordered to reappear, with his medals. Lawrence returned to the parade wearing a row of medals and two decoration stars. The CO immediately ordered Lawrence to remove the decorations. Lawrence refused on the grounds that he had been awarded the decorations by an authority senior to the CO. The indignant CO then conducted an enquiry into the identity of the decorated aircraftman and Lawrence was discovered. Officers and men alike thought he had been planted as a spy. The Secretary of State for Air had no option but to dismiss Lawrence. While pondering his next move, he purchased Clouds Hill in Dorset.

A month later he enlisted as a private soldier in the Royal Tank Corps. In due course word spread through the corps that this diminutive soldier, known as Private Shaw, was Colonel Lawrence of Arabia. He became a figure of curiosity though many of the soldiers sought to protect Lawrence from unwelcome attention. Having served for two years without any undue blemish on his record, friends in the prime minister's office managed to get Lawrence transferred back to the RAF and he was posted to RAF Cranwell. He was given a list of available jobs but chose the most menial work. The officers and men at Cranwell knew full well who he was and respected his wish to be a lowly airman. It was accepted that he worked hard for the betterment of his colleagues and they, in turn, did their best for him. The CO even offered Lawrence his house for Christmas but the offer was politely declined. All the while, Lawrence was working on *Seven Pillars of Wisdom* and only rarely did he relax. On one occasion he took his flight of airmen and their wives in a charabanc, which he paid for, to the annual air show at Hendon. He spent some of 1929 in Afghanistan but, following press reports that he was arranging a rebellion, he was sent back to England where he served in various capacities until his final posting to RAF Bridlington.

Perhaps those in the army and RAF charged with his care understood what he had been through, for they treated him with some compassion and allowed him to work as and where he pleased; he spent his time performing routine tasks, writing and rewriting *Seven*

Pillars of Wisdom and enjoying riding his motorcycle around the lanes. His overall plan was simple, to remain in the RAF for as long as he could and then retire to his cottage, but as his friend Robert Graves wrote, 'whether he will succeed in settling down quietly is another question'. Winston Churchill put it more succinctly: 'A rare beast; will not breed in captivity.' He retired from the RAF in February 1935 and was killed in a motorcycle accident just two months later.

Lawrence was always an enigma to those who knew him and his circle of friends was wide and equally complex; he was popular with reigning monarchs, politicians, senior military officers and private soldiers, yet kept them all in their own 'compartments'. He was able to mix freely with whosoever he chose and he would behave at the appropriate level. During his army service in Arabia, he was well summed up by Major Young who wrote, contrasting Lawrence with the other senior British officers present, 'Lawrence counted more with Feisal and Allenby. He used to flit backwards and forwards between the two as the spirit moved him.' Conversely, there were many, not only fellow officers, who were perplexed by Lawrence and his later fame. One British officer, Colonel Bray, later challenged Lawrence's motives during the latter stage of the war: 'Throughout the war, the chances of allied victory were compromised by the sheer idiosyncrasies of an individual.' Years later, Harold Nicholson wrote for the *Jerusalem Post* of 1961:

> His disloyalty reminded one of the boy who would suck up to the headmaster and then sneak to him about what went on in the school. Even when he became a colonel, he was not the sort of colonel whom one would gladly leave in the office when confidential papers were lying on the desk. So sensitive a man, it seemed to me, ought to have possessed a finer sense of mercy: when, in his gentle voice, he told tales of a massacre, his lips assumed an ugly curl. His habit of telling

fibs was almost pathological. His affectations were so intricate and diverse that they became a nuisance to his friends.

Lawrence always bore a heavy weight on his shoulders. He was only too aware that he had become a hero only at great expense to the Arab people. After the war he repeatedly wrote to the press with warnings of chaos and enmity falling across Arabia if the European allies failed to unite this huge landmass; invariably his warnings fell on deaf ears. One piece of writing that Lawrence left behind is a clear statement of the dangers he foresaw, though it is evident that not even he saw the impact on the world of the great oil finds that would forever change Arabia and the Western world. Jean Beraud Villers recorded that Lawrence wrote about the Iraqis and the Syrians:

> They were weak in material resources, and even after success would be, since their world was agricultural and pastoral, without minerals, and could never be strong in modern armaments. Were it otherwise, we should have had to pause before evoking in the strategic centre of the Middle East new national movements of such abounding vigour.

In the final analysis, not even Lawrence could have foreseen how events would unfurl across the Middle East during the decades following the war and beyond his death, though he gave mankind in *Oriental Assembly* a prophesy for the future: 'Mesopotamia (Iraq) will be the master of the Middle East, and the power controlling its destinies will dominate all its neighbours.'

Following the sudden death of Lawrence, Churchill in *Great Contemporaries* wrote:

> Lawrence had a full measure of the versatility of genius. He held one of those master keys which unlock the doors of many kinds of treasure-

house. He was a savant as well as a soldier. He was an archaeologist as well as a man of action. He was an accomplished scholar as well as an Arab partisan. He was a mechanic as well as a philosopher. His background of sombre experience and reflection only seemed to set forth more brightly the charm and gaiety of his companionship, and the generous majesty of his nature. Those who knew him best miss him most; but our country misses him most of all; and misses him most of all now.

King George V wrote to Lawrence's brother: 'His name will live in history.' Churchill agreed and added: 'That is true. It will live in English letters; it will live in the traditions of the Royal Air Force; it will live in the annals of war and in the legends of Arabia.'

It is fitting to leave the final word on Lawrence, recorded by Mrs Stewart Erskine in her biography, to King Feisal of Iraq who wrote: 'A hundred years hence, perhaps two hundred years hence, he might be understood; but not today.'

APPENDIX A:

Personae

Arab

Hussein, ibn Ali, Emir and Sherif of Mecca: A direct descendant from the prophet Mohammed through his daughter Fatima, Hussein was the most influential Arab leader at the time. Became Grand Sherif in 1908 and in order to render him politically impotent he had been a virtual prisoner of the Turks at Constantinople for fifteen years, having originally been 'invited' to Constantinople as a 'guest' with his three small sons.

On his release by the Turks, he secretly negotiated with Sir Henry McMahon between 1915 and 1917 to commence the Arab Revolt. He supported the Allies with the launching of the Arab Revolt following the British surrender at Kut. In so doing he cut himself, his family and people from the Muslim allegiance of India, Turkey, Afghanistan and Egypt.

After the war, he was largely ignored by the Allies and in 1925 he abdicated in favour of his eldest son, Ali.

HUSSEIN'S SONS

Ali ibn Hussein: Ineffectual during the Arab Revolt and described by Lawrence as being 'too clean'. Post-war, took over from his father, only to be defeated in 1925 by the Wahabi leader, Ibn Saud, founder of Saudi Arabia. Died in Jordan in 1931.
Abdullah ibn Hussein: Distrusted by Lawrence for being 'too clever', served throughout the war, initially by holding the Turks at Mecca, then as his father's Foreign Minister. Later became King of Jordan until his assassination in 1951.
Feisal ibn Hussein: First met Lawrence in 1916 while endeavouring to unite the numerous Arab tribes to revolt against Turkey. Described by Lawrence as 'having fire' he became a firm friend and confidant of Lawrence. He led the Arab Revolt throughout the war and negotiated on behalf

of the Arabs at the Paris Peace Conference in 1920. Later became King of Iraq. Died of natural causes in 1933.

Zeid ibn Hussein: Aged nineteen years at the outbreak of hostilities but a popular and brave Arab leader. Described by Lawrence as being 'too cool' but who was widely recognized as a fearless fighter; joint commander with Lawrence at the battle of Tafileh. Following the war Zeid went to Balliol College, Oxford and became a noted rower. When Feisal became ill, Zeid became Regent of Iraq.

Auda, Abu Tayi, sheikh of the Howeitat tribe from Maan district: a major Arab leader with a fearsome reputation as a fighter. Accompanied Lawrence to take Aqaba and at the fall of Damascus. Post-war he returned to his home village of El Jefer and used Turkish prisoners to build a palace. He died in 1924 while still in his fifties.

Nuri Said: An Arab regular army officer, chief of staff to General Jaafar.

Jaffar, General: Commander-in-chief to Feisal. A Mesopotamian Arab from Baghdad.

Zaal: Nephew of Auda.

Aziz el Masri: A senior Arab who had originally held high command under the Turks, was given overall command of a force of ex-Turkish Army conscripts and Arab townsmen that later gave loyal service to General Allenby in his coastal advance on Damascus.

Nasir, Sherif: Brother of the Emir of Medina and close friend of Feisal.

Maulud Pasha: A former army officer from Mesopotamia who was captured by the British while commanding a Turkish cavalry regiment. Pro-Arab, he and other officers elected to serve under Feisal and he became Feisal's ADC. He defended Aqaba when attacked from Maan and destroyed the Turkish force. Severely injured at Maan in attack on Turks.

British and American

Sykes, Sir Mark: Diplomat. Held honorary posts in Turkey and throughout the Near East. Was secretly tasked by the British government to formulate a policy for the future of the Middle East, so long as it placated France. Author of the Sykes–Picot treaty. A victim of the Influenza Pandemic – he died during the Paris Peace Conference in 1919.

Storrs, Sir Ronald: Oriental Secretary to the British in Cairo from 1909. Met Lawrence in 1915 when both worked for the Arab Bureau; Lawrence accompanied Storrs to Jeddah and Rabegh in 1916, the journey which introduced Lawrence to Feisal. Became Governor of Jerusalem, Cyprus and northern Rhodesia. He died in 1955.

Lowell, J. Thomas: Former professor and later noted journalist. Reported the Arab Revolt for the American media. He presented numerous travelogues and presentations about Lawrence and is credited with making Lawrence world famous. Wrote a number of works on Lawrence, notably *With Lawrence in Arabia.*

Wooley, Sir Charles Leonard: Archaeologist. In 1905 appointed the Assistant Keeper of the Ashmolean Museum in Oxford. Ran the excavations at Carchemish where Lawrence worked as his assistant. Accompanied Newcombe and Lawrence during the Sinai expedition to give the venture a civilian purpose. He co-wrote *The Wilderness of Zin* based on the expedition. Captured by the Turks, he survived the war and went on to run excavations at Ur in Iraq. Died in 1960.

Hogarth, Dr D. G.: Keeper of the Ashmolean Museum, Oxford. An eminent scholar and noted archaeologist, especially of Carchemish where he employed the young Lawrence. During the war he supported Lawrence in the Arab Bureau and later at the Paris Peace Conference. Without doubt, he was Lawrence's 'father figure' and his death was a severe blow to Lawrence.

Clayton, G. F.: Lieutenant Colonel, Director of Military Intelligence.

McMahon, Sir Henry: High Commissioner of Egypt.

Wingate, Sir Reginald: Governor General of Sudan.

Newcombe, Stewart: Colonel Royal Engineers. As a captain in 1913, he and Lawrence conducted a survey of Sinai. He later became Lawrence's commanding officer having been appointed head of the Military Mission in the Hejaz. He was captured by the Turks in a valiant defence, when hopelessly outnumbered, at the battle of Beersheba in 1918. He named his son after Lawrence and was a pall bearer at Lawrence's funeral.

French

Brémond, Edouard: Colonel. French army officer, former ex-chief of staff on the Somme. An experienced French diplomat, he vainly struggled against Lawrence to protect French interests.

Pisani, Captain: French army officer of Artillery. Fought a number of engagements alongside Lawrence. Awarded the Military Cross on Lawrence's recommendation.

Picot, François Georges: French High Commissioner of Palestine and Syria.
Raho, Captain: French army officer, 2nd Regiment Algerian Spahis.

Turkish and German

Fakri Pasha: Turkish military commander at Medina.
von Sanders, Liman: The German commander in Syria 1916–18.

APPENDIX B:

The French Connection

There were a small number of other officers active during the early stage of the Arab Revolt and some are mentioned by Lawrence in *Seven Pillars of Wisdom*, but few have received more than scant recognition. This is especially true of a group of French officers whose activities are virtually unknown beyond France. Yet a few French officers played an undeniably valuable role in the revolt's early stages by actively engaging against the Turks and repeatedly attacking the Hejaz Railway, while others politically encouraged the Arab cause. Until June 1916 neither Britain nor France, the principal European Allies in the Middle East, were unduly concerned about rumours of an Arab uprising in southern Arabia; it was too far from their proposed sphere of campaigning and neither were interested in Arabia's vast empty deserts sparsely peopled by Arab tribes who were more concerned about settling their ancient disputes than removing the Turkish occupiers. In June, and after much consideration of all the implications to his people, Sherif Hussein of Mecca and descendant of Mohammed, finally authorized the Arab attack on the Turkish forces garrisoned in the holy cities of Mecca, Medina and Jeddah and so the Arab Revolt against the Turkish occupation began. Within two weeks, and after much bitter hand-to-hand fighting, both Mecca and Jeddah were retaken by Arab forces, though the determined Turkish defenders managed to hold Medina. Both Allies were aware that Arab attacks against the Turkish-held southern cities had taken place but unless the Arabs could tie down a sizeable Turkish force nearly 1,000 miles away their interest would continue to be minimal.

Instead, Britain and France were concentrating on their advanced preparations for attacking Turkey from the direction of Egypt and to that effect, the situation in Syria and Palestine was of far greater importance to the Allied cause. In effect, neither believed the Arabs could contribute to the overall war effort, even less to the Arabs' possible involvement in governing post-war Arabia; the Allies considered the Arab role to be especially insignificant due to their long-standing internecine struggles. France's prime interest in the Middle East was powerfully focused on Syria and in the event of the Allies' eventual victory, it was mutually agreed between the two main powers that, in return for France being given control of Syria, Britain's reward was to be Mesopotamia and, should Britain want it, the remainder of the Arabian peninsula. This secret pact between Britain and France became known as the Sykes-Picot agreement.[1] At the beginning of the First World War the barren and mountainous region facing the Red Sea, the Hejaz, didn't remotely feature in the initial Allied plan to attack Turkey; even when vague rumours of a possible Hejaz uprising reached Cairo, the news failed to enthuse the Allies. The French Prime Minister merely noted that the Hejaz was too far from Syria to have any political or military influence on French plans.

Being a long-standing major colonial power along the North African coast, France was not interested in the aspirations of the Arab people. Solely to protect her interests in her Muslim colonies by being on the winning side, the French government duly responded to the growing British interest in the area by authorizing the sending to Egypt of a token French military mission to ascertain the military requirements of Sherif Hussein. The mission arrived at Alexandria on 1 September 1916 and consisted of 1,000 troops armed with eight machine guns and a variety of artillery pieces, including field and mountain guns, under the command of Lieutenant Colonel Cadi of the 113th Regiment of Heavy Artillery. Without doubt, the sudden arrival in Egypt of the French military mission alarmed the British to the extent that they swiftly formed their own mission, under Colonel Newcombe of the Royal Engineers, to balance the activities of the French. Newcombe knew the area well as he had accompanied Lawrence on a covert mission to Sinai in 1914.

With the news that the Turks were becoming progressively bogged down at Medina, the Allies suddenly saw merit in sustaining the Arab Revolt. They could see the benefit to be obtained from providing military support for the Arabs; it would greatly assist their own plans if Turkish forces could be held far from their proposed sphere of military operations, which was intended to stretch from Egypt towards and across Palestine into Turkey. The Allies also began to realize that such sustained aggressive action on the part of the Arabs could force Turkey to divert significant military aid away from their main theatre of war opposing the Allies to the distant, inhospitable and irrelevant Hejaz region. Seizing the initiative, the French attaché, the experienced and elderly Colonel Brémond, sent a team of advisers to Mecca and tried, unsuccessfully, to persuade the British to also

---

[1] The agreement specified that northern Syria and Mosul would go to the French with southern Syria, Jordan and Palestine going to the British.

send a joint force to Mecca, via Rabegh, naturally all under Brémond's command. The British actively considered the plan – until Lawrence, now a captain on the staff at Cairo, pointed out that European troops, being Christian, could not enter the holy territory of Islam; the plan was dropped. In addition, had the Allies landed in accordance with French wishes, then the main theatre of the Arabs' war would have remained in the south. This would dash Lawrence's personal aim of leading the Arabs into Damascus, regardless of whether this accorded with the main British objective, which was to destroy Turkey's ability to successfully fight in the war.

With the intention of compounding the Turkish Army's serious problems, Britain began to send both military equipment and large sums of gold to support the Arab uprising; France followed suit but with smaller financial contributions. Brémond nevertheless sought to match the influence of Colonel Wilson, the British Consul at Jeddah, by creating a similar position for himself. Brémond was hoping that once the Arabs had taken Medina, he would take charge of the whole operation on behalf of both Britain and France. Another French officer, Captain Depui, was nominated to serve with Emir Abdullah's forces to the south and Depui rendered the Emir sound advice during the siege of Medina. Other French officers were sent to help organize the Arab military training centre at Mecca. Brémond's plan for a commanding French presence was suddenly cancelled by the French government when they realized that Brémond would be acting against the recently signed, and still secret, Sykes–Picot agreement. It is possible that this French reversal came about following the intervention of a junior British officer at Cairo, locally appointed Captain T. E. Lawrence, who was growing increasingly alarmed by the intense interest of the French. Perhaps due to the worsening situation in France, and his scathing statement that the Arabs would never be able to defeat the Turks, the French recalled Brémond to Paris and reduced the size of their Egypt mission to just 600 military personnel. There can be little doubt the French government thought the Sykes–Picot agreement would alone secure their future interest in the area – without having to commit troops and finance at a time when France was experiencing serious difficulties in Europe.

Nevertheless, the few French officers who remained with the Mecca mission were not idle. A liaison was formed between the two Allied missions to disrupt the Turkish railway line through the Hejaz; both missions saw the strategic significance in disrupting the passage of Turkish troops and supplies. Accordingly, two British officers, Colonel Newcombe and Captain Garland, set to work with one of the French officers, Captain Raho of the 2nd Algerian Regiment of Spahis, to disrupt the railway between Damascus and Medina.

On 1 February 1917 Captain Raho and a team of five NCOs commenced a series of camelry attacks on the Turkish railway near Medina. This series of sharp actions marked the beginning of Allied participation on the side of the Arab uprising. This first attack was a complete success and several miles of undefended railway track were destroyed by landmines. On 26 March, Captain Raho's force, accompanied by Lawrence, set out to attack the railway near Aba el Naam, which lay about ninety miles north of Medina. Lawrence was impressed by what he saw; Raho was clearly an expert in demolishing railway lines and bridges, and the still inexperienced Lawrence took note of Raho's technique though, in typical Lawrence fashion, he inexplicably claimed all credit for the raid in *Seven Pillars of Wisdom*. Lawrence's role in the raid was commented on in a telegram from the French minister in Cairo to Paris that Captain Raho was attacking the station at Aba el Naam in support of Sherif Nasir: 'and Captain Lawrence is accompanying them'.

The next stage of this particular plan was to attack the Turkish position inside the town's railway station. Such fighting was new to the Arabs and although they succeeded in taking the Turkish outposts around the Aba el Naam station, they could not dislodge the main defending Turkish force. The Arabs bombarded the station and contented themselves by dynamiting a mile of track leading from the town and destroying a hastily abandoned train. They then retreated, with some forty prisoners, abandoning the Turkish wounded to their fate under a blazing sun. By now Lawrence and his French colleagues were fully aware that the Turks would not stray far from their heavily defended positions, which left the Allied saboteurs free to roam far and wide without the Turks knowing where they would strike next. The Turks did, though, start patrolling the railway line but only within a few miles of their defended blockhouse positions; they also immediately fortified their trains with troop carriages and specially mounted machine guns.

In the months that followed, Captain Raho completed a number of similar missions, and although the Turks were always able to quickly repair even major damage such raids were a serious nuisance to them. Buoyed with his success, Raho requested approval to undertake a more ambitious raid and it was decided that he should take a force of forty of his own men plus a contingent of over 200 Bedouin raiders to attack the railway bridges near the Turkish garrison town of Mudurij. In the heat of summer, Raho's force had to negotiate over fifty-five miles of unmapped desert and on 24 August they were ready to launch their attack. Unbeknown to Raho, local Arab informers in the pay of the Turks warned the Turkish garrison of the approaching saboteurs who, as they prepared to dynamite the bridges, came under steady fire from the pre-warned Turkish defences. Undaunted, Raho gave instructions for the laying of a number of mines and soon three miles of line and four rail bridges were successfully dynamited. Flushed with their success, and urged on by the accompanying Bedouin Sherif Slima to cause further damage, similar raids were successfully undertaken on 28 and 29 August near the Turkish railway station at Jeddah; several miles of stra-tegically important railway track were dynamited before Raho's patrol returned to their base at Abu Markhan. The whole distance travelled amounted to over 200 miles across difficult desert terrain that was largely unmapped and in searing heat. Over the following months, Raho led a series of equally successful raids on the Turkish railway line near Medina.

Following the successful seizure of Aqaba by Lawence in July 1917, another Frenchman, Captain Rosario Pisani, was sent to Aqaba to take charge of a French-led sabotage group. Pisani had earlier been torpedoed by the Turks just as his vessel, the *Caledonian,* was approaching Port Said, and as he was one of only fifty survivors consequently he felt he had good reason to exact revenge on the Turks. On 26 September 1917 Pisani led an operation, accompanied by Lawrence, to attack a Turkish train near Akabat el Hedjazia. A large landmine was carefully laid and camouflaged under a bridge but, unusually, no train was seen approaching until 5 October when the tell-tale sign of distant smoke could be seen. All excitedly awaited the arrival of the target and as the heavily laden train approached the bridge the detonation sequence was commenced – but there was an unex-pected fault and the mine failed to explode. The saboteurs' disappointment was great but there was nothing they could do; opening fire would have exposed their position to the Turks, and there was always the consolation that another train would arrive in due course, so the unsuspecting Turkish train passed on its way without further molestation. The fault lay within the mine itself and Lawrence replaced it with a newer electric mine. The group settled down to await the next train.

The very next day an unsuspecting train approached the bridge from the opposite direction. The train was lightly guarded and when it reached the centre span of the bridge, the mine was detonated with dramatic results. The bridge collapsed and the train and carriages telescoped into each other before crashing to the ground beneath the shattering bridge. The dazed and terrified Turkish survivors did their best to flee the wreckage as the Arabs noisily charged the train, urged on and led by Pisani. The captured Turks pleaded for mercy but were ignored and the prisoners were quickly despatched; the Arabs showed captured and wounded Turks the same lack of indifferent mercy that they would have received from the Turks. With the last Turk killed, looting and pillaging of the train began in earnest and, in an instant, the Arabs switched from being patient fighters to murdering looters. It was in their nature to behave thus and the Europeans who accompanied them never intervened. Occasionally the looters would find and take trunks of Turkish gold; Turkish paper money was inevitably thrown to the wind or burned. The most popular items of loot were rich colourful clothes, rugs and personal trinkets. On this occasion some thirty Turkish bodies were left at the scene and within quarter of an hour the train had been stripped of all removable supplies. As a result of Pisani's leadership and courage during the action, Lawrence recommended him for the Military Cross, which was presented to Pisani at Aqaba on 12 November, much to Pisani's delight. The citation reads: for 'brilliant conduct and excellent service rendered during operations undertaken against the Hedjaz railway'.

Captain Pisani was then attached to Prince Feisal's force based in Aqaba, where he continued to support the Allies' progress as they advanced further to the north of the Hejaz. By 12 April 1918, he was in command of artillery attached to a force commanded by Nuri Said, an ex-Turkish officer who had crossed over to join the Arab cause. They successfully attacked the Turks at Ghadir el Haj and then moved to occupy Semna – just five miles from Maan, again accompanied by Lawrence. The Arabs' artillery was placed along a sandy ridge overlooking the railway station and their guns commenced firing as Said's attacking force swept into the attack; at that crucial point Pisani's guns ceased firing and the Turks were soon able to repel the Arabs. Watching the battle from his car, Lawrence could see that it had lost its impetus, just as Nuri Said arrived to implore Lawrence to get the guns firing again. Lawrence rushed to the ridge only to find that Pisani's guns had run out of ammunition. Pisani was distressed that the cause of the failed attack was his but without further supplies of artillery ammunition there was nothing more the attacking Arabs could do, other than to call off the attack. Somewhat distressed, the Arabs retreated back to Semna.

The next major French contribution was against the Turkish-held city of Derra; Pisani and his men were detailed to support Nuri Said by attacking the nearby Turkish-held railway bridge at Tell Arar. Having successfully destroyed the bridge, they moved on to Mezerib and blew up the railway line to the west of Derra. At Mezerib the Turks put up a short, spirited fight but so devastating was Pisani's artillery that less than forty severely shell-shocked Turks were able to surrender out of an initial force of nearly 200 men. In French style, Pisani had walked into the Turkish position to personally accept their surrender while Nuri Said's force moved on towards Maan, which had recently been abandoned by the Turkish garrison who had clearly lost the will to fight the Arabs under their British and French advisers. The retreating and now panicking 8,000-strong Turkish column, mainly from the Turkish Fourth Army, was haphazardly strung out across the desert over a distance of more than two miles when, on 27 September, they came across the undefended Arab village of Tafas. For reasons known only to the Turks, and with the Arab army only five miles behind and rapidly closing with them, the Turkish troops attacked the defenceless village, shooting, stabbing, raping and killing everyone they could find, and then burnt the village. Both Lawrence and Pisani accompanied the Arab force as it entered into Tafas and neither they nor the Arabs could comprehend the scale of the Turks' brutality. Houses were still burning, the dead lay about in groups and as a final insult to the Arabs, raped and murdered Arab women had been grotesquely laid out with bayonets left protruding from their genitalia. Nuri Said gathered his incensed fighters and, supported by Pisani's artillery and machine guns, they quickly overhauled then fell upon the disorganized Turkish column. Pisani's shells scattered the head of the fleeing column, which ground to a halt; in desperation the Turkish cavalry swept back towards the rapidly closing Arabs only to be stalled by accurate and devastating fire from Pisani's guns. The bloody chase lasted several days and few Turks were to survive the wrath of the Arabs; Lawrence would later give a detailed account of the battle in *Seven Pillars of Wisdom* (see Chapter 12).

On 28 September the Arabs took Derra and almost without pause advanced upon Damascus, which they reached on 1 October. Pisani was justly proud of his men's achievements and wrote that the French detachment had showed 'an excellent spirit of sacrifice and devotion'. Lawrence was also fulsome in his recognition of Pisani's efforts and achievement, so much so that in *Seven Pillars of Wisdom* Lawrence frequently and generously mentions Pisani, though he doesn't mention Raho. Without doubt, Captains Raho and Pisani and their small band of Frenchmen played an important part in the Arab uprising. Their intelligent support for the advancing Arabs was invaluable and the Frenchmen's enthusiasm for regularly sabotaging the Turkish railway line between Damascus and Medina was most probably the initial spark that fired Lawrence's own subsequent enthusiasm for all his similar activities.

The French mission to the Hejaz remained in support of the main British force until it was dissolved on 1 August 1920. Full details of French attacks can be found in *T.E. Lawrence, la France et les Français* by Maurice Lares.

APPENDIX C:

Special Documents

From Lawrence's letter to *The Times* dated 11 September 1919

Lawrence quoted the existence of four documents that he had seen during the Arab Revolt and which, he claimed, supported King Hussein. Lawrence cited their existence as clear and unambiguous evidence to induce the Arabs to fight in support of the Allies, mainly the British. The documents are:

1. British promise to King Hussein
Dated 24 October 1915
Author: Sir Henry McMahon

This document recorded British recognition of independence of the Arabs, subject to the launch of the Arab Revolt, south of latitude 37 degrees except in the province of Baghdad and Basra, except where Britain is not free to act to the detriment of France. PRO, CAB, 27/24

2. The Sykes–Picot agreement made between England and France
Dated May 1916
Author: Sir Mark Sykes

In dealing with the area, post-war, the document referred to 'the interior' (mainly the provinces of Allepo, Damascus, Urfa, Deir and Mosul) to be 'independent Arab' under two shades of influence:
(i) Between the lines Akaba–Kuweit and Haifa–Tekrit, the French to seek 'no political influence' and the British to have 'economic and political priority, and the right to supply such advisers as the Arabs desire'.
(ii) Between the lines Haifa–Tekrit and the southern edge of French Armenia or Kurdistan, Great Britain seeks no 'political influence', and the French to have political and economical priority and the right to supply 'such advisers as the Arabs desire'.

3. The British statement presented to the Arabs in Cairo
Dated 11 June 1917
Author: Sir Mark Sykes

A document assuring the Arabs that pre-war Arab states, and Arab areas freed by the Arab military action during the war, shall remain entirely independent.

4. Anglo-French Declaration
Dated 9 November 1918
Author: Lord Robert Cecil

Britain and France agree to encourage native governments in Syria and Mesopotamia, without interfering in the working of any local government.

Note: By this stage, the American government were becoming sensitive to possible British control of the newly discovered oilfields in Iraq and it was felt by both British and American governments that a British monopoly would not be good for American-British long-term relationships.

INSTRUCTIONS FROM LT COL DAWNAY TO LAWRENCE, 16 JULY 1918

Savoy Hotel
Cairo
16 July 1918

Special Instructions
1. Two companies, Imperial Camel Corps (Commander Major R. Buxton; strength 16 officers, 300 other ranks, 400 camels, with 6 Lewis guns) have been placed temporarily at the disposal of Hejaz Operations, for the purposes of carrying out the following operations of the Hejaz Railway:
    a. To seize Mudawra [sic] with the primary object of destroying the enemy's valuable water supply at that place.
    b. To destroy the main railway bridge and tunnel at Kissela, 5 miles south of Amman, or
    c. The demolition of the railway bridge immediately north of Jurf Ed Derwish, and the destruction of the enemy's supply dumps and wells at Jurf Station.

2. The following instructions and attached march programme are based on the assumption that the objectives a. and b. will be carried out.

Should it prove necessary, as the second phase of the operations, to substitute c. for b., which will be decided solely at the discretion of the O.C. Imperial Camel Corps, these instructions will be amended, and a revised plan prepared by the officer responsible for its execution.

3. Marches

The column will march, subject to such modifications as may be imposed by circumstances at present unforeseen, in accordance with the march programme and time table attached.

4. Operations

a. The operations, both at Mudawra and at Kissela (or Jurf Ed Derwish) will be carried out as night attacks, under cover of darkness. In each case, the precise plan of attack will be decided, after personal reconnaissance of the positions to be assaulted by the O.C., I.C.C. In this connection, stress is laid upon the value to be obtained by the element of surprise, the Turks in the Hejaz area being, hitherto, unaccustomed to attack by night, and therefore, probably ill-prepared to resist an operation of this nature.

b. To provide artillery support during the operation against Mudawra, the Hejaz ten-pounder section will be placed by the O.C. Troops, Northern Hejaz, temporarily at the disposal of the O.C., I.C.C. On the completion of the operation, the section will not proceed east of the railway, but will return independently to Guweira or elsewhere, under the orders of the O.C. Troops, Northern Hejaz.

c. For the operation against Kissela, the O.C. Troops, northern Hejaz, should arrange for the co-operation of a detachment of armoured cars, to be held in readiness at a suitable point east of the Railway to cover the retirement of the column to Bair in the event of pursuit by hostile cavalry from Amman.

5. Supplies

The column will march from Aqaba, carrying three days' supplies and water for men, and forage for animals. In addition, each man will carry one day's emergency iron ration, to be consumed only by direct order of the O.C. Column.

Dumps for the replenishment of supplies and forage will be established, in advance, under arrangement to be made by the O.C. Troops, Northern Hejaz, as under:

a. At Rum, 5 days' ration for men and forage for animals.
b. At El Jefer, 4 days' ration for men and forage for animals.
c. At Bair, 14 days' ration for men and forage for animals.

6. Water

Plentiful drinking water for men and animals will be found at the following localities:

Rum, Modawra, El Jefer, Bair, Wadi Dakl.

7. Medical

A casualty hamla, with capacity for dealing with 24 cases (12 sitting and 12 lying) will be organized at Aqaba, to accompany the column, by Major Marshall, M.C., R.A.M.C., under instructions to be issued by the O.C. Troops, Northern Hejaz.

A general scheme for the evacuation of casualties during the operations will be prepared by Major Marshall and forwarded through O.C. Troops, Northern Hejaz, to this office as early as possible.

8. Ammunition

260 rounds Small arms ammunition per man, and 2,000 rounds per Lewis gun will be carried.

9. Explosives

a. Under arrangements to be made by the O.C. Troops Northern Hejaz, an explosives hamla, carrying 2,500 lb. of gun-cotton, will accompany the column from Aqaba to Mudawra. Empty camels and drivers should return from Mudawra to Aqaba on the conclusion of that phase of the operations.
b. For the operations at Kissela, arrangements should be made for an explosives hamla carrying 6,000 lb. of gun-cotton to meet the column on the arrival of the latter at Bair, whence it will accompany the column to Kissela.

10. Guides

a. For the first phase of the operation (from Aqaba to El Jefer, inclusive) the following arrangements should be made by the O.C. Troops, Northern Hejaz, through Sherif Feisal.

(i) Guides to meet the column at Aqaba and to conduct it thence to Rum.

(ii) A suitable Sherif selected by Sherif Feisal, together with the requisite party of guides to join the column at Rum, and to conduct it thence to Mudawara, and subsequently from Mudawara to El Jefer.

(iii) Provision of food for Arab guides, and forage for their camels, whilst employed with the column, should be included in the arrangements to be made in accordance with para. 5 above.

b. The provision of guides required for the march of the column north from El Jefer to Kissela, will be arranged, on his arrival, by Lieut. Col. Lawrence.

11. Communications

The O.C. Troops, Northern Hejaz, should arrange for the closest possible touch to be kept with the column whilst operating east of the Railway, as far north as El Jafer (inclusive) by aeroplanes of the Hejaz flight. If possible, similar arrangements will be made direct with G.H.Q. for the maintenance of communication by aeroplane from the Palestinian brigade during the second phase of the operations, north of Bair.

Acknowledge by wire.
A.C. Dawnay
Lt. Col.
General staff,
Hejaz Operations.

Daily Telegraph news item January 2006

Lawrence's flag flown over Aqaba

Mark Sykes may be best known for his role in the Sykes-Picot Agreement but he was also partly responsible for the design of the Arab flag. Its purpose was to unite the many disparate and feuding Arab tribes. The very first flags were used by the Arabs in the Arab Revolt, mainly in the Hejaz area where the revolt first took hold. The colours of the flag represent the four earliest Islamic dynasties.

One of these early flags was carried by Lawrence when he and the Arab leader, Auda, crossed the desert to take the Turkish-held port at Aqaba. The flag was raised above the old ruined fort overlooking the small port and flown there until it was lowered and taken into custody by an Australian naval officer, Capt. Harold Bedwell who was visiting Aqaba in late 1918. The flag comes with provenance in the form of a note which states: 'Flag of Sheik of Aqaba presented to me by the sheik'. The identity of this sheik is unclear; it could have been Auda, though why he would present an Arab flag to an Australian naval captain is equally unclear.

Nevertheless, the flag was recently auctioned by Sotheby's and the princely sum of £165,000 was paid on behalf of the Jordanian Royal palace. How this particular flag can be labelled as Lawrence's flag remains a mystery. Lawrence certainly owned one of these flags and it is more likely that he brought his home to Oxford. The flag was frequently seen flying from a spire at All Souls College in Oxford during periods when he was in residence there. The whereabouts of this particular specimen is unknown – and probably languishes in a tin box somewhere, its existence and value unknown to the current owner.

In any event, the 'Bedwell' flag will be taken on a tour of Jordan prior to being permanently exhibited in Amman later in 2006.

Bibliography

Brémond, Edouard, *Le Hedjaz dans la Guerre Mondial*, Paris 1931

Churchill, Winston, *Great Contemporaries*, Macmillan 1941

Doughty, C. M., *Travels in Arabia Deserta* (Vols I & II) Jonathan Cape 1936

Erskine, Mrs Steuart, *Feisal*, Hutchinson & Co 1933

Gardner, Brian, *Allenby*, Cassell 1965

Garnett, David, *The letters of T.E. Lawrence*, Jonathan Cape 1938

Graves, Robert, *Lawrence and the Arabs*, London 1927

Harrap, Sir Archibald, *Allenby: A Study in Greatness*, Wavell 1940

James, Lawrence, *The Golden Warrior: The Life and Legend of Lawrence of Arabia*, London 1995

Knightly & Simpson, *The Secret Lives of Lawrence of Arabia*, Literary Guild 1969

Lares, Maurice, *T. E. Lawrence, La France et les Français*, Lille 1978

Lawrence, M. R., (edited by), *Letters of T.E. Lawrence*, Oxford 1954

Lawrence, T. E., *Revolt in the Desert*, Jonathan Cape 1927

Lawrence, T. E., *Oriental Assembly*, London 1939

Lawrence, T. E., *Seven Pillars of Wisdom*, Alden Press 1935

Thomas, Lowell, *With Lawrence in Arabia*, New York 1925

Toynbee, Arnold J., *The Treatment of the Armenians in the Ottoman Empire, 1915–1916*, London 1919

Villars, Jean Beraud, *Le Colonel Lawrence ou la Recherche de l' Absolu*, Paris 1955

Villars, Jean Beraud, *T.E. Lawrence*, London 1958

Wavell, Gen. A., *Allenby*, Harrap 1940

Wilson, H. W., *The Great War* (Vol III), Amalgamated Press 1915

Wooley, Charles Leonard, *Lawrence By His Friends*, London 1937

TV

Yardley, Michael, in interview with Channel 4 TV, *Lawrence of Arabia*, 2004

NEWSPAPERS AND JOURNALS

New York Times, 1915
The Journal of the Victoria Cross Society, Crowborough UK

Index